岸 和郎の建築

WARO KISHI

First published in Japan on January 27, 2016

Author／Waro Kishi
Publisher／Toru Kato
TOTO Publishing (TOTO LTD.)
TOTO Nogizaka Bldg. 2F, 1-24-3 Minami-Aoyama
Minato-ku, Tokyo 107-0062, Japan
[Sales]　　　Telephone　+81-3-3402-7138
　　　　　　Facsimile　+81-3-3402-7187
[Editorial] Telephone　+81-3-3497-1010
URL　http://www.toto.co.jp/publishing/
Art Director／Nobuhiro Yamaguchi
Designer／Rei Miyamaki
Printed／Tosho Printing Co., Ltd.

Except as permitted under copyright law, this book may not be reproduced, in whole or in part, in any form or by any means, including photocopying, scanning, digitizing, or otherwise, without prior permission. Scanning or digitizing this book through a third party, even for personal or home use, is also strictly prohibited.
The list price is indicated on the cover.

ISBN978-4-88706-356-3

WARO KISHI

岸 和郎の建築

目次
Contents

006 序文　岸 和郎
　　Introduction　Waro Kishi

009 岸和郎をつくった14の出来事
　　14 Incidents that shaped Waro Kishi

Selected Works 1982-2016

026 京都芸術短期大学高原校舎
　　Kyoto College of Art, Takahara Campus

034 KIM HOUSE 1987/2011

050 京都科学・開発センター
　　Kyoto Kagaku Research Institute

060 日本橋の家
　　House in Nipponbashi

072 下鴨の家
　　House in Shimogamo

080 紫野和久傳
　　Restaurant "Murasakino Wakuden"

086 山口大学医学部創立50周年記念会館
　　Memorial Hall in Yamaguchi

096 苦楽園の家 I
　　House in Kurakuen I

106 朱雀の家
　　House in Suzaku

116 かづらせい・寺町
　　Antique Gallery "Kazurasei"

124 文京の家
　　House in Bunkyo

132 苦楽園の家 II
　　House in Kurakuen II

144 深谷の家
　　House in Fukaya

160 堺の家
　　House in Sakai

168 和歌山の家
　　House in Wakayama

178 Hu-tong House

190 子午線ライン 明石船客ターミナル
　　Akashi Meridian Line Ferry Terminal

200 京都・小野
　　Zen Lounge I

204	熊野古道情報センター Kumano-kodo Information Center project	368	歴史の中の岸和郎　　髙橋康夫 Waro Kishi_within the context of History　Yasuo Takahashi
210	ライカ銀座店 Leica Ginza Showroom	376	作品データ Project Data
214	Suzhou Vanke Villa	388	略歴 Profile
222	紙屋HOUSE Kamiya House	390	クレジット Credits
232	Tearoom project in the Center of Tokyo		
234	書院 / Penthouse Zen Lounge II		
238	書院 / Third-place Zen Lounge III		
242	KIT HOUSE		
256	御所西の家 House near Kyoto Gosho		
268	日東薬品構内景観整備計画 NITTO PHARMA Landscape project		
274	Wujiang New City Planning project, China		
280	象彦漆美術館 Zohiko Urushi Museum		
288	Spiretec Office Headquarters project		
292	曹洞宗 仏光山 喜音寺 Kionji Temple		
306	GLA近畿会館 GLA Osaka Hall		
318	京都大学北部グラウンド運動部部室棟 Kyoto University Student Clubhouse, north campus		
322	山野井の家 House in Yamanoi		
338	白鳳堂京都本店 Hakuhodo		
348	Warehouse Renovation at Minsheng-road		
354	京都市美術館新館計画案 Kyoto City Museum Annex project		
358	南泉禅寺再建計画 Nanquan Temple project		

Introduction

Waro Kishi

I have been designing architecture for quite some time now. The earliest project in this monograph, the Kyoto College of Art Takahara Campus, dates back to 1982, so more than three decades have gone by since then. To me, the most momentous architectural incident that has occurred during this time is the terrorist attack on the World Trade Center (WTC) in New York on September 11, 2001. I had been watching television a little after 11 at night when the screen abruptly switched to show images of the WTC. Images of smoke rising from the mid-level floors. Images of the passenger jet as it came crashing in. The critical moment came when the skyscraper suddenly collapsed some minutes later.

I may be mixing up my memories of the live broadcast that I watched that night with the recorded footage aired during the same period. In any case, when I saw the television footage that ran for several tens of minutes—and, in particular, the sight of the WTC towers collapsing instantaneously—I felt like I was watching the architectural values that I believed in crumble.

I did not think that I was one who believed somewhere in my heart in the image of architecture that lives perpetually through time, like the Acropolis or Pantheon and Toshodaiji or Horyuji. I thought this was something that only held true for those exceptionally fortunate works of architecture. Yet, after seeing the WTC collapse and realizing just how much the event unsettled my mind, I felt like I finally came to understand what I actually believed to be the meaning of architecture.

I will no doubt be told that these are 15th-century values, but I believed that architecture was something that brought about a certain order to the world and, furthermore, that this manifested order took on a permanent form that transcended the existence of the architecture itself. But it was revealed to me right

1990年代はソ連の崩壊に始まり、湾岸戦争、阪神・淡路大震災、2001年の9.11と社会の在り方を揺るがす事件が続く。それもあって意識的に古典主義、20世紀的な価値観で言えば〈近代主義〉に回帰するようになったのか。〈近代主義を偽装する〉、〈とりあえずの近代主義〉などと言いながら、近代という時代、その背後に在る古典主義的価値観との距離を測ることを続ける。

1990年代以降、コミュニケーションの手段も変わった。電話からFAXに移り、今やメールにSNSが主流だ。図面もトレーシングペーパーに鉛筆で描かれたものの青焼きから、紙に出力されたCADの図面へと変化し、今やBIMらしい。我々の設計図面も1980年代には手描きでスタートし、1990年代中頃にはCADへと変わっている。そう考えると、1990年代は理念的には自分自身の立ち位置の見出せない時代だったが、建築の設計表現方法にも大きな変化が訪れ、それは結果的に建築の価値観を当たり前のように変化させる。

それでも妄想してしまう。そんな時代でさえ、変わらない建築的価値観というものが存在するというのだろうか？

WTCの崩壊が教えてくれたのは〈ない〉という答えだった。

でも時に思う、いや、思いたい。〈存在する〉に違いないと。

なぜ建築設計などということを生業としているのかという質問を自らに投げ掛けつつ、その答えを探そうとしたこともある。そんな時、建築を目指そうとする自分にきっかけを与えてくれた建築、元気にしてくれる建築を想い出すようにしている。〈原点〉という言葉はあまり好きではないので、建築を信じさせてくれる建築、というのが正直な言

before my eyes that when architecture lost its actuality, the order that had existed where it stood also vanished with it. That day, September 11, was when I realized that I was a backward classicist.

The 1990s opened with the Soviet Union's collapse and was followed by a string of incidents that shook the very framework of society, such as the Gulf War, Kobe Earthquake, and then September 11 in 2001. Possibly because of this, I made a conscious shift to classicism and reverted to what in a 20th-century sense was Modernism. I told myself that I was just "assuming the guise was Modernism" and turning to "Modernism just for now" while measuring my distance from the era called the Modern age and the classicist values behind it.

Since the 1990s, even our modes of communication have changed. The telephone shifted to fax, and now email and SNS are dominant. Architectural plans also have evolved from blueprints made with pencil drawings drawn on tracing paper to CAD drawings plotted on paper, and apparently now they are generated from BIM. We started out by hand-drawing architectural plans in my office in the 1980s, but we also shifted to CAD in the mid-1990s. Thinking about this now, I realize that the 1990s had been a time when I could not determine where I stood conceptually, but the drastic changes to the modes of representation in architectural design transformed my architectural values as a matter of course.

Yet, I still wonder: Does there exist such a thing as an unchanging sense of architectural value even in such an age?

The collapse of the WTC taught me that the answer is no.

Even so, I sometimes think—or rather, I hope—that it does indeed exist.

There have been times when I asked myself why I

い方だろうか。

　この書籍の最初にはそんな、自分が迷った時に確認に戻る建築を12個まとめようと思った。自分がアジア人であるということを意識させられることが最近多いため、アジアに共通する数字として12項目にしたかったのだが、数えてみると外せない建築ばかりで、結果、14項目になってしまった。

　ここではその14の建築を、さながら百科事典のように並べてみる。その建築のわたし個人とのかかわり合い、それぞれの建築が如何にわたし自身に元気を与えてくれたか、について語るところから始めたい。

　わたしにとって14個の建築に意味があるのは、自分自身のアリバイ確認であることはもちろんだが、もし可能ならば、以前と同じように建築的価値観の存在を見せて欲しい、あるいは、改めてもう一度建築を信じさせて欲しい、というのがわたし自身の切なる想いなのだ。

practice architectural design and attempted to come up with an answer. At such times, I have made myself recall the works of architecture that brought me to pursue architecture and that give me energy. I do not really like to use the word "origins", so "architecture that gives me faith in architecture" might be a more genuine way for me to describe such works.

I wanted to start this book with a compilation of 12 such works of architecture that I go back to when I feel lost. I wanted there to be 12 because recently I am often made aware of the fact that I am Asian, and 12 is a number used commonly throughout Asia. However, I found that there were too many works that I could not leave out when I started counting them, so I ended up with 14 items.

I have laid out the 14 works of architecture here in an encyclopedic manner. I want to begin by speaking about my personal interactions with these works of architecture and about how they have each inspirited me.

The reason why the 14 works of architecture hold meaning for me is certainly partly because I see them as my alibis. But if possible, I earnestly hope that they will show me the presence of architectural value in the same way as they did for me before, and I want them to give me faith in architecture once again.

岸和郎をつくった14の出来事
14 Incidents that Shaped Waro Kishi

岸和郎をつくった14の出来事
1

孤児養育院
Ospedale degli Innocenti

31才の時、建築家としてひとり立ちし、最初に訪ねた街がフィレンツェだった。他の街を訪ねることなど、考えられなかった。建築家としてひとり立ちしたらまずフィレンツェを訪ねると決めたのは、大学院の建築史研究室に在籍していた時代だった。そのフィレンツェでは最初にフィリッポ・ブルネレスキの孤児養育院に行こうと決めたのもその大学院の時代だ。その決心から5年の時が流れた。同じブルネレスキ設計のドゥオモの横を抜け、孤児養育院を探した。そこでその孤児養育院に初めて出会った時、これは本物じゃない、後年に建ったレプリカだろう、と思った。本物はどこだろうと改めて探してみたのだが、結局目の前に在るそれがまさしく本物であることが分かる。何故、レプリカだと思ったか。それはその建築があまりにも新しく思え同時代的＝contemporaryに感じられたからだ。建築を支配する幾何学とそれがもたらす明快な世界観と秩序、それを支える鋳鉄というテクノロジーの導入、抽象化された光と影、など、そうした建築の在り方が600年近く前に実現されていたとは信じられなかった。それ以来、孤児養育院は私のアイドルになった。

Florence was the first city I visited when I started out on my own as an architect at the age of 31. I could not imagine going to any other city. I was still researching architectural history at graduate school when I decided that Florence would be my first destination when I became an independent architect. That was also when I decided that I would go to Filippo Brunelleschi's Ospedale degli Innocenti. Five years after making this resolve, I was walking past the Duomo, also designed by Brunelleschi, looking for the orphanage. When I made my first encounter with the building, I thought, *This can't be the real thing—this must be a later replica*. I resumed my search, wondering where the real one was, only to find out that the building standing before me was indeed the original after all. Why did I think that it was a replica? Because the building seemed much too new and felt so *contemporary*. I could not believe that that mode of architecture—i.e. an architecture that was ruled by geometry which established a clear worldview and order, embedded with technology in the form of cast iron, articulated by abstracted light and shadow, etc.—had already been realized some 600 years ago. The Ospedale degli Innocenti became my idol from that point on.

孤児養育院(1427)。
Ospedale degli Innocenti (1427).

岸和郎をつくった14の出来事

2

CSH #22

ポストモダニズムの嵐が吹き荒れる1970年代、大学院建築史研究室の時代には図書館の書庫にこもるのを常としていた。そこで出会った建築のひとつに南カリフォルニアの1960年代を代表する一連のケーススタディハウス（CSH）やその建築家達、クレイグ・エルウッド、ピエール・コーニッグ、それにエドワード・キリングスワースといった人達の仕事がある。1970年代時点では既に遠く忘れ去られていた、それらのモダニズムの建築家の仕事とその書庫で出会ったのだ。カビ臭く薄暗い書庫での、一見すると能天気に見える"sunny california"との出会い。ほとんどシュールリアリスティックな瞬間だった。その建築群を象徴するアイコンの建築だったのがCSH#22であり、さらに言えばジュリアス・シュルマンが撮影した1枚の写真、ロサンゼルスの夜景の上に浮遊する夕方の風景、透明なリビングルームでパラシュートスカートを履いた女性が談笑する姿こそが〈ケーススタディハウス〉だった。

ほとんど官能的と言っていい風景、そんな建築空間が1960年代に存在していたことを知る。どんなに反時代的であろうと、自分自身がモダニズムを継承しようと決心したのはこの時、その書庫の中だった。

1990年代になってたまたまコーニッグ氏に会い、CSH#22を訪ねるチャンスを得る。現実に南カリフォルニアの陽光の中に存在するCSH#22はあの官能性からはほど遠く、20年間の想いとは違ってとても健康的に見えた。しかしその同じ建築がまったく異なる様相を見せる瞬間は必ず在ることを、シュルマンの写真は確実に物語っているのだ。

I spent much of my time holed up in the library stacks as a graduate student of architectural history in that era of the 1970s when the storm of Postmodernism was sweeping through the world. Among the architectural works that I came across in there were the Case Study Houses (CSH)—the emblematic works of 1960s Southern Californian architecture—and other buildings by their architects, which included the likes of Craig Ellwood, Pierre Koenig, and Edward Killingsworth. I encountered in those stacks the works of Modernist architects who were long forgotten by then in the 1970s. But to think that I happened upon the seemingly carefree "Sunny California" air there in those dim, musty stacks. It certainly made for a surrealistic moment. The most iconic building that emblematized that group of architecture was CSH #22. Or one could go further and say that Julius Shulman's photograph of the house, with women in parachute skirts, chatting inside the transparent living room suspended above Los Angeles' evening skyline, essentially embodied what the Case Study Houses were all about.

I so discovered that there existed such a sight and architectural space in the 1960s that could even be described as sensual. It was then and there in those stacks that I resolved to commit myself to Modernism, however backward a thing it was for me to do.

In the 1990s, I happened to meet Mr. Koenig in person and had the chance to visit CSH #22. The CSH #22 that stood under the Southern Californian sun in real life was far from sensual; it had a very healthy feel to it, unlike how I had been picturing it in my mind for two decades. Yet, Shulman's photograph gives us certain proof that there are moments when that same building will show a completely different face.

ケーススタディハウス#22（1960）。
Case Study House#22 (1960).

土浦亀城自邸

Kameki Tsuchiura Residence

大学院での建築史研究室在籍時代、同じ図書館の書庫で、『国際建築』の1935年の合本と出会う。日本の戦前にこんな抽象的な建築が存在していたことに驚愕する。同時にその頃心酔していたコーリン・ロウやピーター・アイゼンマンの建築形態の読解や形態分析の延長上に土浦亀城の建築を分析するというアイデアを思い付いて興奮していたのは、やはりそのカビ臭い書庫で、それも夕方の光の影が長く伸びた大学院1年目の秋だった。

同じ頃アメリカの雑誌、『Architectural Forum』の表紙に載ったピーター・アイゼンマンのHOUSE1は衝撃だった。そのアイゼンマンが土浦亀城と同時代の建築家、ジュゼッペ・テラーニの建築カサ・デル・ファッショを分析している論文とも出会う。

カサ・デル・ファッショと土浦亀城自邸、そのふたつの建築へのオマージュとして、アイゼンマンの分析論文に私自身の土浦の作品分析を重ねてみたいという、大それた試みから始まったのが自分の修士論文だったのだ。ところがそれは最後には気持ちが変化してしまい、フィリップ・ジョンソンのガラスの家、それも『Architectural Review』での1950年の発表形式へのオマージュへとすり替わってしまう。この辺りの思考の横滑りや逡巡する思考態度、それに皮肉な韜晦趣味は今も変わらない。自分はこの頃からまるで進歩していないし、何も変わっていないな、と改めて思う。

Back when I was a student of architectural history in graduate school, I happened upon a volume of the 1935 issues of *Kokusai Kenchiku* in those same library stacks. I was amazed to discover that a work of architecture as abstract as this had existed in pre-war Japan. I became excited at the same time as I had the idea to extend the approaches of formal interpretation and formal analysis employed by Colin Rowe and Peter Eisenman—who I was infatuated with at the time—to analyze Kameki Tsuchiura's architecture. This all took place in those musty stacks in my first year of graduate school; it was an autumn day and the afternoon light was casting long shadows.

It was also around that time when I was shocked by Peter Eisenman's HOUSE I, which I saw on the cover of the American magazine *Architectural Forum*. I also came across a paper in which Eisenman gives an analysis of the Casa del Fascio designed by Giuseppe Terragni, who was a contemporary of Kameki Tsuchiura.

I started my graduate thesis with an audacious attempt to overlay my analysis of Tsuchiura's work with Eisenman's analytical paper as an homage to both the Kameki Tsuchiura Residence and Casa del Fascio. I changed my mind in the end, however, and my thesis ended up turning into an homage to Philip Johnson's Glass House—specifically, to the way it was presented in the *Architectural Review* in 1950. My tendencies to sideslip and vacillate in my thinking and to cynically hide my ideas have not changed to this day. I really have not changed or grown up at all since then.

土浦亀城自邸(1935)。
Kameki Tsuchiura Residence (1935).

4 パンテオン

岸和郎をつくった14の出来事

Pantheon

パンテオンを初めて訪ねたのは、意気込んでフィレンツェを訪れたのと同じ時だった。レンタカーでフィレンツェからローマまで走り、ローマに着いて駐車した途端に他の車にぶつけられたのを覚えている。

ローマはバロックの都市だし、やっぱり自分の好みはルネッサンスでありフィレンツェが好きな都市だな、と思いながらローマに入った。そうは言いながらジャン・ロレンツォ・ベルニーニとフランチェスコ・ボッロミーニには大いに心を動かされるのだが、それよりも何よりも、パンテオンには驚愕させられた。高さ14mの円筒形の上に直径45mの半球ドームが載り、その真ん中に直径5mの円形の穴が穿たれる。それだけだ。ただそれだけのことでそこに〈建築〉が出現すること、そのことを初めて知る。幾何学と光、それだけで建築的秩序が実現し得ること。文字にすると簡単で歯がゆいこと極まりないのだが、そういうことだ。

それからしばらく、ヨーロッパを訪ねる旅には必ずローマ・トランジットのフライトを選び、乗り継ぎの時間の間に空港からパンテオンまでタクシーを走らせることが続いた。私の心への建築エネルギー注入装置だったのだ。

I went to the Pantheon for the first time on that same trip that I eagerly visited Florence. I recall taking a rental car from Florence to Rome and being hit by another vehicle as soon as I arrived and parked the car.

I arrived in Rome thinking that I would not like it as much as Florence because I was more partial to the Renaissance, and Rome was a Baroque city. Despite what I thought, I was greatly moved by the works of Gian Lorenzo Bernini and Francesco Borromini. More than anything else, however, I was awed by the Pantheon. A 14-m-wide cylinder capped by a 45-m-wide hemispherical dome with a 5-m-wide circular hole at the center. That was all it was. I learned for the first time that that was all it took for *architecture* to emerge. Geometry and light are all that are needed for the realization of architectural order. It is quite vexing to put it in words, yet this is all it is.

For a while after that, I always chose transit flights through Rome whenever I traveled to Europe, and I made a habit of taking a taxi out to the Pantheon from the airport between my connecting flights. It became a device for pumping architectural energy into my soul.

パンテオン (128)。
Pantheon (128).

香港という都市

The City of Hong Kong

友人が住んでいるというだけの理由で香港を最初に訪ねたのは、1980年代の中頃だったか。でも何回か訪ねているうちに、どうも自分はこの都市が好きなのだ、と気付く。それは都市空間をルール違反ギリギリで使い切り、さながら都市という空間をジャングルで暮らすターザンのようなライフスタイルで使い切る人達に共感するからだ。違法とおぼしき屋上増築されたペントハウスや、高層ビルから隣のビルへと渡っていく"building hopping"、いわゆるビル渡りや、香港中の高層ビルを使って午後8時から始まるレーザーショーや、オーダーすると何でも作ってくれるローカルのレストランなど、香港の人達のライフスタイルから都市空間の愉しみ方を随分学んだ。

香港が英国から中国へと返還された1997年には誰もが香港は終わったと言い、さらに空港がカイタック空港から新しいチェプラックコック空港へと移った1998年にはあの刺激に満ちた着陸の体験が出来なくなり、この時には香港も遂に終わったのか、と思ったのだが、そうではなかった。今でもあの街は相変わらず刺激に満ちた都市で在り続けている。少なくとも私にとっては。

でも、時々昔の香港の都市空間が懐かしくて、チョウ・ユンファの『男たちの挽歌』に1980年代の香港を見たり、ウォン・カーウァイの映画に1990年代の香港を思い出す。時代は現在、場所は新幹線の中、しかもiPadの画面の中で、だ。

I visited Hong Kong for the first time in the mid-1980s based just on the reason that my friend lived there. After making several visits, however, I realized that I seemed to have taken a liking to the city. I was drawn to how the inhabitants utilized the city's spaces in ways just barely within the rules; they made full use of the spaces of the city through living a lifestyle like that of Tarzan in his jungle. There was much that I learned about ways of having fun with urban space from the lifestyle of the Hong Kongers, who built seemingly illegal penthouse additions to rooftops; practiced "building hopping", where they literally hopped between neighboring high-rise buildings; made use of towers throughout the city to put on a laser show from 8 PM; and ate at local restaurants that seemed to serve anything one wished to order.

Everyone said Hong Kong was done for when it was returned to China from the UK in 1997. I thought the real end for Hong Kong came when the moving of the airport from Kai Tak to Chek Lap Kok in 1998 took away that thrilling landing experience. But this was not the case. The city is still exciting as ever today, at least for me.

From time to time, however, I will become nostalgic for the urban spaces of the old Hong Kong, and I will look at the Hong Kong of the '80s in Chow Yun-fat's *A Better Tomorrow* and reminisce about the Hong Kong of the '90s in Wong Kar-wai films—all through the screen of my iPad and in the comfort of a Shinkansen in the year 2016.

香港の町並み（1860〜現在）。
Hong Kong (1860–present).

岸和郎をつくった14の出来事

6

バリ島の棚田
Rice Terraces of Bali

初めてバリ島を訪れたのは1980年代中頃。昼間は人が行き来している集落や稲田でも夜になると人工の光の無い、真の暗闇が訪れる。真の暗闇、それが実は既視の体験だったこと、自分の幼少時の風景、夏休みの臨海学校の記憶だったことを思い出させてくれたのがバリ島だった。電気の光の無い風景、虫の音だけが聞こえる暗闇を何十年振りかで体験したことで、その同じバリ島で人工の光とエアコンのおかげで明るく涼しい環境に身を置いている自分とは誰だろう、自然とは何だろうと考え始めた。

そんなバリ島で、キンタマーニ高原からの帰り、見渡す限りの山肌に階段状の棚田が拡がる風景に出会う。まだ稲が植えられておらず、水が張られただけの棚田を見ながら、これは自然の風景なのか、いや、人間がつくり上げた終極の人工的な風景なのか、と考え込んでしまった。その時以来、自然でもあり、同時に人工的でもあるこの棚田の風景こそが目指すべき建築の有り様ではないか、と考え始める。同時に、自然を構成する要素のひとつでありながら、樹木や風と違って、唯一幾何学的な形態＝水平面を取る〈水〉という物質に興味を持ち始める。それは幾何学とは人間がつくり上げた建築的秩序の象徴だと考えていたからだ。自然の一部である〈水〉が水平という幾何学に従う物質なのであれば、この〈水〉が自然と建築とを結び付ける触媒となるのではないか、棚田がこれほど自分を魅了するのは自然と人間との新しい関係を生み出す鍵となるからではないか。そんな〈暗闇〉と〈水〉との出会いこそが私にとってのバリ島だった。

The first time I visited the island of Bali was in the mid-1980s. When night fell, even the villages and rice paddies where people passed to and fro during the day were engulfed in total darkness, as there were no artificial lights. Bali brought back memories of a time when I went to summer school by the sea as a child, and it reminded me that I actually had already experienced total darkness before. Experiencing again, after so many decades, that landscape absent of electric lights and that darkness in which all I could hear were the sounds of the insects made me ask myself, *Who am I, sitting here on the same island in a bright, cool environment thanks to artificial light and air conditioning? What does it mean to be natural?*

While I was there in Bali, I made a trip out to the Kintamani Highland. On my way back, I came across a landscape of rice terraces that covered the mountainsides for as far as I could see. I lost myself in thought as I looked out at the unplanted, water-filled rice paddies. *Is this a natural landscape? Or might this be the ultimate artificial landscape created by humans?* From that point on, I started to believe that the landscape of rice terraces, which was both natural and artificial at once, embodied the state that I wanted to achieve with my architecture. At the same time, I developed an interest in *water*, which, unlike the trees or wind, has the ability to assume a geometric form—a flat horizontal plane—despite being an element of nature. This interested me because I had always thought of geometry as a symbol of artificial architectural order. It occurred to me that if *water* is a natural substance which conforms to geometry in the form of horizontal planes, then *water* should be able to be used as an agent for tying together nature and architecture. The rice terraces fascinated me so much because they were the key for generating a new relationship between nature and humans. Bali, to me, was all about these encounters with *darkness* and *water*.

バリ島の棚田（9世紀頃〜現在）。
Rice Terraces of Bali (9th century–present).

大徳寺孤篷庵

Daitokuji Kohoan

1981年から、1人の建築家としての活動を京都で始めた。それまで東京で暮らしていたこともあり、京都を愉しむ余裕などなく、ただただこの街の時間の流れる速度の遅さに焦りだけを感じていた。そんな訳だから、京都に居ながら京都の伝統建築にはまったく興味が無く、それが自分に関係あることだとはまったく考えていなかった。そんな時、外国の編集者から、あなたの建築は日本的だね、と指摘される。人に指摘されて初めて、自分の建築が持つ〈日本的〉な要素とは何か、と考え始める。

避け続けていた日本の伝統建築を体験しよう、見なければ始まらないと思い、ようやく日本建築を訪ね始める。そのひとつが大徳寺孤篷庵だった。特に忘筌。障子の浮遊するスクリーンがもたらす拡散光面と縁側のエッジのずれ。さながら舞台装置のような庭の扱い。室内からの低い視線の位置と、下から入って来て天井面にバウンスする光。そのための砂摺り仕上げの天井面。さらにアプローチ導線とランドスケープデザインの論理性など。

孤篷庵が教えてくれたのは、伝統的な日本建築であっても現代建築を見るように見てもいいということだ。歴史的な建築とはそういう現代的な視線にも答えてくれる建築であり、それは自分にとっては、フィレンツェの孤児養育院との出会い以来の出来事だった。

このしばらく後に同じ大徳寺の真珠庵、その庭玉軒と出会い、明快な論理性の対極、官能的で感性的な空間もまた日本建築の特性なのだ、と知ることになる。孤篷庵を真珠庵より先に訪れていた偶然をこの時は感謝したものだ。

I started my activities as an independent architect in Kyoto in 1981. Because I had lived in Tokyo prior to that, I did not have a mind to enjoy Kyoto—the slow pace of the city just made me restless and impatient. Thus, despite living in Kyoto, I was not interested in Kyoto's traditional architecture, and I did not think that it had anything to do with me. But then one day a foreign editor pointed out to me how very Japanese my work was. It was only after being told so that I began thinking about what elements of my architecture might be considered to be "Japanese".

I decided that to understand this I needed to start off by seeing and experiencing the traditional architecture that I had been avoiding all along, and I finally began visiting works of Japanese architecture. One such work was the Daitokuji Kohoan. I looked particularly at its Bosen tearoom—noting the suspended *shoji* screen, which created a light-diffusing surface in a position shifted off from the edge of the *engawa*; the garden treated as if it were a stage set; the low viewpoint from inside the room; the light that entered from below and bounced up into the ceiling; the ceiling surfaces that were given a sand-polish finish for this very reason; and the logicality behind the approach route and landscaping.

The Kohoan taught me that I could look at traditional Japanese architecture in the same way that I looked at modern architecture. It reminded me that historical architecture is that which is capable of answering to a modern gaze. This was something that I personally had not experienced since encountering the orphanage in Florence.

It was some time later when I encountered the Teigyokuken tearoom of the Shinjuan, also at Daitokuji. There I learned that sensual, visceral spaces—completely opposite of the clear, logical spaces—were also an attribute of Japanese architecture. I blessed my luck then for having visited the Kohoan before the Shinjuan.

大徳寺孤篷庵(1612)。
Daitokuji Kohoan (1612).

8 岸和郎をつくった14の出来事

西本願寺対面所／白書院
Nishi Honganji Taimensho / Shiroshoin

孤篷庵を体験した後、自分はどうも数寄屋の空間よりも書院の空間の方が好きなのではないか、と思い始める。小堀遠州の孤篷庵は書院への原型回帰のように思えたからだ。

大学院時代、在籍していた建築史研究室ではルネッサンスから近代までが自分の興味の対象だったのだが、その頃、日本建築には少ない〈柱〉の内部空間を持つ建築として、西本願寺対面所を知る。ルネッサンスで出現する付け柱=pilasterを見ながら、建築とは柱なのか、という思いを強くしていた自分にとって、柱の内部空間を持つ西本願寺対面所は、何時かは訪ねなければいけない建築リストに入っていた。

さらに極めて個人的な日本建築史の概念理解、それは均質空間としての寝殿造りから、所作=activityに全ての要素が対応するような、言い換えると終極の機能主義建築である数寄屋=茶室建築への遷移の中間段階として書院を考えるという、建築史の先生からは怒られそうな極私的日本建築理解から、書院への興味は増すばかりだった。

対面所、上段に向かって右側の障子スクリーン=水平連続窓が上段、付け書院に繋がる辺りで乱調をきたす感じは、私にとっては寝殿造りから書院へと変化する空間の有り様を象徴するかのようだし、西洋建築の列柱空間と比べると、その木柱の列柱空間はどこかひ弱であるものの、その西洋建築の英雄的な列柱空間とは異なる柱列の在り方には興味が尽きない。対面所の裏にある白書院は、空間としては〈建築（architecture）〉と〈装置（instrument）〉の中間にあり、同じ西本願寺の飛雲閣を思い出させるが、こちらも西欧的な建築の構築性からは遠い場所に在る。こうした書院の持つ、西洋建築のものとは違うどこかひ弱な〈構築性〉といったものが私は好きなようだ。

After experiencing the Kohoan, I realized that I seem to favor the spaces of *shoin* architecture over *sukiya* architecture. The reason behind this was that I felt like Enshu Kobori's Kohoan represented a return to an original form of *shoin* architecture.

During my graduate school years, my area of interest in the architectural history laboratory I belonged to ranged from the Renaissance to the Modern period. I learned about the Nishi Honganji Taimensho around that time as a rare example of Japanese architecture that possessed an interior space with *columns*. As one who was convinced that architecture was all about columns through looking at the *pilasters* that emerged during the Renaissance, I could not leave out the Nishi Honganji Taimensho from my list of must-see buildings.

My interest in *shoin* architecture has only grown stronger based on a very personal reading of Japanese architectural history that certainly will anger my history teachers. As I see it, *shoin* architecture represents an intermediate phase in the transition from the uniform spaces of *shinden-zukuri* architecture to the ultimate functionalist spaces of *sukiya* architecture (i.e. tearoom architecture), in which every element responds to the actions of its occupants.

To me, the way that the Taimensho's band of *shoji* screens (i.e. ribbon windows)—on the right-hand side when facing the raised floor—breaks out of rhythm in the area where it meets the alcove seems to represent the transition from *shinden-zukuri* space to *shoin* space. And however frail the space's timber colonnades may feel in comparison to the colonnades of Western architecture, I have an inexhaustible interest in this colonnade space that differs in nature from that of the heroic colonnade spaces of the West. Similarly, the Shiroshoin behind the Taimensho, which as a space is something between *architecture* and *instrument*—and which brings to mind the Nishi Honganji Hiunkaku—also stands poles apart from the highly constructed architecture of the West. I seem to have a liking for the rather delicate nature of construction that *shoin* architecture expresses, which differs greatly from that of Western architecture.

西本願寺対面所／白書院（江戸初期頃）。
Nishi Honganji Taimensho / Shiroshoin (early Edo period).

9

ラ・ロッシュ-ジャンヌレ邸

Villa La Roche-Jeanneret

サヴォア邸はこれまで数回、訪ねている。1992年冬、様々な想いを抱えていた時期、改めてサヴォア邸を訪ねた。細かな印象はともかく、ここに〈建築〉が在る、という想いを強くした。ポアッシーからパリへと戻る電車の車中で、あれこそが〈建築〉なのだ、そうだとすれば、自分が日常的にやっている設計という営為、そしてその結果生み出されているものとは何か、それを〈建築〉と呼んでいいのか、自分自身が作っているモノなど、限りなくゴミに近いではないか、設計という仕事は自分は止めた方がよいのではないか、という最悪の精神状態に落ち込んでいた。

次の日、念のためにと思い付き、ラ・ロッシュ-ジャンヌレ邸を見に行く。建築的な秩序そのものと言っていいサヴォア邸の厳しさと比べると、ラ・ロッシュ-ジャンヌレ邸はロマンティックで、限りなく優しい。これもまた〈建築〉で在るのか、という安堵。あの優しい〈建築〉に癒されて、今も建築家を続けている。

I have been to the Villa Savoye several times now. I revisited the building in the winter of 1992, which was a time when I was dealing with many thoughts in my mind. Detailed impressions aside, it left me with the strong feeling that *This is architecture*. During the train ride back to Paris from Poissy, I thought to myself, *If that's what architecture is, then what am I to make of the work called design that I engage in every day? What am I to make of the things that I've been producing? Can any of it really even be called architecture? Isn't it all pretty much just trash? I probably shouldn't even be doing design work.* I fell into a miserable state of mind.

The next day, I decided that I should go look at the Villa La Roche-Jeanneret, just in case. Compared to the strictness of the Villa Savoye that seemed to be a direct embodiment of architectural order, the Villa La Roche-Jeanneret was romantic and utterly benign. I felt relieved, realizing that *This, too, is architecture*. I stuck to being an architect thanks to this benign architecture that comforted me.

ラ・ロッシュ-ジャンヌレ邸(1925)。
Villa La Roche-Jeanneret (1925).

10 ル・トロネ修道院

Le Thoronet Abbey

サヴォア邸やラ・ロッシュ=ジャンヌレ邸と同じ時、1992年冬に、ル・トロネ修道院を訪ねた。フランスには、建築に迷ったらル・トロネに行け、という言葉があるそうだ。それならば今こそ行くべき時だ、と思い、プロヴァンスまで車を走らせる。12月の冬の日の朝、ル・トロネには我々以外にはイタリア人が2人居ただけだった。幾何学的な建築をその場所のランドスケープに合わせ、しかもそこで採掘された石で造るというシトー派の建築だが、セナンクの青い石に比べると、温かい色調の石のル・トロネは厳しくも優しい。もっとも室内の温度でさえ摂氏0℃に近く、19世紀までは修道士の平均寿命が30才を超えなかったという逸話も了解可能なほど寒かったが。物理的には凍え死ぬほど寒くても、それでもどこか人間を許容してくれる建築であること、厳密に幾何学的な平面がその場所特有の起伏に出会った時に聖堂や回廊に出現する階段とレベル差、そこに導入される光とそれが際立たせる石という素材の質感、たったそれだけのことがその厳密な幾何学を人間に優しくしてくれることを知ったのはこの場所だった。

I visited Le Thoronet Abbey on the same trip I visited the Villa Savoye and Villa La Roche-Jeanneret in the winter of 1992. The French supposedly have a saying that goes, "When at a loss with architecture, go to Le Thoronet". I took a car out to Provence that winter, thinking, *Well then, this is the time for me to go*. The only other people at Le Thoronet on that cold December morning were two Italians. The warm-toned stone of Le Thoronet—a work of Cistercian architecture, recognizable by its geometric form adapted to the site's landscape and by its use of locally quarried stone—had a strict yet gentle feel compared to the blue stone of Sénanque Abbey. That being said, the temperature inside the rooms was actually close to 0 °C—cold enough for me to understand why it was said the average life expectancy of the monks did not exceed 30 years until the 19th century. However, even if physically it was lethally cold, the architecture somehow gave the feeling of being tolerant and receptive towards humans. It was here where I learned that those steps and level differences that appeared in the sanctuary and corridors at moments where the rigid geometric plan encountered the site's unique undulations, the light that was drawn into the spaces, and the textures of the stone that were brought out under the light were all it took to make the strict geometries feel benign to humans.

ル・トロネ修道院(1230)。
Le Thoronet Abbey (1230).

11 ロックフェラー・ゲストハウス

Rockefeller Guest House

ミース・ファン・デル・ローエやル・コルビュジエの次の世代の建築家の仕事に興味があり、アメリカ東海岸に残るマルセル・ブロイヤーやフロリダのポール・ルドルフ、ロサンゼルスのリチャード・ノイトラなどの建築を精力的に見て歩いていた時期がある。その時代も、そして今も、見たくても見られない憧れの建築として在るのが、フィリップ・ジョンソンのロックフェラー・ゲストハウス、ニューヨーク、マンハッタンの真只中に在るあの建築だ。ニューヨークを訪れるたびにあの建築の前では何時も立ち止まっているし、見学のアポイントメントが取れたこともあった。ただ、約束の3日前にキャンセルになったのだが。

意外に大きな建築だということや、しかも結構即物的なファサードだということは、外からも分かる。しかし、中央に水盤の中庭を挟んだあの平面のプロポーションや、多分、図面から想像するよりも大振りであろう内部空間など、自分の身体で体験し刻み込みたいと思い始めて、もう半世紀近い。ニューキャナンのガラスの家を訪ねながら、その彼方にロックフェラー・ゲストハウスを夢見ていたのはわたしだけだろうし、悔しくなって、ジョンソンの処女作、ハーバードでの学生生活のためにケンブリッジの街中に建てたコートハウスを覗き見に行ったのもわたしだ。これを称して韜晦趣味と言うのだろうか。

この建築を現実に体験した人の数は結構多い。ただ、わたしにとってはどうやってもたどり着けない夢の建築であるようだ。

There was a period in my life when I spent time industriously walking around the US to look at the existing buildings of Marcel Breuer on the East Coast, Paul Rudolph in Florida, and Richard Neutra in Los Angeles because I was interested in the work of the generation of architects that came after Mies van der Rohe and Le Corbusier. One work of architecture that I longed to see then and still do now is Philip Johnson's Rockefeller Guest House, which stands right in the middle of Manhattan, New York. I have always stopped in front of the building when I have gone to New York, and I have even once managed to make an appointment to look inside—only to be cancelled on three days before the scheduled date.

I can tell from the outside that the building is actually rather large and that it has quite a matter-of-fact façade. However, for almost half a century now, I have wanted to experience the spaces on the interior, which are probably larger than I have been imagining from the drawings, and to absorb the proportions of its plan that encloses a courtyard with a reflecting pool. I am probably the only person who has ever dreamt about the Rockefeller Guest House while visiting the Glass House in New Canaan, and I am also that person who, after becoming so disgruntled, went to peep into Johnson's debut work—the courtyard house he built in Cambridge as a student at Harvard. This is no doubt the sort of thing that people call a secret obsession.

There are actually many who have experienced this building in reality. Yet, to me, it seems to be a work of architecture of my dreams that I will never be able to reach.

ロックフェラー・ゲストハウス (1950)。
Rockefeller Guest House (1950).

岸和郎をつくった14の出来事
12

ブロイヤー自邸

Breuer Houses

どうもニューヨークという都市には、特別な想いがあるようだ。2004年の秋、MITで大学院のスタジオを持っていた時、毎週末ごとにアムトラックかパンダバスでニューヨークに通っていた。ひとつは耳も千切れそうなほど寒いクリスマス前のニューヨーク、そのロックフェラーセンターの雰囲気が好きだったこと、もうひとつは時間を見つけては地元の友人とマルセル・ブロイヤーの住宅を見に行っていたからだ。彼は元のブロイヤー事務所に勤めており、過去のブロイヤー・アーカイブを管理していたため、2人で現状調査のつもりで住宅を訪問し続けていたのだ。

そのブロイヤーの3番目の自邸。既に取り壊されてしまい、今はもう存在しないが、その空間を体験出来たのは幸甚だった。緩やかに起伏するランドスケープの中に注意深く埋め込まれた壁の建築。決して、"英雄的"な建築ではない。その絶妙なランドスケープと建築との関係を通して、"understatement"という言葉を知った。大きな声で自らの存在を叫ぶ建築ではなく、その場所に昔から在ったかのように、穏やかに存在する建築を創りたいという想いを確認出来たのは、あのニューイングランドを毎週のようにさまよった2004年冬の日々の最大の成果だった。

I seem to have special feelings for the city of New York. When I was running a graduate studio at MIT in the fall of 2004, I used to take the Amtrak or Panda Bus down to New York every weekend. One reason I did this was because I liked the atmosphere at the Rockefeller Center before the arrival of New York's ear-freezing Christmas season. Another reason was that I was using any time I could find to look at Marcel Breuer-designed houses with a local friend. My friend, who used to work at Breuer's office, managed the Marcel Breuer Archive, so we kept visiting the houses together with the intention of surveying their condition.

I feel very grateful to have been able to experience the spaces of Breuer's third house, which no longer exists having been demolished. It was an architecture of walls that was carefully embedded into the gently undulating landscape. It was by no means a work of "heroic" architecture. In fact, it was through the exquisite relationship the building established with the landscape that I learned the English word "understatement". The greatest thing that I gained from those days I spent traveling around New England almost every week of the winter of 2004 was the opportunity to confirm that what I wanted to make was not an architecture with a big voice that screams out its presence but an architecture that exists quietly as though it had always been there from long ago.

ブロイヤー邸（1951：3番目の自邸）。
Breuer House (1951: Breuer's third personal residence.).

岸和郎をつくった14の出来事

13

アルテス・ムゼウム

Altes Museum

カール・フリードリッヒ・シンケル（1781-1841）。この人の建築に魅力を感じるようになってから久しい。建築家がベルリンを訪ねる目的は概ねミース・ファン・デル・ローエの新国立ギャラリーを見に行くというのが第一だろうけれど、わたしが最初にベルリンを訪ねた時にまず行こうと想っていたのはこのアルテス・ムゼウムと、それにポツダムのシャルロッテンホフまで足を伸ばし、庭師の家を見に行こうと想っていた。

パンテオンが半球形の内部空間＝ロトンダにペディメントの付いた列柱が付加された建築だとすれば、アルテス・ムゼウムでは逆にギリシャ的な列柱のファサードの奥にロトンダが隠されている。さらにここにもうひとつ、パラディオの2軸対称の建築であるヴィラ・ロトンダを置くと、これら3つの建築だけでローマからルネッサンスを経て、様式建築へと至る古典主義建築の通史が出来上がる。そんなふうに古典主義建築を通してみると見えてくるアルテス・ムゼウムの印象、それはその身近さ、現代との距離の近さだった。アルテス・ムゼウムとシャルロッテンホフの庭師の家を同じ建築家が構想したという事実、さらにその同じシンケルがゴシック様式の教会まで設計していたことなど、クラシシズムとロマンティシズムが隣り合わせで存在しているような19世紀建築の感覚は、自分にとって極めて今日的に感じられたのだ。

それは西本願寺対面所、書院の建築が与える印象に近い。

その建築の背後で何かがダイナミックに動いているように思える感覚、それがつくられた時代に大きく動いていた世界がたまたま建築の姿で凍結されたかのような感覚である。アルテス・ムゼウムからさほど遠くない場所に建つミースの新国立ギャラリーとの類似性もそんなところにあるという気がしてならない。

Karl Friedrich Schinkel (1781–1841). It has been quite some time since I first became fascinated by his architecture. For most architects, the primary aim for visiting Berlin is probably to see Mies van der Rohe's Neue Nationalgalerie, but the place that I wanted to visit first when I went to Berlin was the Altes Museum. I also wanted to make a trip out to the Charlottenhof in Potsdam to see the Gardener's House.

If the Pantheon should be described as a building comprising a circular interior space (i.e. *rotunda*) with a pedimented colonnade appended to it, the Altes Museum should be described oppositely as a colonnaded façade of Greek columns with a rotunda concealed behind it. If we bring Palladio's biaxially symmetrical Villa Rotonda into this set, the three buildings will complete a historical overview 0f Classicist architecture that illustrates the transition from Roman to Renaissance to stylistic architecture. When I look over the range of Classicist architecture in this way, the impression that I have of the Altes Museum is that it is actually rather familiar and not so distant from our present age. The sense of how Classicism and Romanticism existed side-by-side in the 19th century—as exemplified by the fact that Schinkel conceived both the Altes Museum and Gardener's House in Charlottenhof, and that the same architect also designed Gothic-style churches—feels very contemporary to me.

I get a similar impression from the *shoin* architecture of the Nishi Honganji Taimensho.

These works of architecture give me a sense that there is something moving dynamically behind them; it is as though the world that was changing dynamically at the time of their construction just happened to be frozen in the form of architecture. I have the feeling that this is also where the similarity lies between the Altes Museum and Mies' Neue Nationalgalerie that stands not so far away from it.

アルテス・ムゼウム（1828）。
Altes Museum (1828).

14 京都、あるいは歴史都市の憂鬱

Kyoto (or the Despair of the Historical City)

最後は京都について語らなければならない。1969年から78年まで大学生活を京都で過ごした。東京で仕事を始めた後、1981年に再び京都に戻ったのだが、そのまま今日まで京都に居ることになるとは夢にも考えてもいなかった。現代の建築家がこの街でなし得ることは限りなく小さく思えたからだ。東京の友人達の、何時東京に戻って来るの、という声を聞きながらの1980年代だった。ちょっと歩けば桂離宮や大徳寺真珠庵といった歴史的な傑作建築が在る街で、どんな顔をして現代建築家だと言えるのか、と思っていた。京都という場所に押しつぶされた80年代だった。

1990年代に入り、スペインの出版社から作品集を出そうというオファーが舞い込む。その時にスペインの編集者から言われた言葉、あなたの建築は日本的だね、という言葉に驚愕する。自分の建築を日本的だなんて思ったことは一度だって無いし、むしろこの京都という都市からは逃げ出したいと考えていたのだから。

しかし、その言葉に勇気付けられ、京都に居続けることを決めた。自分なりのやり方で京都と関わろうとようやく決心したのだが、それは既に1990年代も半ばになろうとしていた頃だった。

アイデンティティ、という言葉がある。自分の建築家としてのアイデンティティを京都という都市に定めること、その決心のためには自分は10年以上の時間を必要としたのだ。

それ以降、プロジェクトの場所そのものは海外にまで拡がっていったのだが、せっかく決心したにも関わらず、結果として京都でのプロジェクトは多くはない。それは建築の神様からの皮肉なのだろうか？

I shall end by speaking about Kyoto. I spent my university years from 1969 to 1978 in Kyoto. I started out working in Tokyo, only to return to Kyoto again in 1981, but I never imagined then that I would still be in Kyoto to this day. This was because it seemed like there was very little that a modern architect could achieve in the city. Throughout the 1980s, I listened to my friends in Tokyo ask me, "So when are you coming back?" I wondered how I could possibly call myself a modern architect and keep face in this city where there were historic masterpieces like the Katsura Villa and Daitokuji Shinjuan just a few steps away. I spent the '80s feeling crushed under the weight of this place called Kyoto.

When the 1990s came around, a Spanish publisher offered to publish a monograph of my work out of the blue. That was when the Spanish editor told me, "Your architecture is very Japanese". I was astonished. I had never once thought that there was anything Japanese about my architecture—indeed, if anything, I just wanted to get away from Kyoto.

Those words emboldened me, however, and I decided to remain in Kyoto. I finally resolved to commit myself to the city in my own way. By that time almost half of the 1990s was already over.

There is a thing that people call "identity". It took more than a decade for me to decide to root my identity as an architect in this city.

Dcspitc having finally made up my mind, however, I do not actually have that much work in Kyoto because my projects have since spread out to sites overseas. Could it be that the architecture gods have played an irony on me?

京都の町並み (794〜現在)。
Kyoto (794–present).

Selected Works
1982-2016

京都芸術短期大学高原校舎
Kyoto College of Art, Takahara Campus

1982, 京都市左京区
Sakyo-ku, Kyoto

フリーの建築家となって初めて設計したプロジェクト。当時教鞭を執っていた京都芸術短期大学（現在の京都造形大学）の日本画と洋画のための校舎だった。同じく教鞭を執っていた大石義一先生との共同設計。意図的に4棟に分けた建築の外部空間、中庭や露地、それに屋上庭園などの設計に眼が向いていて、内部空間は教室や研究室などの機能空間のみ、外部での学生生活の多様性を許容するようなキャンパスとしたいと考えていた。設計を始めたのは1982年。建築界ではポストモダニズムの嵐が吹き荒れる中、意識的にモダニズムに興味を集中させていた自分が透けて見えるのは、今から思うと少々面映い。当時自分の中で教科書としていたのはアリソン・アンド・ピーター・スミッソン設計のハンスタントン中学校であり、あの即物的な空間（ザッハリッヒカイト）に魅了されていたからだ。構造も外壁もスティールで、開口部は工場のように古臭い網入りのガラスという建築で、スタイルの議論なんてどうでもいい、確実なモノがそこに在ればそれでいいし、在って欲しいという、当時の自分の切羽詰まった気分を想い出す。私の仕事の中で、多分、最も即物的な建築だろう。今でも、だ。

This was the first project that I designed as a freelance architect. It was a school building for the departments of Japanese painting and Western painting of the Kyoto College of Art (now Kyoto University of Art & Design), where I taught at the time. This was a joint design with Yoshikazu Oishi, who also taught at the school. I wanted to create a campus that would tolerate the diverseness of the students' outdoor activities, so I deliberately separated the building into four volumes and put the focus of the design on the exterior spaces, such as the courtyard, paths, and roof gardens, while reserving the interior for programmed spaces such as classrooms and laboratories. We started design work in 1982. Looking back now, I feel slightly embarrassed by how the design clearly shows how I had consciously focused my tastes on Modernism at a time when the storm of Postmodernism had been sweeping over the architecture world. I considered the Hunstanton School by Peter and Alison Smithson to be my bible at the time because I was fascinated by its *sachelichkeit* (matter-of-fact) spaces. I was in such a despairing mood back then that I believed that buildings should just be built as steel structures with steel envelopes and those old-fashioned wire-glass windows like in factories. I felt that discussions of style were utterly trivial. I was fine if buildings just existed as sound constructions, and that was all I wanted them to be. This was probably the most matter-of-fact building that I ever did. It still is, even now.

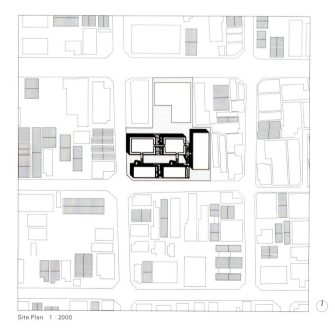

Site Plan 1 : 2000

ハンスタントン中学校（1954）。構造や設備配管は言うに及ばず、排水の流れまで露出し、可視化されている建築。レイナー・バンハムの言う"beyond aesthetics"を体験する。

右頁／南側正面。鉄骨の架構を露出し、スティール・パネルと安価な網入型板ガラスの開口部による工場のような外観。

Hunstanton School (1954). The architecture revealed everything from the structure to the ducts and even showed the flow of drainage water. I experienced what in Reyner Banham's terms was "beyond aesthetics".

opposite / South face. The building gives the outward appearance of a factory with its exposed steel frame structure, steel panels, and cheap wire mesh glass openings.

左が2階建ての研究室棟で右が階高の高い平屋のアトリエ棟。アトリエ棟の屋上庭園と中庭を階段が結ぶ。住宅地の中に建つ校舎のため、可能な限り広い外部空間を確保することが必要だと考えた。

The two-story research wing is on the left, and the single-story atelier wing with a high ceiling is on the right. Stairs link the atelier wing's roof gardens with the courtyard. I felt it necessary to provide as much outdoor space as possible because the school building stands in a residential district.

1	専攻科室	classroom
2	制作室／アトリエ	studio
3	研究室	office
4	既存建物	existing building

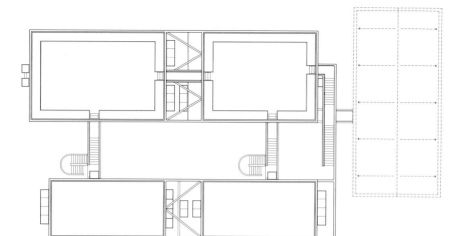

Roof Plan

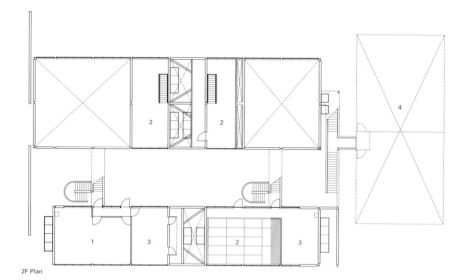

2F Plan

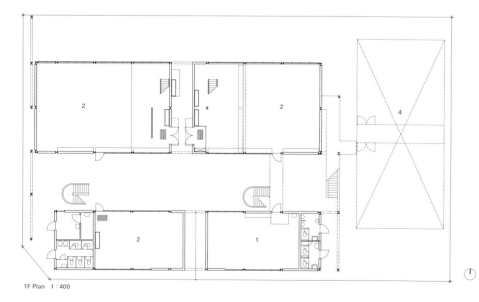

1F Plan 1:400

● Kyoto College of Art, Takahara Campus

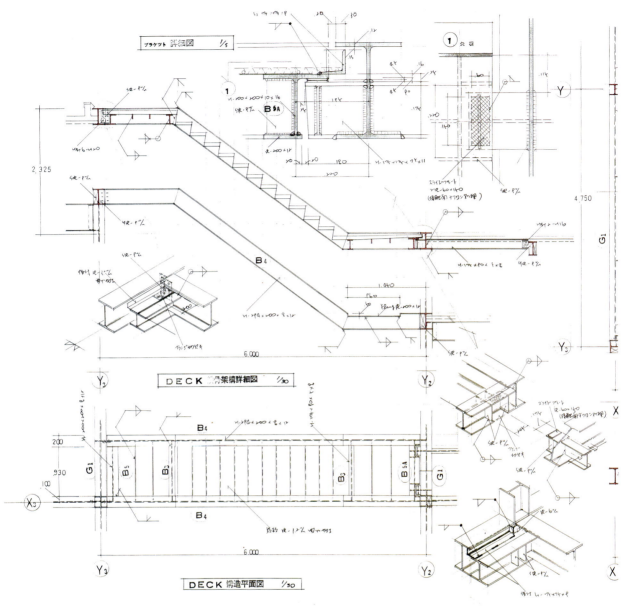

Detail Drawing of Steel Stairs

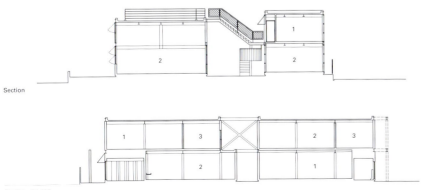

Section

Section 1 : 400

1 専攻科室　classroom
2 制作室　アトリエ　studio
3 研究室　office

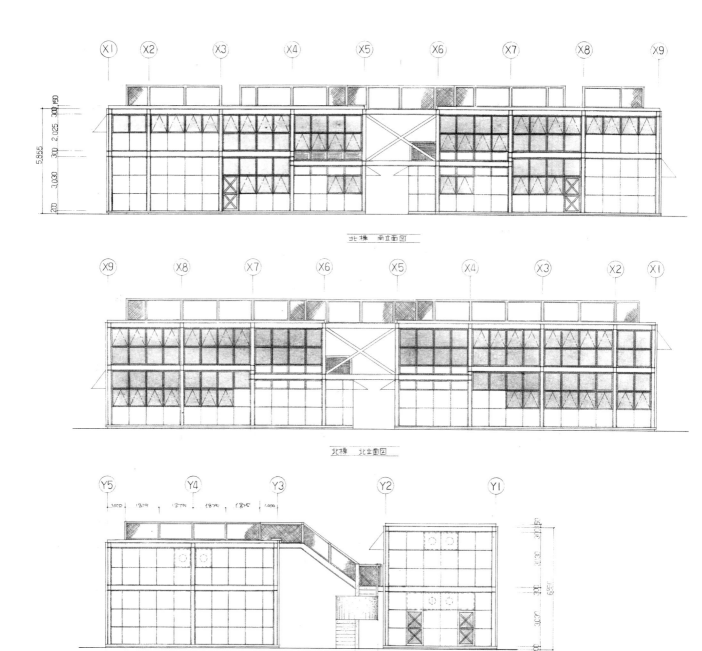

上から、北棟南面立面図、北棟道路内西立面図、北棟北立面図、北棟道路内東立面図、北・南棟西立面図。

From top to bottom, left to right: South elevation of north wing, west elevation of north wing, north elevation of north wing, east elevation of north wing, west elevation of north and south wings.

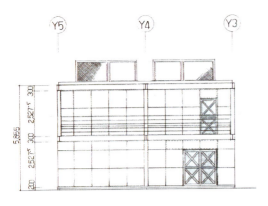

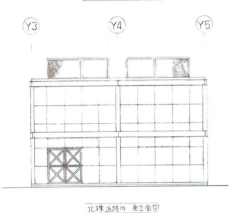

上／北棟(アトリエ棟)端部。H形鋼を構造体として用いる時、常に問題となるのは出隅の考え方である。ここでは東西方向、南北方向どちらをも等価に扱うディテールとした。
下／全景。住宅の中にある小さなキャンパス。この大学の主なキャンパスは緑の山の中、自然と共に在る。こちらの別キャンパスは都市の中、しかも住宅地の中のキャンパスとして建物を4ブロックに分割し、中庭、露地などが連続する外部空間を計画した。

below / End of north wing (atelier wing). The treatment of the corner is always a problem when using I-beams for the structure. Here I detailed them in a way that gives equal weight to the east-west and north-south directions.
bottom / General view. A small campus surrounded by houses. The main campus was located within nature on a lush mountain. For this separate campus situated in an urban residential district, I divided the buildings into four volumes and made a series of interconnected exterior spaces comprising courtyards and walkways.

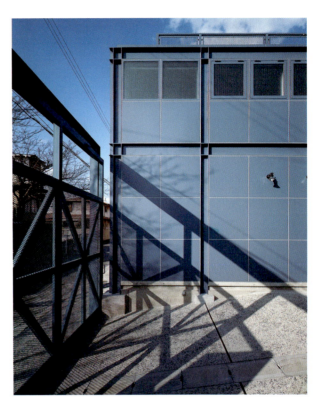

KIM HOUSE 1987/2011

1987/2011, 大阪市生野区
Ikuno-ku, Osaka

1987年。
　若い夫婦とその母親、それにお子さんが3人という合計6人、それも3世代同居のための住宅の設計を依頼された。間口3mで奥行き18m、敷地面積50m²弱という大阪に典型的な〈鰻の寝床〉の敷地、しかも重機が入れない軟弱地盤にローコストというプロジェクトだった。建物の荷重が敷地全体に平均するような形態とし、それをスラブ全体で受けて地面に浮遊するという構造、短辺方向の日の字の鉄骨架構を工場制作し、現場に仮固定した後に床スラブを打設することで固定する、短辺方向をラーメン構造、長辺方向をブレース構造とするという解決案はそうした条件から決まったものだ。出来上がった当時は安藤忠雄の住吉の長屋の模倣だと言われることもあったが、どちらもギリギリの限界条件が導いた解答である故に結果として似ているのだ、という思いがあり、特に気にならなかった。
そして2011年。
　望外の喜びはそれから24年の年月が経ち、クライアントからの封書を受け取る。それにはこの住宅の住まい手が夫婦2人だけになり、改めて2人だけの住まいとして改装したい旨が記してあり、さらにもっともうれしかったのは、この家で大きくなった子供達が改装設計をわたしに依頼すべきだ、と言っていると記されていたことだ。折版の屋根の上を歩いていたあのいたずらっ子達がわたしを推薦してくれたのなら、やるしかないではないか。それが2011年だった。それから数年後、再び会った彼は立派な医師になっていた。今度はわたしが彼に面倒を見てもらう順番なのだ。

The year was 1987.
　I was asked to design a house for a three-generation family of six members consisting of a young couple, their mother, and their three children. Not only was the site one of Osaka's typical "eel's nest" lots that measured roughly 50 m2 with a width of 3 m and depth of 18 m, but the soft ground prevented the use of heavy machinery, and the project also had a limited budget. These conditions were what determined my decisions to shape the building so that it would evenly distribute its weight across the site, to make a floating slab structured to support the building's weight across its entire surface, to prefabricate the double-square steel frames in the short direction in a factory, to temporarily erect the frames on site before fixing them into place by pouring the floor slab, and to employ a truss structure in the short direction and a brace structure in the long direction. When the building was completed, some called it a copy of Tadao Ando's Row House in Sumiyoshi, but I was not particularly bothered by this because I believed that their similarities were the result of the severely restrictive conditions that they both had to address.
Fast forward to 2011.
　I was pleasantly surprised when the client sent me a letter 24 years later. It informed me that the couple were now the only residents of the house and that they wanted to remodel the house as a home for two. What made me even happier was the note that their children who had grown up in the house were urging them to ask me to do the redesign. I could not decline knowing that those little rascals who used to climb onto the corrugated roofs had nominated me. This was in 2011. When I met the son several years later, I found out that he had become a doctor. It was now my turn to be taken care of by him.

Site Plan 1 : 1800

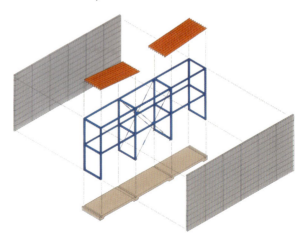

Axonometric Drawing

右頁／ファサード。構造スパンで2,580mmというスケール。
opposite / Façade. It has a structural span of 2,580 mm.

1987

ダイニング・テーブル越しに中庭を見る。中庭に面した開口部は100％開放可能な形式とすることで中庭と連続する空間を実現する。

View of the courtyard beyond the dining table. The opening facing the courtyard can be opened by 100% to create a single space that is continuous with the courtyard.

左／中庭からダイニング・ルームを見返す。
右／階段ディテール。ブレースと勾配を揃えた階段。
右頁／中庭夕景。

left / View back towards the dining room from the courtyard.
above / Stair details. The angle of the stairs and braces match.
opposite / Evening view of the courtyard.

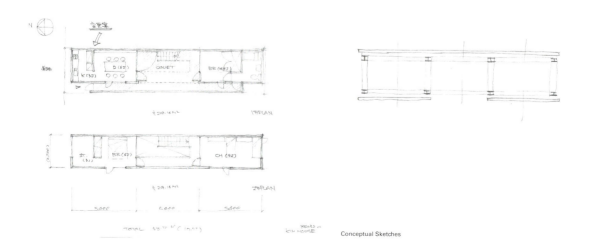

Conceptual Sketches

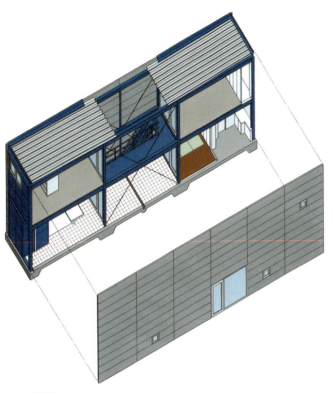

Axonometric Drawing

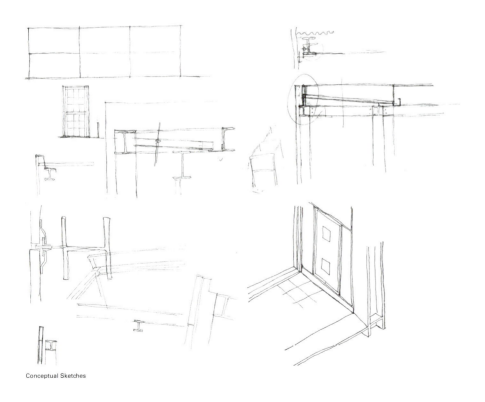

Conceptual Sketches

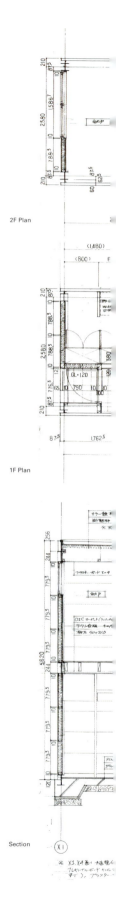

2F Plan

1F Plan

Section

● KIM HOUSE 1987/2011

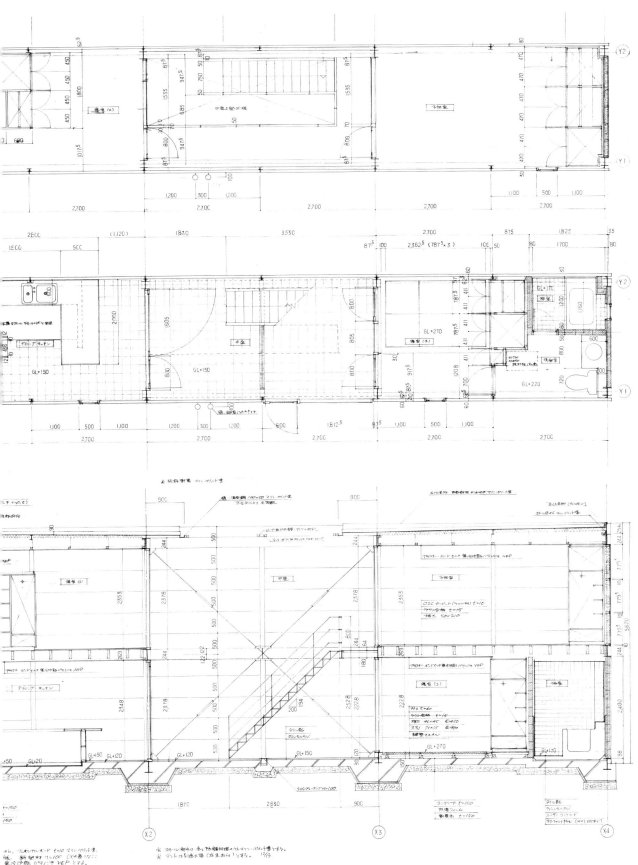

2011

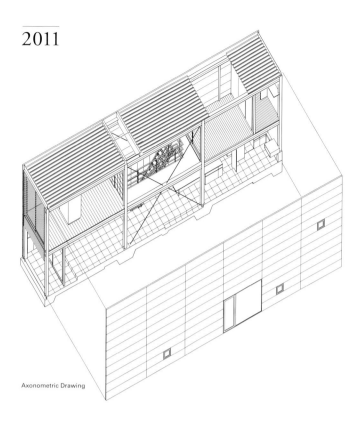
Axonometric Drawing

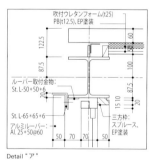
Detail "ア"

Detail "ウ"

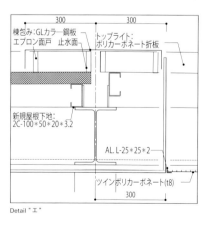
Detail "エ"

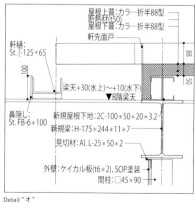
Detail "オ"

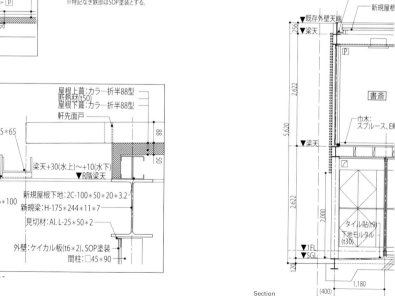
2F Plan / 1F Plan / Section

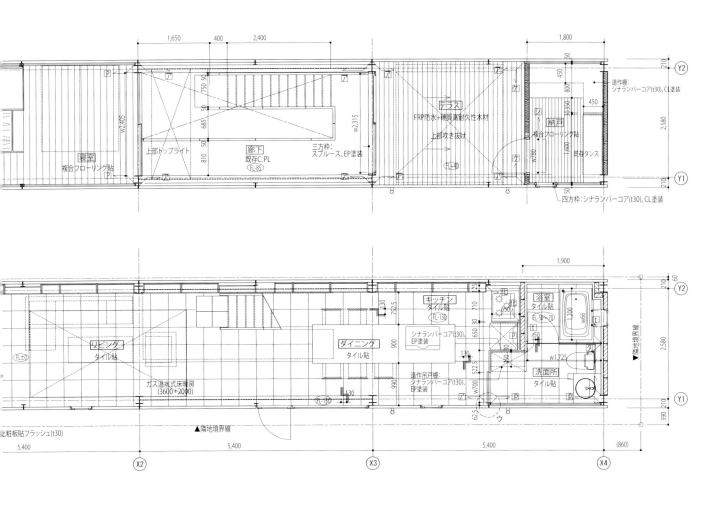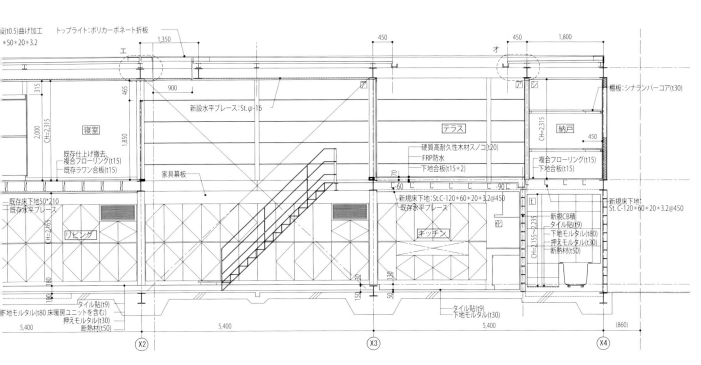

44-45頁／ファサードから奥行方向を見る。右側壁面と階段はオリジナルのまま。
左／ファサード・ディテール。
右／前面道路方向を見る。
下／新しくつくったダイニング・キッチンと壁面収納。
右頁／階段部の詳細。オリジナルの階段と新しく設けた1階の壁面収納。

pp. 44–45 / View into the back from the façade. The right-hand wall and stairs are the originals.
far left / Façade details.
left / View towards the front street.
below / The new dining/kitchen room and wall storage.
opposite / Stair details. The original stairs and the newly added wall storage on the first floor.

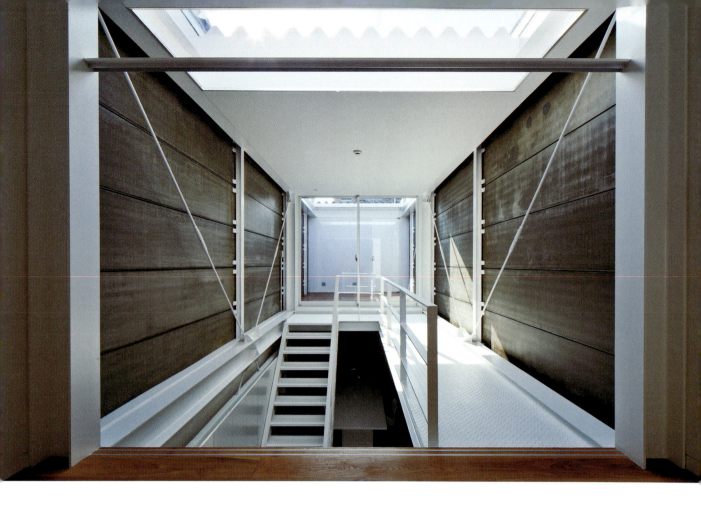

上／2階寝室からテラス方向を見る。手前は新しく設けたスカイライト。
左／新しく設けた2階テラス。
右／スカイライトと寝室。
右頁／ファサード夕景。

above / View towards the terrace from the second-floor bedroom. The skylight in the foreground was newly added.
far left / The new second-floor terrace.
left / Skylight and bedroom.
opposite / Evening view of the façade.

京都科学・開発センター
Kyoto Kagaku Research Institute

1990, 京都府木津町
Kizu-cho, Kyoto

この頃から、柱の建築、壁の建築ということを考え始める。柱こそが建築であり、壁はロマンティックな2次的要素ではないのか、ギリシャの神殿でも外周に列柱があり、壁はその内側にメガロンとしてあるだけではないのか、その壁を改めて建築の主題としたのがミース・ファン・デル・ローエ、例えばバルセロナ・パヴィリオンだと考えてみたらどうだろう、といったことだ。

この研究所は古い美術工芸品の補修などを行うための場所であり、緻密な作業の合間に眼を休めるための緑や、休憩して見上げる時に見える空の形といった、自然との出会いを創り出すことが最初に決めた主題だった。

一方自分自身にとっての課題、それは〈柱〉そのものは自分が取り扱うにはまだ荷が重過ぎるので、とりあえずはスティールのフレームとコンクリートの壁との関係を主題としたい、しかし遠くにアクロポリスの丘を見るような建築を構想したいと思っていた。今から思うと、赤面するほど壮大な想いだが、久しぶりに敷地60m²の都市住宅ではなく、広く、しかも道路や隣地とレベル差のある敷地を初めて前にして、気負い立っていたのだろう。

そんな気負いはともかく、結果については満足している。棟が上がり、コンクリートの連続する壁の上に鉄骨フレームが浮遊した時、この場所を支配する建築的秩序が出現したと思った。もっともパネル壁やサッシュで仕上げられていくに連れて、場の支配力が弱くなっていくことに焦ったことを覚えている。

I started thinking about the ideas of an architecture of columns and an architecture of walls from around this time. I pondered: Is the column not the very essence of what architecture is, and is the wall not just a romantic secondary element? Is the Greek temple not lined with columns along its perimeter, while the walls merely demarcate the megaron inside? Could Mies van der Rohe be considered as one who reinstated the wall as the main subject of his architecture, say, for example, through the Barcelona Pavilion?

This research institute was to be a place where people would repair old artwork. I decided from the outset to focus on setting up encounters with nature, such as by providing greenery and shaping the sky for the staff to relax their eyes on during their breaks from the painstaking work.

I also gave myself a separate problem to deal with. The problem of the *column* itself, I decided, was still too hefty for me to handle, so I sought to instead address the problem of the relationship between the steel frame and concrete walls—whilst envisioning an architecture that would bring to mind the sight of the Acropolis in the distance. It makes me blush to think of the grandiosity of my vision now. I undoubtedly was emboldened by the site, which for once was not a 60 m² lot for an urban house and even had a level difference from the street and adjacent lots.

However emboldened I may have been, I am satisfied with the outcome. When the building was topped out and the hovering steel frame took its position above the concrete walls, it really felt as if an architectural order had emerged and taken hold of the site. I also recall how I grew anxious as the strength of the architecture's hold over the site weakened as it got covered up with wall panels and sashes.

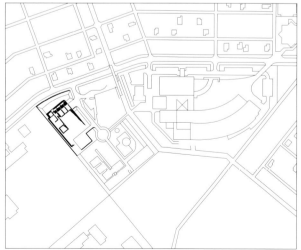

Site Plan 1:6000

右頁／1階のコンクリート壁。それに載せられた2階のスティール・フレームがこの場所に新しい〈秩序〉を導入する。建築とは〈秩序〉の別名か、とこの時考えた。

opposite / Concrete wall on the first floor. The steel frame placed on top of it brought a new order to the site. It dawned upon me here that Order is another name for Architecture.

Section 1 : 800

● Kyoto Kagaku Research Institute

長く延びる壁の上に直交グリッドが載る。そこに導入される外部空間と切り取られた内部空間の対比。
The orthogonal grid sits atop the long walls. The exterior spaces introduced into the composition contrast to the interior spaces framed within it.

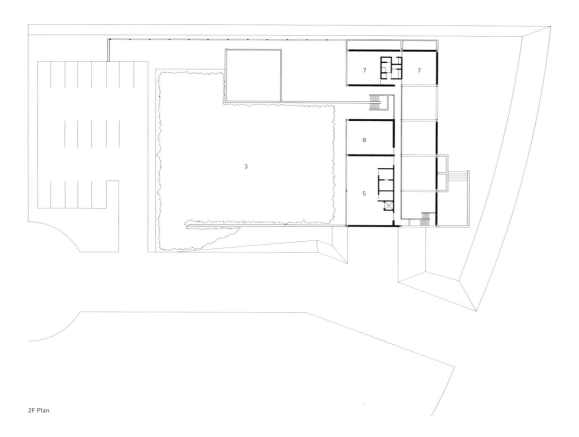

2F Plan

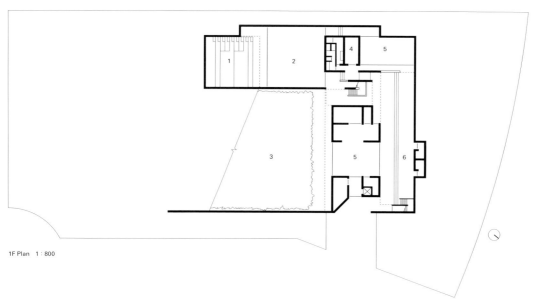

1F Plan 1:800

1 屋外展示　outdoor exhibition space
2 展示室　exhibition room
3 前庭　front garden
4 倉庫　storage
5 研究室　research room
6 中庭　courtyard
7 事務室　office
8 会議室　conference room

上／RCの壁とスティールのフレーム。そこに侵入する緑の斜面。
左／アプローチ。
右／屋外展示スペースとその向こうにアプローチの屋根を見る。
top / The RC wall, steel frame, and encroaching green slope.
above / Approach.
right / View of the outdoor exhibition space with the roof of the approach behind it.

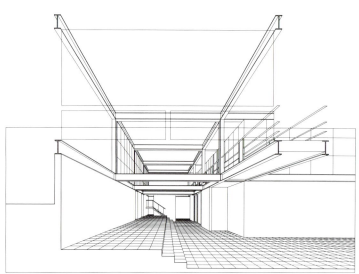

Perspective Drawing

● Kyoto Kagaku Research Institute

左／山城国の穏やかに延びるランドスケープの中に屹立する〈秩序〉をつくり出すこと。
右／中庭から研究室越しに前庭を見る。

left / I sought to create an order that would rise up above the gently rolling landscape of the Yamashiro Province.
right / Forecourt beyond the research rooms as seen from the courtyard.

1 前庭　front garden
2 事務室　office
3 中庭　courtyard
4 展示室　exhibition room
5 屋外展示スペース　outdoor exhibition

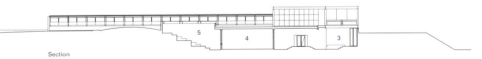

Section

Section

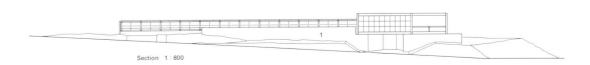

Section　1：800

● Kyoto Kagaku Research Institute

上／東側全景。
左頁／北側立面。斜面の上に載せられた箱。ただし内側はヴォイド。
above / General view of the east side.
opposite / North façade. A box placed atop a slope. The inside is actually a void.

日本橋の家
House in Nipponbashi

1992, 大阪市浪速区
Naniwa-ku, Osaka

ちょっとした病気で入院していた時、その病室に、当時のスタッフがぼやぼやしてないで仕事して下さいね、と言って届けてくれた資料がこの住宅だった。既に幾つか都市住宅の設計経験を重ねていた当時、〈中庭〉だけが都市住宅の鍵なのだろうか、他に可能性はないのだろうか、と新しい屋外空間の発見の可能性を模索していた。

その頃、香港という都市が面白くてよく通っていた。ある時友人の家で食事を共にすることになり、ハッピーバレーを訪ねる。競馬場に面した20数階建てのビルの屋上増築住居が友人の家だった。夕方、屋上のテラスで風に吹かれながら競馬場を見下ろす。疾走する馬やレースに興奮する人達の表情はよく見えるのだが、その騒音は聞こえず、ただ風の音が聞こえるのみ。そこで初めて〈屋上庭園〉の意味を知った。ル・コルビュジエの定義を知ってから既に20年近くが経ち、ようやく屋上庭園の体験をしたわけだ。シャンゼリゼに面する建物への屋上増築住居、ベイステギ邸の新しさ、屋外に設えられた暖炉の向こうに見える凱旋門の意味がようやく分かったのだ。

それ以来、熱に浮かされたように、屋上庭園、屋上庭園、と繰り返し念ずるようになる。屋上庭園とそれを可能にした近代という時代、さらに屋上庭園が葬り去った〈屋根〉の持つ意味、特に歴史的意味について考えるようになり、さらに基壇──あるいは、ルスティカ、と言ってもいい──やピロティの意味にまで思いを致すようになる。それは全て、このハッピーバレーの体験から始まったし、それはアジアの都市空間について考えるきっかけでもあった。そんな体験をひとつの建築に集約したのが、「日本橋の家」だった。

I once fell ill and was hospitalized. My staff delivered documents to my hospital room, telling me to not be idle and to do some work. Those documents were for this house.

At the time, I had already gained experience with designing several urban houses, and I had been seeking for a new kind of outdoor space. I questioned whether the *courtyard* was the only key to urban housing and wanted to know if there were other alternatives. That was also a time when I frequented Hong Kong, which fascinated me. I once went to Happy Valley when I was invited to a friend's house for a meal. The house was an addition built onto the roof of a 20-something-story tower that faced the racecourse. In the evening, I looked down at the racecourse from the windy rooftop terrace. I could clearly see the sprinting horses and the excited expressions of the spectators, but I could not hear them. All I could hear was the sound of the wind. That was where I first understood what a *roof garden* was. I finally experienced a roof garden almost two decades after I had learned about Le Corbusier's definition of it. I could finally appreciate the innovativeness of the Beistegui Apartment that he built on the rooftop of that building on the Champs-Élysées and the meaning of that outdoor hearth with the Arc de Triomphe visible beyond it.

I started chanting "roof gardens, roof gardens…" in my mind after that as if taken by a fever. My musings on the roof garden extended to the Modern period that made its existence possible; to the significance of the *roof* that was ousted by the roof garden (particularly the historical significance); and even to the meanings of the podium, or rusticated base, and pilotis. This was all sparked by that experience at Happy Valley, which also led me to think about urban space in Asia. I condensed the experience into a single work of architecture with the House in Nipponbashi.

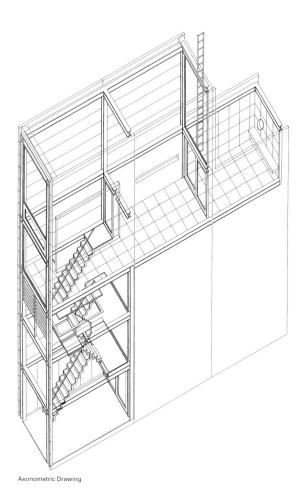

Axonometric Drawing

右頁／ファサード夕景。ファサードが半透明な素材で構成されているため、夕暮れには都市に開いた表情になる。

opposite / Evening view of the façade. At dusk, the façade made of a translucent material gives the house an open appearance to the city.

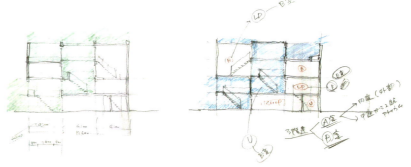

62-63頁上／立面・断面ドローイング。最終の実施案。
62-63頁下／最終に至るまでの別案スケッチ。
pp. 62-63 top / Elevation and section drawings of built scheme.
pp. 62-63 bottom / Sketches of alternative schemes.

● House in Nipponbashi

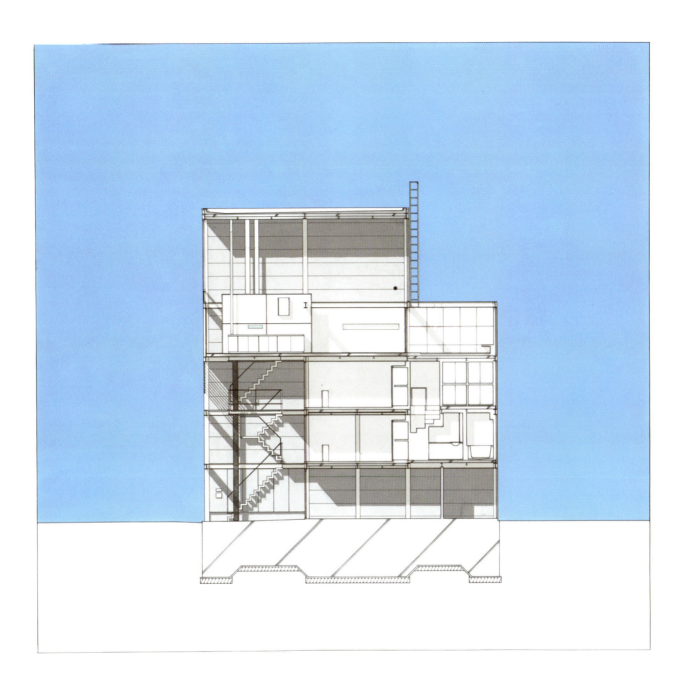
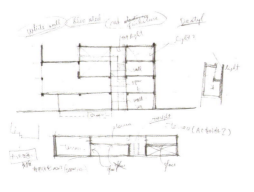
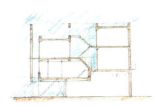
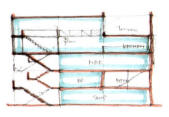

左上／都市に開いた階段部。
above / Stair area that is open to the city.

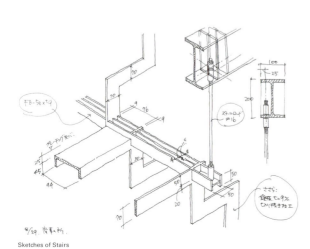

Sketches of Stairs

● House in Nipponbashi

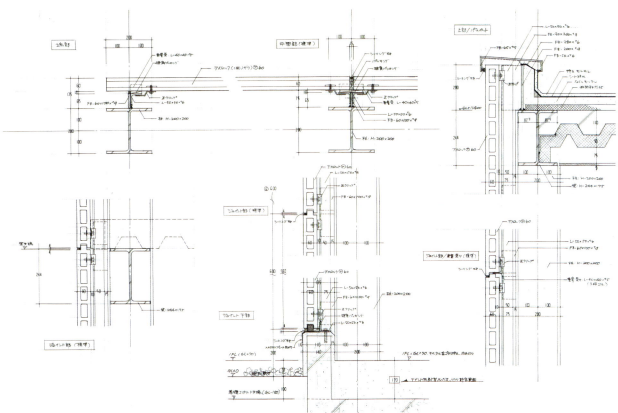

Wall Details

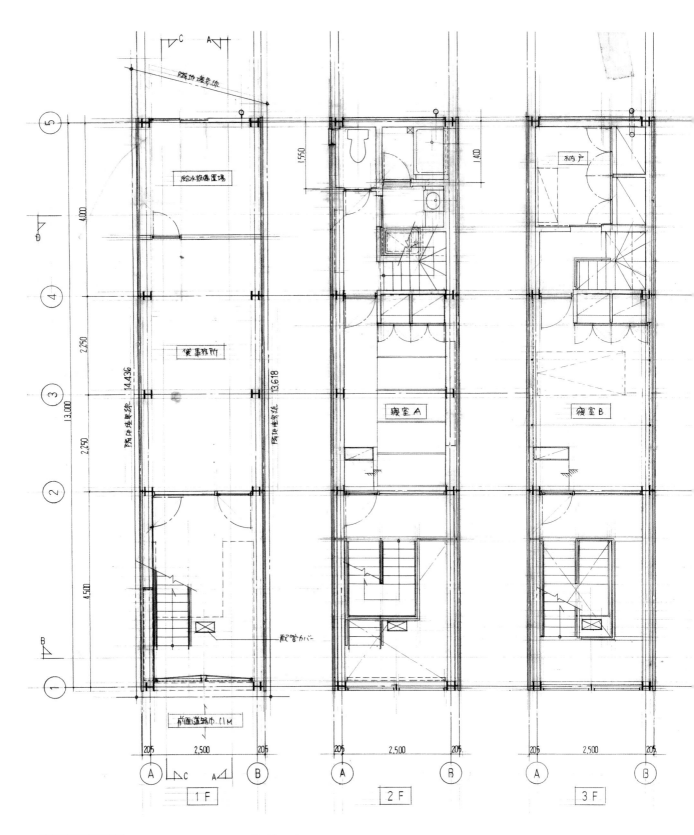

実施設計図の各階平面図。
68-69頁／最上階のインテリア。

Final floor plans.
pp. 68-69 / Interior of top floor.

House in Nipponbashi

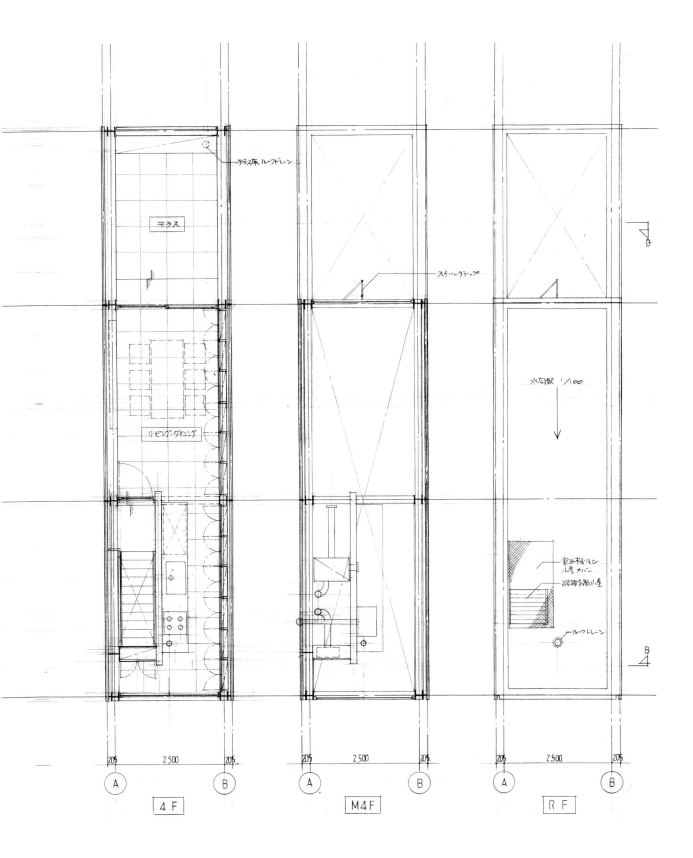

House in Nipponbashi

左頁／建物裏側の立面。
上／全景。
いずれも都市空間とこの建築との関係の在り方のヴァリエーションを見る。
下／そのきっかけを与えてくれた香港のハッピーバレー競馬場。

opposite / Back elevation.
above / General view.
These images illustrate two variations in the way this building relates to the urban space.
below / The Happy Valley Racecourse gave me the inspiration for this design.

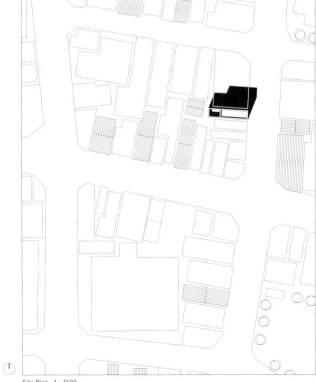

Site Plan 1 : 1500

下鴨の家
House in Shimogamo

1994, 京都市左京区
Sakyo-ku, Kyoto

1980年代の初め、フランク・O・ゲーリーの自邸や初期の作品を見に行った時、その金網や成形合板の使い方、DIYストアから持って来たままのような素材の使い方に衝撃を受けたことがある。それを畏友である渡辺真理が〈チェーンリンク・トランスペアレンシー〉、金網の透明性、と呼んだ時はうまい、やられた、と思った。コーリン・ロウの言葉でゲーリーをまとめるなんて、カリフォルニア以外ではあり得ないだろう。

ゲーリーのような素材の使い方は出来ないが、自分らしいやり方で圧倒的に〈即物的〉な建築は出来ないか、と考えてきたことの答えがこの建築だった。

工場制作としての溶接と現場での構法であるボルト接合を組み合わせることで実現するH形鋼の構造フレームに成形セメント板の外壁とガラスを〈即物的〉に取り付けるだけで出来上がる建築。これ以前の「KIM HOUSE」や「日本橋の家」と同じ構法ではあるのだが、それらには中庭や屋上庭園といった、別の主題があった。この「下鴨の家」には中庭も無ければ、屋上庭園も無い。敷地と呼ばれる限定された場所の中に可能な限り大きな気積を持つ内部空間を確保することが主題であり、そのためには架構と外皮が主題とならざるを得なかったのだ。その結果として思いもかけず〈即物性〉が立ち現れるのではないか、と考えていた。

When I went to look at Frank O. Gehry's house and his early work at the start of the 1980s, I was shocked by how he used wire netting, molded wood, and other materials that seemed to have come straight out of a DIY store. When Mari Watanabe, my respected friend, described Gehry's work as "chain-link transparency", I thought, *touché*. Only in California would Gehry be summed up with the words of Colin Rowe.

I could not use materials in the same way as Gehry, but I wondered whether I could create an architecture so powerfully *sachelichkeit* (matter-of-fact) in my own way. This project was the result of my pondering.

This architecture of cement panel exterior walls and glass fixed *matter-of-factly* to an I-beam structural frame was realized through a combination of factory welding and on-site bolting. The earlier KIM HOUSE and House in Nipponbashi were built in the same way, but they dealt with other themes, such as the courtyard and roof garden. The House in Shimogamo has neither a courtyard nor a roof garden. The theme here was to secure an interior space with the largest possible volume in the confined place described as the site, and this inevitably made the structure and skin the main subjects. I believed that this just might be able to bring about that quality of *matter-of-factness*.

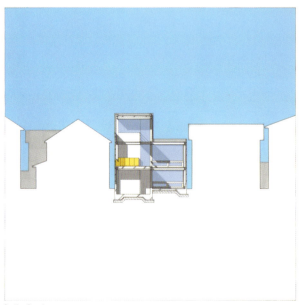

Section Drawing

建築が〈即物的〉であることを教えてくれたゲーリー自邸 (1978)。
右頁／前面道路方向の見返しで都市との関係を示す。
The Gehry Residence (1978) taught me how "matter-of-fact" architecture can be.
opposite / The view back towards the front road illustrates the house's relationship with the city.

鉄の構造体、成形セメント板の外壁、スチールサッシュとガラスといった素材をそのまま組み合わせ、アッセンブルすることで建築をつくりたいと夢見ていた。

I envisioned creating an architecture made by assembling the steel structural components, extruded cement panel siding, steel sashes, and glass panes just as they are.

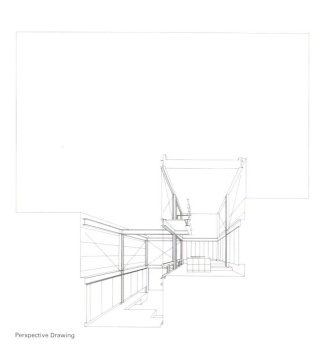

Perspective Drawing

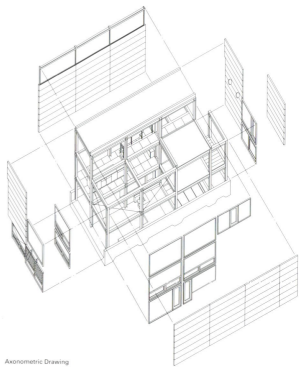

Axonometric Drawing

● House in Shimogamo

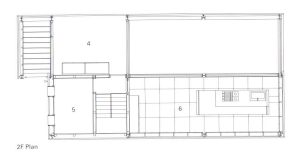

2F Plan

Section

1 中庭   courtyard
2 和室   tatami room
3 ワークショップ workshop
4 寝室   bedroom
5 書斎   study
6 ダイニング   dining room

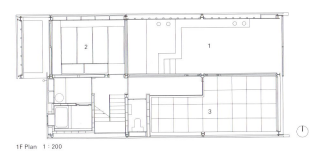

1F Plan 1:200

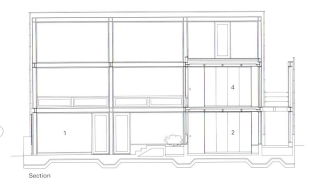

Section

76-77頁／2階リビングのキャットウォークから都市を望む。
上／街路とファサードの関係。
左／建築の内部空間と都市との関係を見る。
右頁／ファサードの構成。

pp. 76-77 / View out to the city from the catwalk in the second-floor living room.
above / Relationship between the street and façade.
left / Relationship between the interior and the city.
opposite / Façade composition.

Site Plan　1 : 1000

● House in Shimogamo

紫野和久傳
Restaurant "Murasakino Wakuden"

1995, 京都市北区
Kita-ku, Kyoto

数寄屋大工である中村外二工務店と創った建築。京都に居ながら〈和〉の世界とはなるべく距離を置いていようと決心していたわたしに、その世界を教えてくれた1人が中村義明さんだった。大徳寺真珠庵所有の建物に高台寺にある料亭の和久傳が入り、施工はその中村外二工務店というプログラムを聞いただけで、そこに設計で加わるというのは、現代建築家としては身構えてしまわざるを得ないのは正直なところだろう。でもその時考えたのは、京都から逃げてばかりいても逃げ切れるものではないだろう、いつの時点かで京都と関わるのだとすれば、今こそが最良の機会ではないか、そう決心して関わることを決めた仕事だった。

コンクリートと栗の外装、土のたたきの床に左官の中村塗り仕上げや障子の使い方、それに構法としての数寄屋的プレファブリケーションなど、このプロジェクトで初めて試みたことは数多い。自分がものを知らないことに絶望し、でもその中から生まれた想い、仕上げや構法を中村外二工務店に相談すると、出来ないと言われたことなど一度も無かった。こちらもだんだんこれは出来ないだろうと言われそうなことを探して、提案するようになる。その度にいとも簡単に、出来るよ、と言われた時、日本建築の伝統、それに数寄屋大工の心意気を知ることになる。今から考えると、出来ないなんて絶対言わない、というのが中村さんの意地だったのではないか、とも思うのだが。

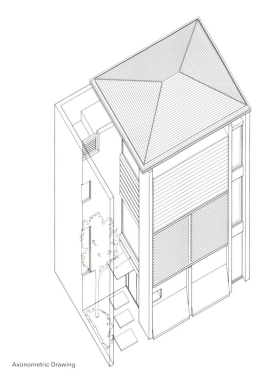

Axonometric Drawing

I made this building with Nakamura Sotoji Komuten, a company specializing in *sukiya* carpentry. Yoshiaki Nakamura was one of the people who opened my eyes to the world of *wa* [Japanese-ness], which I had been determined to keep a distance from despite living in Kyoto. Even just hearing the program—which entailed making a new location for Wakuden, a Japanese restaurant at Kodaiji, in a building owned by the Daitokuji Shinjuan, with Nakamura Sotoji Komuten handling the construction—any contemporary architect would surely have braced themselves at the thought of taking part in it as the designer. But this was the job that brought me to realize that I was never going to be able to elude Kyoto even if I kept running, and it made me decide that if I was going to get involved with Kyoto at some point anyway, there should be no better opportunity than this for me to do so.

There were many things that I experimented with for the first time through this project, such as the exterior of concrete and chestnut, the earthen floors with an exposed troweled underlayer finish, the treatment of the *shoji* screens, and the method of prefabricated *sukiya* construction. I despaired over my lack of knowledge, but this led me to come up with my own ideas for finishes and construction methods. When I consulted Nakamura about them, he never once told me that something could not be done. I eventually started to look for ideas to pitch to him that I thought he would not be able to do. Every time he readily told me that he could do it, my appreciation grew for the tradition of Japanese architecture and for the spirit of the *sukiya* carpenters. Thinking about it now though, I also suspect that Nakamura might just have been determined to never say he could not do something.

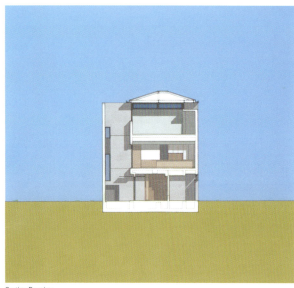

Section Drawing

左／小さな中庭と内部空間を見る断面ドローイング。
右頁／中庭からのアプローチ。
left / Section drawing showing the small courtyard and interior spaces.
opposite / Approach from the courtyard.

1階はさながら地下のような、光の限定された空間。主階である2階は中庭と道路向かいの大徳寺の両方に開いた空間とした。

The ground floor with limited light has a subterranean feel. I opened up the main floor above to both the courtyard and Daitokuji temple complex across the road.

● Restaurant "Murasakino Wakuden"

Section 1:200 South Elevation

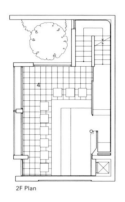
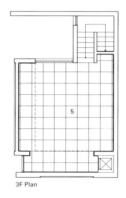

1F Plan 1:200　　2F Plan　　3F Plan

1　中庭　courtyard
2　店舗　store
3　事務室　office
4　ダイニング　dining room
5　厨房　kitchen

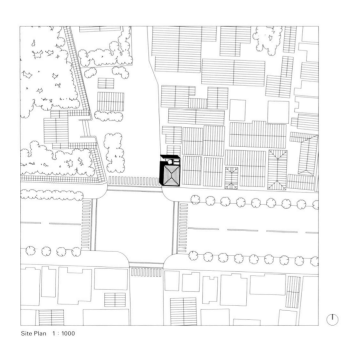

Site Plan 1:1000

左下／西に拡がる大徳寺との関係を示す配置図。
右頁／主階である2階が夕刻には都市から垣間見える。ちなみに2階を主階としたのはこの前面道路を通る観光バスの屋根越しに大徳寺を眺めるため。

left / Site plan showing the building's relationship to the Daitokuji complex to the west.
opposite / One can glimpse into the second level from the street in the evening. I put the primary floor on the second level in order to secure a view of Daitokuji over the passing sightseeing buses on the front road.

● Restaurant "Murasakino Wakuden"

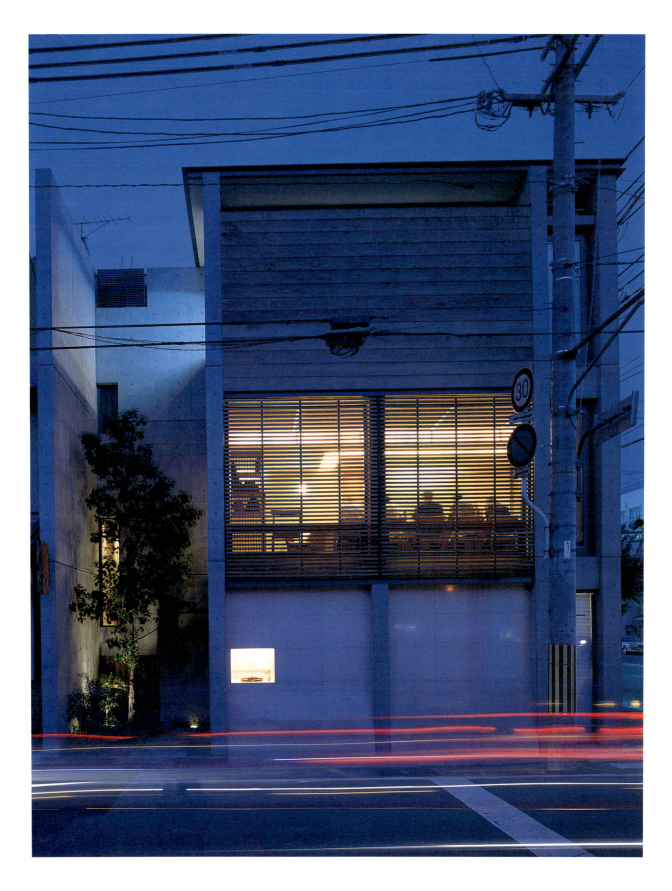

山口大学医学部創立50周年記念会館
Memorial Hall in Yamaguchi

1997, 山口県宇部市
Ube, Yamaguchi

戦後に新制大学となった山口大学、その医学部の創立50周年を記念して大学構内に建設する記念会館のプロジェクトである。

山口県宇部市の医学部キャンパスを訪ねると、その敷地の西端に荒れ果てた日本庭園があった。それが20年近く前に創立30周年を記念して卒業生から寄贈された庭園であり、20年の間手を入れられず、荒れ果てたままで、まったくメンテナンスされていない。その場所に50周年の記念会館を建設するのであれば、荒れ果てたままで放置されていた日本庭園を再生すること、新しい建築はせいぜいその背景となるようなものでいいだろうというのが、最初の想いだった。昔読んだフランシス・バーネットの『秘密の花園』〈Secret Garden〉の壁に囲まれ閉鎖されていた庭園、それを再生したメアリーに自分をなぞらえる訳ではないが、誰もが見向きもしなくなっていた庭園を再生するという主題に興奮していたことを覚えている。

建築はその日本庭園からアプローチする計画とし、既存の庭園を再生した上に新しくウッドデッキを重ねる。過去の卒業生達の寄贈した庭園をそのままにするのではなく、現代の視点を重ねながら改めて体験してもらうこと。

その庭からの導線はそのまま建築の内部まで続き、スロープが最上階まで連続する。庭園を経験するように建築を体験してもらいたい、そのことが30周年を記念する庭園と新しく50周年を記念して計画された建築とを繋ぐだろうと考えていた。

This was a project to build a memorial hall to commemorate the 50th anniversary of the founding of the medical school at Yamaguchi University, which had been reinstituted after the war.

When I visited the medical school campus in Ube, Yamaguchi, I found a dilapidated Japanese garden at the west end of the project site. The garden had been endowed by alumni to mark the school's 30th anniversary almost two decades earlier, but it had not been maintained at all and had fallen into ruin. My first thought was that the garden needed to be revived if a memorial hall for the 50th anniversary was going to be built beside it and that, if anything, the new building should be nothing more than a backdrop for the garden. I recall being excited by the idea of reviving this forgotten garden, identifying myself with Mary, who revives the closed walled garden in Frances Burnett's *The Secret Garden*, which I had read a long time ago.

I planned to lay down a new wooden deck in the revived garden so that the building would be approached from the garden. Rather than simply restoring the garden to how it used to be when it was endowed by alumni, I wanted it to be experienced anew from a present-day perspective.

The circulation through the garden leads directly into the building and continues up to the uppermost level via ramps. I wanted the building to be experienced like a garden because I believed that this would link the garden commemorating the school's 30th anniversary with the new building commemorating its 50th anniversary.

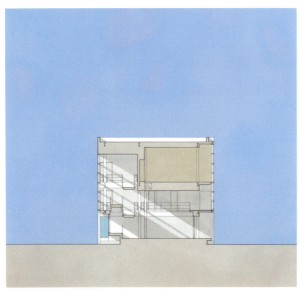

Section Drawing

緑が建築のすぐそばに存在する実例を想う時、ソウルの昌徳宮（1405）がまず頭に浮かぶ。昌徳宮の英語名は〈Secret Garden〉。

The Changdeokgung (1405) in Seoul is the first example that comes to mind when I think about architecture encompassed by greenery. In English, it is called the Secret Garden.

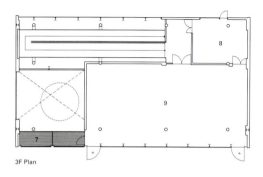
3F Plan

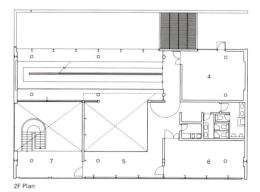
2F Plan

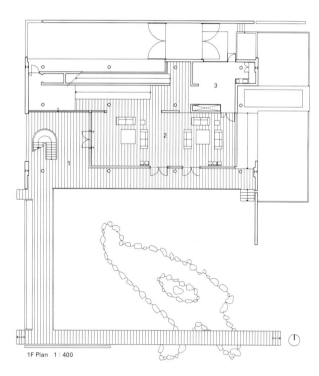
1F Plan 1:400

1	テラス terrace	6	会議室 conference room
2	エントランスホール entrance hall	7	バルコニー balcony
3	事務室 office	8	準備室 preparation room
4	資料室 archive room	9	多目的ホール large hall
5	サロン salon		

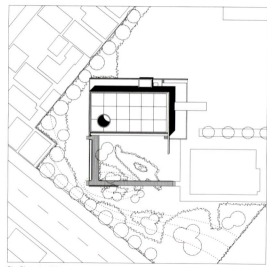
Site Plan 1:1200

Axonometric Drawing

87頁／建築内部まで導入された屋外空間や散策路としてのスロープを見る。

上／既存の日本庭園との関係を示すアクソメ。

右頁／建築内部まで導入された庭園散策路の延長としてのスロープ。

p.87 / View of the exterior spaces continuing into the building and the ramps that provide a walking trail.

above / Axonometric showing the building's relationship to the existing Japanese garden.

opposite / The ramps extend the garden path into the building.

● Memorial Hall in Yamaguchi

90-93頁／1階エントランスホールと2階サロンの内部空間。テラスや日本庭園などの屋外空間との関係を示す。

pp. 90-93 / Relationship between the interior spaces of the first-floor entrance hall and second-floor salon and the exterior spaces of the terrace and garden.

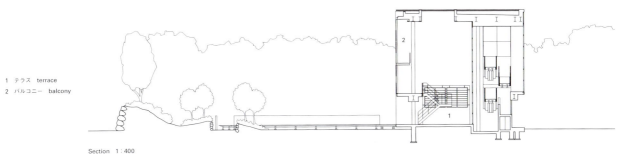

1 テラス　terrace
2 バルコニー　balcony

Section 1:400

上、左／建物西側のテラス。
右頁／日本庭園からテラス方向を見る。
above and left / West terrace.
opposite / View towards the terrace from the Japanese garden.

● Memorial Hall in Yamaguchi

苦楽園の家 I
House in Kurakuen I

1998, 兵庫県西宮市
Nishinomiya, Hyogo

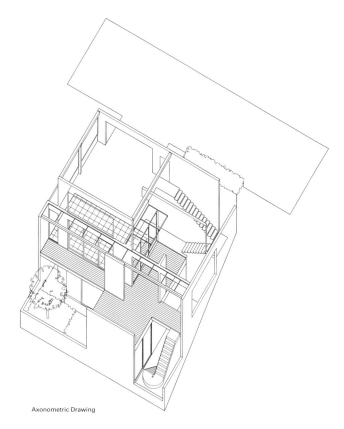

Axonometric Drawing

前面道路から約3m下がった所から南面する約30°の勾配の斜面、その先は擁壁で終わり、川の向こう側には緑に溢れる自然が拡がるという敷地である。道路面と同じレベルにはパーキング、そこからランプを下がると上階のリビング・ダイニング・スペース、もう一層下がると下階は個室階であり、下に下がるほどプライベートな空間へと変化する。その変化に合わせて、上階のリビング・ダイニング・スペースは開口部が全て引き戸で100%開放可能な形式とし、内部空間を外部空間であるテラスに積極的に繋げ、その上階全体を一室の屋外空間化が可能なように設計した。そうすることで南側の川向こうに拡がる緑とも一体化すると共に、川のせせらぎと鳥の声だけが聞こえてくる。

それと対比的に下階は閉じた空間とし、それぞれの寝室や浴室は閉じた中庭を持つことで上階とは違うプライベートな雰囲気を演出する。

このリビング・ダイニング・スペースの開放的な空間構成は、この頃通っていたバリ島の伝統住居の形式、敷地全体を壁で囲み、そこに独立した屋根だけのパヴィリオンが何棟か建つが、基本的には敷地全体でひとつのオープンな屋外空間となるという形式に魅了されており、それを現代住宅の空間として再解釈したいという少々強引な想いの結果でもあった。結果として少し大きくはあるが基本的には都市住宅であるこの建築が開放的な、どこか汎アジア的な雰囲気を持っているとすれば、この強引な引用の結果だと思う。

The site is a south-facing slope of about 30° that begins its descent from roughly 3 m below the fronting road and terminates at a retaining wall. Beyond it there is a river with lush greenery spread out on the other side. The house's spaces become more private as one descends further down the site, so the parking area is on the same level as the road, a ramp leads down into the living/dining room on the upper floor, and the bedrooms are located another level down at the bottom. Accordingly, I have actively connected the interior space of the living/dining room with the exterior terrace space by fitting all of the openings in the room with sliding doors that can be opened 100% to turn the entire upper floor into a single open-air space. When this is done, the space also merges with the greenery across the river to the south, and one can hear the murmuring of the water and the songs of the birds. The spaces of the lower floor, by contrast, are more closed. The bedrooms and bathrooms each have their own courtyards, giving the spaces a private feel different from the upper floor.

The airy spatial composition of the living/dining space is in part the outcome of my slightly farfetched idea to create a space for a modern house by reinterpreting a type of traditional housing found in Bali, which I often visited at the time of the project. The houses are built as walled compounds that contain several free-standing pavilions that are nothing more than roofs. I was fascinated by how these entire compounds essentially form single open-air spaces. So, if this building—which, though quite large, is still basically an urban house—seems to have somewhat of an airy Pan-Asian feel to it, that is probably the result of the forced reference.

右頁上／遠くに神戸を見る夕景。
右頁下／前面道路からのファサード。

opposite, top / Evening view with Kobe in the distance.
opposite, bottom / Façade as seen from the front road.

1 ガレージ garage
2 テラス terrace
3 リビング・ダイニング living/dining room
4 個室 private room
5 中庭 courtyard

East Elevation

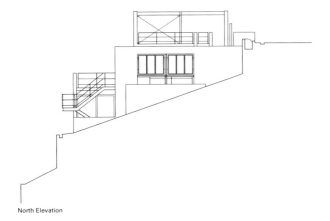

North Elevation

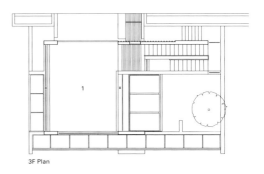

3F Plan

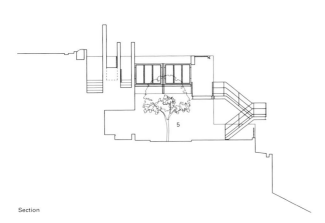

Section

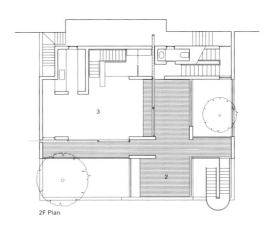

2F Plan

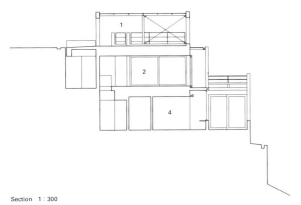

Section 1:300

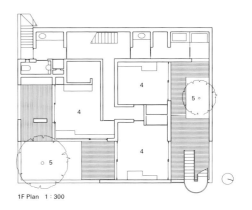

1F Plan 1:300

● House in Kurakuen I

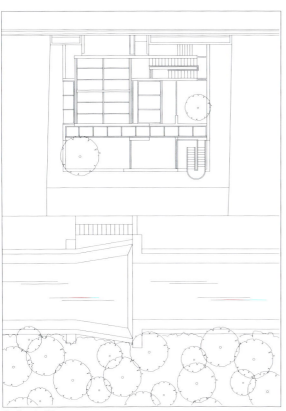

Site Plan 1 : 400

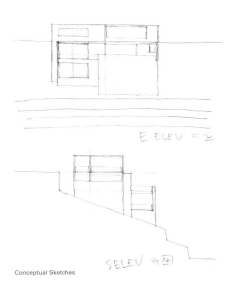

Conceptual Sketches

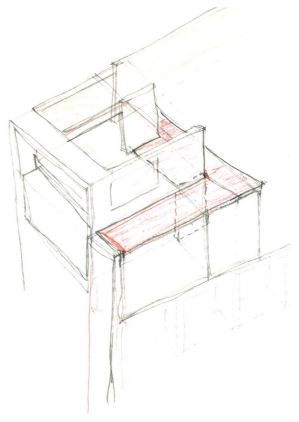

前面道路から約3m下がった場所から東方向に約30°の勾配で下がる敷地形状。下がった所の水路に水が流れ、その向かい側には緑の自然が残るという環境に建築が沈み込む。

The ground drops 3 m from the front road and slopes down to the east at about 30°. The architecture sinks into the environment that overlooks a flowing waterway with greenery beyond.

上、下／リビング・ダイニングとは対照的に閉じた階段の空間。
101-103頁／自然に開いたリビング・ダイニングとテラスの空間。

left and bottom left / The stair space is closed in contrast to the living/dining room.
pp. 101–103 / Spaces of the living/dining room and terrace that open up to the nature.

自然や都市と建築との関係を示す。
Relationship of the building to nature and the city.

● House in Kurakuen I

朱雀の家
House in Suzaku

1998, 奈良県奈良市
Nara, Nara

奈良郊外に建つ住宅である。

　クライアントはわたしの過去の仕事である「紫野和久傳」をご存知で、当初から中村外二工務店との協働で茶室を設けることが決まっていた。現代的な住宅の中に場違いに茶室が挿入されているかのような仕事にはしたくない、むしろどこから茶室の空間が始まっているのか分からないような、住宅全体が現代的であると同時に日本的な空間の雰囲気を持っているようなものにしたいと考えていた。

　従って、茶室を含めて住宅の中でそれぞれの機能を持った空間が連続的に繋がるような構成としたいというのがコンセプトであり、〈階〉によって空間が切れ切れにならないようふたつに分けたヴォリュームを半階ずらし、それをスロープで繋ぐこととした。階段を持たず、幅の狭い通路であるスロープが外部から内部まで全体を繋ぎ、その途中に天井高の高いリビング、それにそのスロープの行き着く先としての茶室など、それぞれの機能を配置し、場所によって変化させた光と開放性に従って空間形状は変化するものの、全体はひとつの連続的な空間として体験される。

　また、典型的な都市郊外の風景が拡がる外部から見ると、コンクリート打ち放しと木材の壁面、それに木製ルーバーによって閉じた表情に見えるが、茶室へのアプローチにも使う中央の中庭には全ての部屋が面しており、そこに対しては開放的な表情としている。

Elevation Drawing

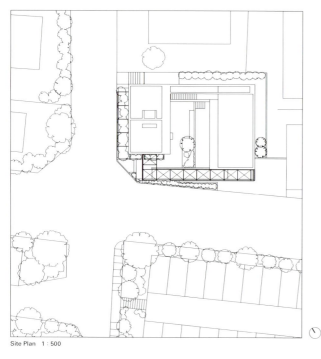
Site Plan 1:500

This is a house in the outskirts of Nara.

　The client was familiar with my earlier work for Murasakino Wakuden, and he had decided that I should work with Nakamura Sotoji Komuten to make a tearoom from the start. I did not want to make a modern house that looked like it had an out-of-place tearoom inserted into it. Rather, I wanted the whole house to feel modern and to have qualities of Japanese space at the same time so that it would not be clear where the tearoom space begins.

　My concept thus was to create a composition in which each of the various functional spaces in the house, including the tearoom, would be seamlessly linked together. In order to prevent the spaces from being chopped up into *stories*, I separated the house into two volumes, staggered them by half a floor, and connected them with ramps. I arranged the narrow stairless ramps so that they would tie the interior and exterior of the entire composition together as they passed through the various functional spaces, such as a high-ceilinged living room and the tearoom at the terminus. This enabled the whole composition to be experienced as a single continuous space even though the individual spaces took on different forms according to their different qualities of light and levels of openness.

　When seen from its typical suburban surroundings, the house appears reclusive with its exposed concrete and timber walls and wooden louver screens. However, it appears very open from the central courtyard, which all of the rooms face. The courtyard also serves as an approach to the tearoom.

右頁／南側道路向かいには集合住宅が建っているため、木製ルーバーで視線を切りながら中庭に光を導入する。

opposite / The wooden louvers screen views from the apartment across the street to the south while bringing in light from the courtyard.

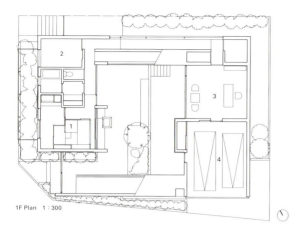
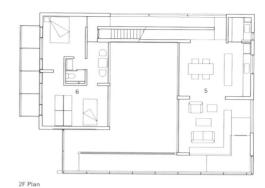

1F Plan 1:300

2F Plan

1 茶室　tearoom
2 趣味室　hobby room
3 書斎　study
4 ガレージ　garage
5 リビング・ダイニング　living/dining room
6 個室　private room

左、右／リビング・ダイニングへと至るアプローチ。
右頁／リビング・ダイニング。

below / Approach to the living/dining room.
opposite / Living/dining room.

● House in Suzaku

左／中庭から南方向を望む。
右／中庭から半階下がったレベルにある書斎から中庭方向を見る。
右頁／南側から中庭を見返す。

left / Southward view from the courtyard.
below / View towards the courtyard from the study located a half level down from the courtyard.
opposite / View back towards the courtyard from the south side.

1 茶室　tearoom
2 書斎　study
3 個室　private room
4 リビング・ダイニング　living/dining room

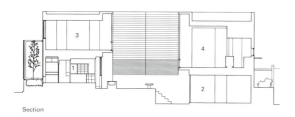

Section

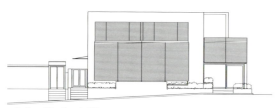

Northwest Elevation　1：300

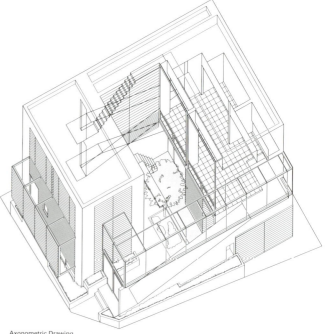

Axonometric Drawing

● House in Suzaku

上2点／茶庭へと至るアプローチのスロープ空間。
下2点／茶室内部。
右頁／茶室から中庭を見る。自分なりに孤篷庵(1793)を理解しようとした試み。左に見える手小鉢はルイス・バラガンのカプチン派修道院(1955)中庭の写し。
left / Ramp spaces on the approach to the tea garden.
below / Interior of tearoom.
opposite / I designed the basin on the left-hand side as an homage to the one at Luis Barragán's Convent of the Capuchinas Sacramentarias.

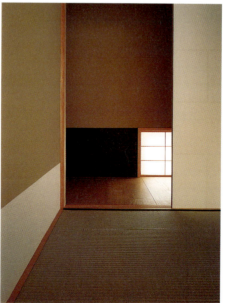

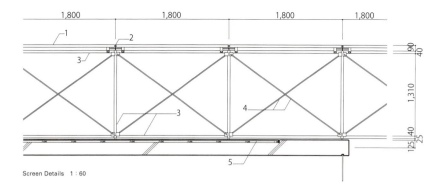

Screen Details 1:60

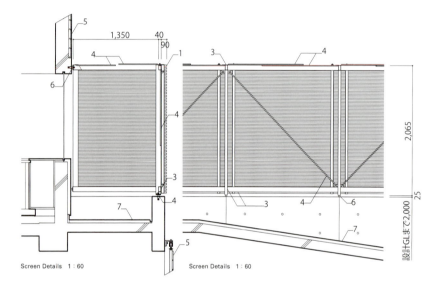

Screen Details 1:60   Screen Details 1:60

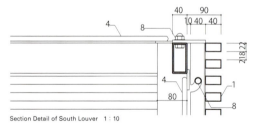

Section Detail of South Louver 1:10

1: 木製ルーバー
2: Fb6×90□P
3: □-40×80×3.2
4: 丸鋼ブレースΦ13
5: 横羽目板(米杉)
6: ケミカルアンカー
7: 豆砂利洗い出し
8: ボルトM12

上3点／都市とのインターフェイスとなる木製ルーバーのディテール。
下／西側の開口部に付く遮光のために突き出す木製ルーバー。

above / Details of the wooden louvers that serve as interfaces to the city.
left / The wooden louvers fixed to the west-side openings push outwards to block the light.

● House in Suzaku

右／リビング・ダイニング夕景。
下／南側夕景全景。都市との関係を示す。
right / Evening view of the living/dining room.
below / General view of the south side in the evening showing the house's relationship to the city.

かづらせい・寺町
Antique Gallery "Kazurasei"

2000, 京都市中京区
Nakagyo-ku, Kyoto

京都御所近く、寺町通りに面した骨董のギャラリーである。

1階、2階がギャラリー、3階が倉庫という構成で、平面中央に中庭と階段室を配置する。街並みに対しては少しファサードを後退させ、さらに1階を地盤面から少し下げることで導入のための数段の階段を設け、さらに導線を90°曲げることでアプローチの距離を取る。本当に数歩のことではあるのだが、骨董と出会うための演出空間、心の準備をするための空間を用意した。

内部に入ると左側に水庭、右にはスカイライトからの光を受ける階段があり、建物中央部には上方からの光が降り注ぐ。

展示される骨董は数百年の歴史をそれぞれ持っているものであるため、その背景となる建築の仕上げも視覚的のみならず、触覚的な次元でも質感の在る素材を採用することにした。コンクリート打ち放し、インド・シルク貼り、ブビンガ枠ヴェネチアン・スタッコ仕上げの展示パネルなどの壁面、木製パネルや紙貼りの天井など、使用する素材の決定には極めて神経質になったのを記憶している。

それぞれの素材がきちんと存在を主張出来るように、その取り付けディテールは可能な限り単純に見えるように考えた。例えば階段部分、スカイライトの和紙による光拡散面の天井など、一見するとごく簡単そうに見える天井面だが、その和紙パネルは意外に大きく、きちんと水平を保ちながら固定するのは簡単なことではない。そんな舞台裏の苦労がまったく見えないように、何事も無いかのように単純なディテールとするというのが、このプロジェクトで素材を扱う時の基本だった。

This is an antique gallery on Teramachi Street near the Kyoto Imperial Palace.

I made a composition with gallery spaces on the first and second floors, storage spaces on the third floor, and a courtyard and stairwell in the middle of the plan. I pulled the façade back slightly from the street, lowered the first floor slightly below grade to create a short set of preludial stairs, and bent the entry path by 90°, all in order to extend the approach. It was only a matter of adding several steps, but I wanted to set up a theatrical space for visitors to prepare their minds for encountering the antiques.

Upon entering, one sees light pouring down from above into the central part of the building, where there is a water garden to the left and a stairway illuminated by a skylight to the right.

I chose to use materials that would offer both a sense of visual and tactile texture for the architectural finishes that needed to provide a backdrop for the displayed antiques, which each had hundreds of years of history. I recall becoming very picky when deciding on what materials to use, such as for the walls of exposed concrete, wall cloth of Indian silk, display panels framed in Bubinga and finished with Venetian stucco, and ceilings finished with wood panels and paper.

I gave thought to how to make the joint details appear as simple as possible so that each of the materials would be properly expressed. For instance, the light-diffusing *washi*-paper skylight ceiling by the stairs may appear to be uncomplicated at first glance, but the *washi* panels are actually quite large, and it was not easy to fix them in place while keeping them flat. My basic attitude with respect to handling the materials in this project was to create simple details that would give no sign of such struggles that went on behind the scenes.

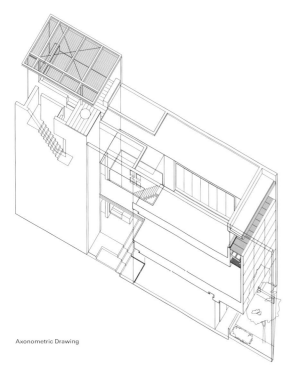

Axonometric Drawing

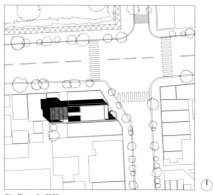

Site Plan 1 : 1500

右／配置図。北西は京都御所という交差点に建つ。
右頁／水と樹木を導入した小さな中庭と土のたたきで仕上げた床。

above / Site plan. The building stands at an intersection with the Kyoto Imperial Palace to the northeast.
opposite / The small courtyard with a water feature and tree and the earthen floor.

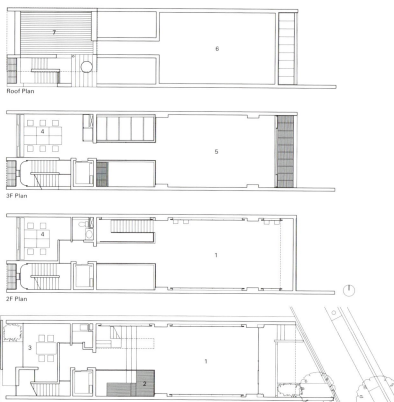

Roof Plan
3F Plan
2F Plan
1F Plan 1:300

上／1階入口から中庭方向を見る。
右頁／中庭横から前面道路方向を見返す。

above / View towards the courtyard from the first-floor entrance.
opposite / View back towards the front road from beside the courtyard.

1　ショールーム　showroom
2　中庭　courtyard
3　接客室　reception room
4　事務室　office
5　予備室　spare room
6　屋上庭園　roof garden
7　屋外接客スペース　outdoor reception space

● Antique Gallery "Kazurasei"

土、木材、鉄、布、左官仕上げ、紙、水、樹木など、それぞれの素材を自然のままに生かしながら構成したディテール。

I composed the details to preserve the intrinsic qualities of each material, such as the earth, wood, metal, fabric, plaster, paper, water, and trees.

1 ショールーム　showroom
2 事務室　office
3 予備室　spare room

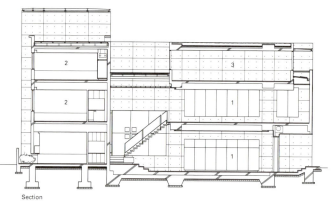

Section 1:300

Section

右頁上／2階中庭横から正面方向を見る。左の階段上は障子のスカイライトで石の中庭と対をなす。
右頁下／2階正面から中庭、階段を見返す。左に中庭、右に障子越しのスカイライトの光の対比が見える。

opposite, top / View towards the front from beside the courtyard.
opposite, bottom / View back towards the courtyard and stairs from the front. One can see the contrast between the light of the courtyard on the left and the skylight with the shoji panels on the right.

● Antique Gallery "Kazurasei"

上／屋上庭園から東山方向を見る。
左／中庭見上げ。
右／数段下がるアプローチの階段と版築でつくった腰壁。
右頁／ファサード。エントランスは道路からは少し下げてある。

above / View towards Higashiyama from the roof garden.
far left / View up through the courtyard.
left / The approach stairs and waist-height wall made of rammed earth.
opposite / Façade. The entrance is located slightly below the street.

● Antique Gallery "Kazurasei"

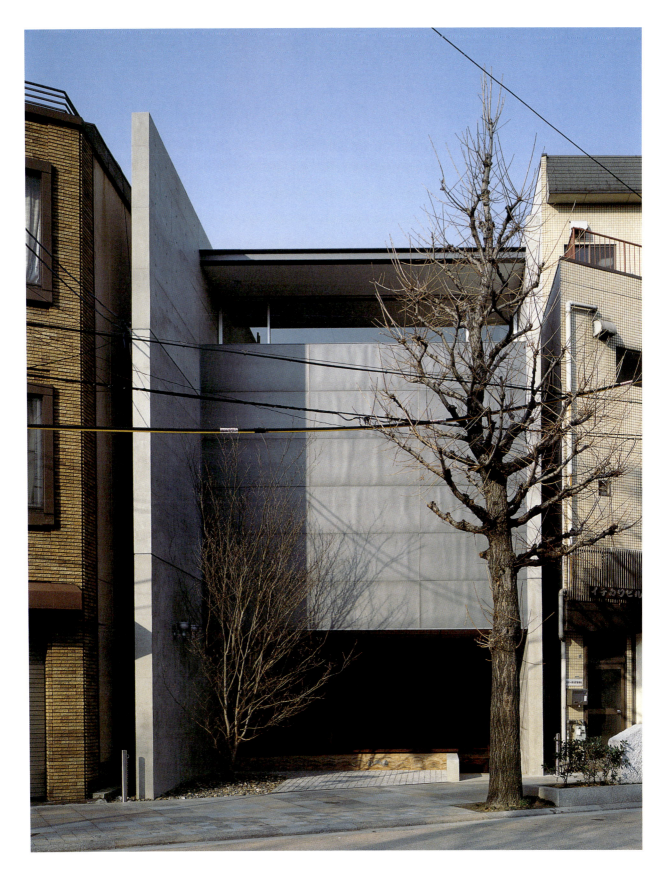

文京の家
House in Bunkyo

2000, 東京都文京区
Bunkyo-ku, Tokyo

東京都心部文京区内に計画した2世帯住宅である。

第2次世界大戦後に分割された住宅街の中の敷地に建つ住宅の建て替え計画だったが、敷地内には戦前から育っていたと思われる樹木が残っており、その緑は隣の敷地の緑へと連続的に繋がっていた。隣は新しく建て替えられた銀行の寮だったが、幸いその緑を残してくれており、こちらもその樹木を残せば本来はひと繋がりであった樹木群を保全することが出来ると考えた。

従ってこの場所の歴史を生き延びてきた緑を残すことを最重要条件とし、設計を始めた。検討してみると、木造の平屋の建築を2棟平行して配置する計画がその残された緑と建築との関係にもっとも無理が無く、しかもその2棟間を中庭とすることで保全された樹木と新しい中庭との関係を創り出すことが出来る。さらに平屋の内部空間と中庭や緑との相互関係も成立しやすいということで、現在の形に落ち着いた。

出来上がった姿だけを見ると、東京の都心部に在るにもかかわらず、緑の樹木に囲まれた木造平屋の建築という、どこか牧歌的でアナクロニスティックにも見える結果となったが、都心部に残る自然を可能な限り保全し、新しい建築の中に生かしていきたいと考えた結果がこういう形態に落ち着いただけである。

This is a two-family house that I designed in the Bunkyo ward of central Tokyo.

This was a project to rebuild a house on a lot in a residential district that had been subdivided after World War II. The site had trees that probably had been growing since before the war, and they formed a continuous belt with the trees on the adjacent property. The neighboring trees fortunately were preserved when a new dormitory building for a bank was built on the property. I realized that I would be able to save the whole belt of trees if I could also preserve the trees on my lot.

When I started on the design, I made it my utmost priority to preserve the trees that had managed to survive through the site's history. As I developed the plans, I found that I would be able to establish the most natural relationship between the exiting trees and architecture if I made two single-story timber structures arranged in parallel. I saw that this would also enable me to set up a new relationship between the trees and the new courtyard that would be created between the two wings. I settled on this as the final scheme because it also worked well for relating the interior spaces of the single-story volumes to the courtyard and trees.

Looking only at the completed form, one may think that the single-story wooden house that stands surrounded by trees despite being in central Tokyo feels somewhat pastoral and anachronistic. However, its form is simply the product of my wish to preserve as much of what little nature still survives in the city center and to give it a place to live within the new architecture.

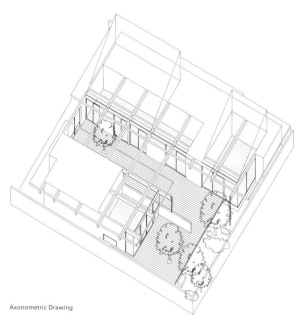

Axonometric Drawing

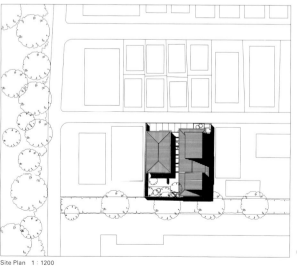

Site Plan 1 : 1200

右頁／中庭から東方向に残る樹木群を見る。
opposite / View towards the preserved stand of trees to the east from the courtyard.

SW-NE section 1

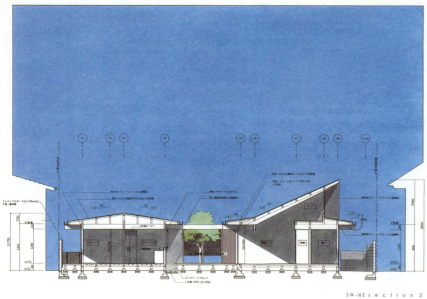

SW-NE section 2

HOUSE IN BUNKYO 02

Section Drawing

126-127頁／中庭西方向を見る。
右頁／この敷地に残っていた樹木群と新しく計画した建築との関係を示す。

pp. 126-127 / View towards the west end of the courtyard.
opposite / Relationship between the existing trees and the new building.

● House in Bunkyo

上／南棟を北棟より見る。
中／2棟の間の中庭とそれに繋がる手前のテラスを西方向に見る。
下／同じ場所から北を見る。いずれも樹木と新しい建築との関係を示す。

left / North wing as seen from the south wing.
below left / Westward view of the courtyard between the two wings and its adjoining terrace.
bottom left / Northward view from the same location. These images show the relationship between the trees and the new architecture.

中庭部分だけが少し開いたファサード。
The façade opens up just a little bit in the area of the courtyard.

Southwest Elevation 1:300

1 個室　private room
2 和室　tatami room
3 リビング・ダイニング　living/dining room
4 書斎　study
5 納戸　storage

1F Plan 1:300

苦楽園の家 II
House in Kurakuen II

2001, 兵庫県西宮市
Nishinomiya, Hyogo

「苦楽園の家 I」では、モダンデザインの衣装を着ながら空間の性格はアジア的な空間となることを指向したのだが、こちらはモダンデザインの継承と分析が主題だった。

「苦楽園の家 I」と対照的に、こちらは前面道路の北側、擁壁が約5m立ち上がった上に、南面する約30°の傾斜面の地盤がある。「苦楽園の家 I」が周辺に溢れる緑の自然にどう開くか、環境に開くことが主題だったのに対し、こちらはその敷地条件から周辺の自然との対応関係は成立しない。むしろ彼方に見える芦屋浜や大阪湾の風景、関西空港に着陸しようとする飛行機の姿、といった南に拡がる都市と彼方に見える瀬戸内海の風景を距離を持って見下ろすこと、その風景を如何に切り取るのか、ということが主題だと考えた。それを建築的に翻案すると、建築のenclosureやframingといった概念が鍵になると考え、大きなガラスの開口部を安易に採用するのではなく、如何に開口部を絞るか、を主題とした。主空間であるリビング・ダイニング・スペースにひとつのボックス、個室群用にもうひとつのボックス、半階ずらしたそのふたつのボックスを繋ぐスロープ部分にさらにもうひとつの、3つのボックス状ヴォリュームの構成とし、それに内部からの視線を優先して決定した開口を穿ち、同時にその開口部とずらしながらガラススクリーンや構造体を配置することで、内外空間のインターフェイスに変化を与える。

結果として、ル・コルビュジエのエスプリ・ヌーヴォー・パヴィリオンに似た表情を持つに至ったが、それはヴォリュームの壁面に穿つ開口部と内外を仕切るガラス面や構造体との関係を積極的にずらすことで内外空間の新しい関係を作り出すという戦略が、ル・コルビュジエ的な発想だったということだろうか。

In the House in Kurakuen I, I aimed to create a space that was dressed in modern design but had an Asian personality. This house was about inheriting and analyzing a modern design approach.

In contrast to the House in Kurakuen I, this house's site was a south-facing slope of about 30° that began its ascent from roughly 5 m above a retaining wall on the north side of its fronting road. While the House in Kurakuen I addressed the problem of how it should open up to the abundant greenery and environment of its surroundings, the site conditions of this house did not allow it the opportunity to respond to the nature immediately around it. I instead put the focus on how it should behold and frame from a distance the landscape of the sprawling city and Seto Inland Sea beyond it to the south, which offered sights of Ashiya Beach, Osaka Bay, and airplanes preparing to land at Kansai Airport. Translating this architecturally, I identified *enclosure* and *framing* as the key concepts for the architecture, and I decided to carefully restrict the openings rather than simply making large glazed openings. I thus set up a composition consisting of three box-shaped volumes—one box for the main living/dining space, one box for the group of bedrooms, and one box for the ramps connecting the two staggered boxes—and then made openings in them that were dictated by the views from the inside. At the same time, I arranged glass screens and structural elements in positions shifted off from the openings in order to add variation to the interfaces between the interior and exterior spaces.

The outcome turned out to resemble Le Corbusier's Esprit Nouveau Pavilion. Perhaps my strategy of relating the interior and exterior spaces in a new way by deliberately not aligning the wall openings of the volumes with the structure and glazing that defined the inside and outside was actually just a Corbusian idea.

Section Drawings

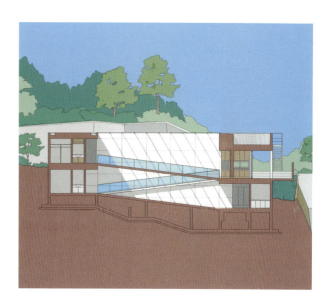

1 リビング living room
2 寝室 bedroom
3 ランプ ramp
4 ダイニング dining room
5 キッチン kitchen

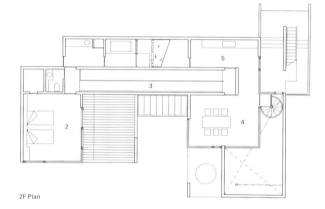

2F Plan

1F Plan 1:300

132頁／敷地との関係(左)と2棟の関係(右)を示す。
133頁／前面道路からの全景。右はリビング・ダイニング棟で左は個室棟。半階ずれているこの2棟はスロープで繋がる。

p.132 / Relationship between the house and site (left) and between the two wings (right).
p.133 / General view from the front road. The living/dining wing is on the right and the bedroom wing is on the left. A ramp connects the two wings that are staggered by a half floor.

● House in Kurakuen II

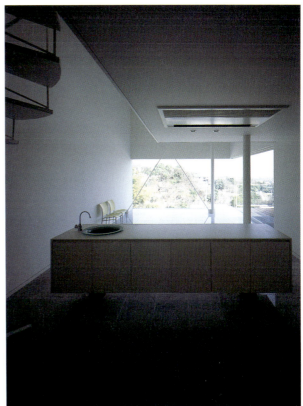

左頁／アプローチからリビングルームへの流れ。
左／リビングルームとダイニングルームの関係。
右／リビングルームから東方向を見る。

opposite, top / Sequence from the approach to the living room.
above left / Relationship between the living room and dining room.
above right / Eastward view through the living room.

Conceptual Sketch

House in Kurakuen II

136-137頁／リビングルームと外部との関係。
上／リビングルームとダイニングルームの関係。
右頁／テラスから遠くに大阪方向を見る。

pp. 136-137 / Relationship of the living room to the outside.
above / Relationship between the living room and dining room.
opposite / View from the terrace towards Osaka in the distance.

左、右／ダイニングルーム。
右頁／ダイニングルームからリビングルームを見下ろす。
left and above / Dining room.
opposite / View down into the living room from the dining room.

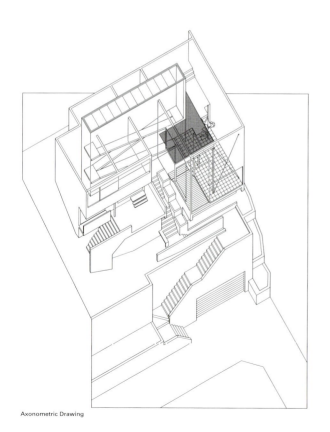

Axonometric Drawing

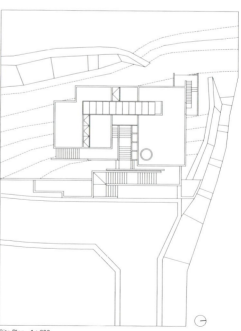

Site Plan 1 : 600

上／寝室とテラス。
下／浴室。
右頁／2棟を繋ぐスロープの空間とスカイライトからの光。
below / Bedroom and terrace.
bottom / Bathroom.
opposite / Ramp space connecting the two wings,
and the light from the skylight.

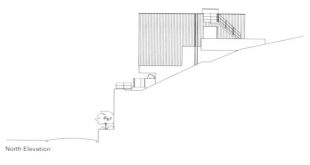

North Elevation

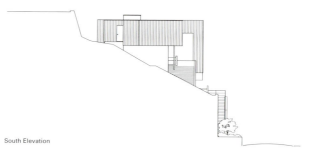

South Elevation

East Elevation　1：500

● House in Kurakuen Ⅱ

深谷の家
House in Fukaya

2001, 埼玉県深谷市
Fukaya, Saitama

この住宅は、クライアントからの突然の電話から始まった。

住宅の設計依頼ではあったのだが、ユニークだったのはその内容だった。

クライアントはアメリカの建築家であるピエール・コーニッグの仕事、1960年代のロサンゼルスを代表する建築であるケーススタディハウスの熱烈なファンであり、日本でそういう建築を設計出来るのはあなたですよね、というものだったのだ。簡単に言うと、もう21世紀になっているというのに、1960年代のピエール・コーニッグを演じて欲しいという依頼である。

わたし自身はケーススタディハウスの本をまとめてもいるし、もちろんそのファン。1981年にはガイドブック片手にレンタカーを運転し、ケーススタディハウスの何軒かは訪ねてもいる。新しいケーススタディハウスを設計して欲しいという話に乗らないわけはない。そんなふうにして始まったのが、このプロジェクトだった。

この住宅の設計期間中に偶然の機会でコーニッグさんと会うことが出来、ケーススタディハウスの#21と#22の案内図を自ら書いていただいた。それから暫くしてコーニッグさんの訃報を聞き、その時の直筆の案内図はわたしの家宝となっている。

この住宅は埼玉県深谷市に建つごく普通の住宅だが、その中庭にプールが在るのはそんな訳で、クライアントと建築家からのケーススタディハウスへのオマージュ、その象徴だと考えていただければいい。何時そのプールで泳ぐのかが重要なのではなく、プールの在る中庭を見ながら毎日の生活を送ることを夢見るライフスタイルも在る、ということだ。そこに流れている音楽は1950年代のクールジャズ、それもジェリー・マリガン以外には考えられないのはもちろんだ。

This house project started when the client called me out of the blue.

He had called to ask me to design a house, but what was unique was what he wanted.

The client was an ardent fan of the work of American architect Pierre Koenig—namely the Case Study Houses that defined 1960s Los Angeles architecture—and he wanted to know whether I was the one who could design him that kind of architecture in Japan. Simply put, he wanted me to act as Pierre Koenig from the 1960s despite the fact that it was already the 21st century.

I have put together a book on the Case Study Houses myself, and I am of course a fan of them. With guide book in hand, I even took a rental car out to visit several of the houses in 1981. There was no way that I was going to let the opportunity to design a new Case Study House go by.

And so, that was how this project started.

I had the chance opportunity to meet Mr. Koenig while I was designing this house, and he personally drew me a guide map for the Case Study House #21 and #22. I heard the news of his passing a little while later. His hand-drawn map has now become one of my personal treasures.

Although this is just an ordinary house in Fukaya, Saitama, the above is why it has a swimming pool in its courtyard. It should be thought of as symbolizing an homage to the Case Study Houses by way of the client and architect. It is not important whether one ever uses the pool; there is such a thing as a lifestyle where one dreams of living their everyday life beside a courtyard with a pool. The only music that could be playing in this house is 1950s cool jazz. In fact, I cannot imagine it being anything other than Gerry Mulligan.

ケーススタディハウス#22 (1960)。
Case Study House #22 (1960).

右頁／平面・断面ドローイング。
146-147頁／中庭のプール越しにリビング・ダイニング・スペースを見る。

opposite / Plan and section drawings.
pp. 146-147 / Living/dining room as seen from across the courtyard pool.

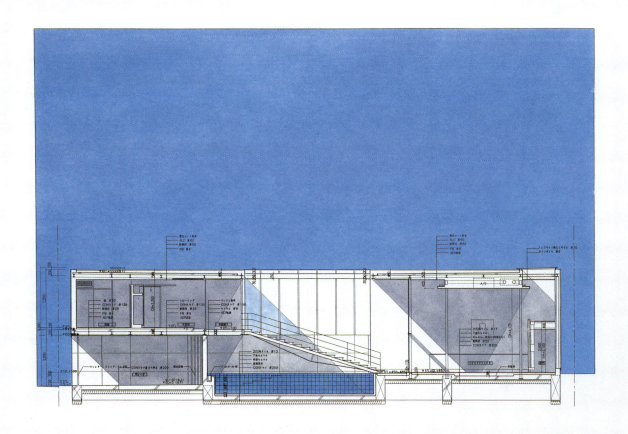

HOUSE IN FUKAYA 02

section
plan

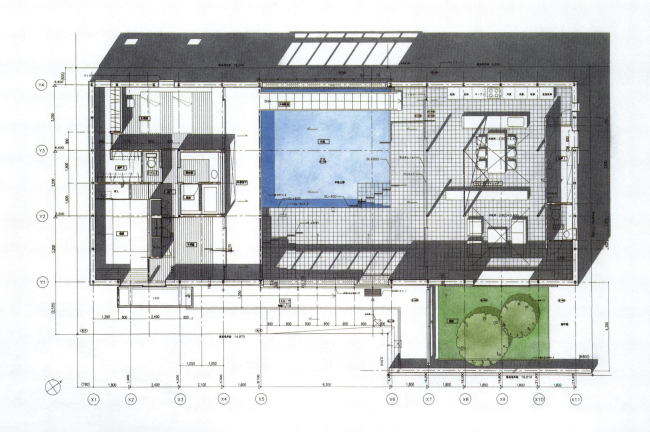

中庭全景。中央左はプール越しに2階へと繋がる鉄骨階段。
General view of the courtyard. The steel stairs spanning the pool at center left lead to the second floor.

左／東側からの中庭全景。
右頁／リビング・ダイニング側から2階寝室方向を見る。

left / General view of the courtyard as seen from the east side.
opposite / View towards the second-floor bedroom from the living/dining room.

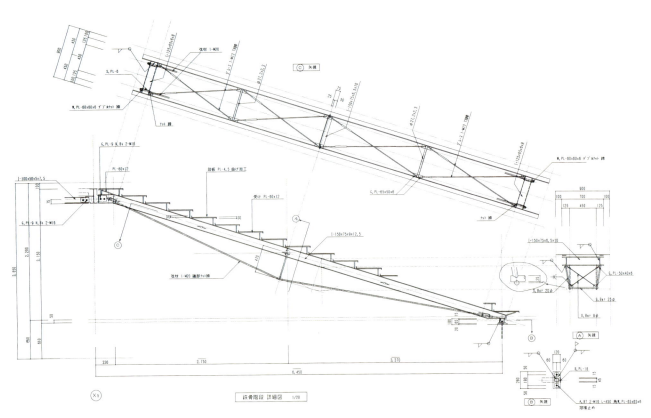

Detail Drawing of Steel Stairs

● House in Fukaya

1 ガレージ　garage
2 書斎　study
3 中庭　courtyard
4 プール　pool
5 リビング・ダイニング・スペース　living/dining space
6 寝室　bedroom
7 子供室　children's room
8 和室　tatami room

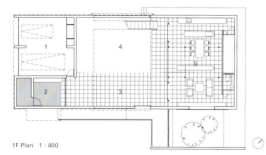

1F Plan　1:400

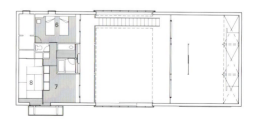

2F Plan

● House in Fukaya

左／リビング・ダイニング・スペースから中庭越しに寝室方向を見る。
右上／寝室からの見返し。
右下／リビング・ダイニング・スペース。中庭からの光とスカイライトからの光。

above left / View towards the bedrooms beyond the courtyard from the living/dining space.
above right / View back from the bedroom.
right / Living/dining room. Light shines inside from the courtyard and skylight.

リビング・ダイニング・スペース全景。
General view of the living/dining room.

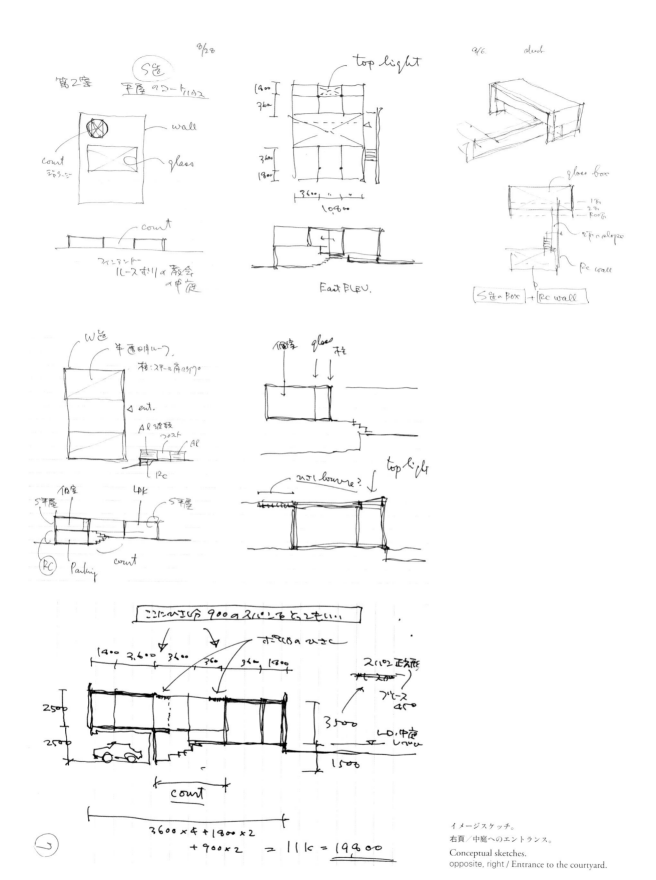

イメージスケッチ。
右頁／中庭へのエントランス。
Conceptual sketches.
opposite, right / Entrance to the courtyard.

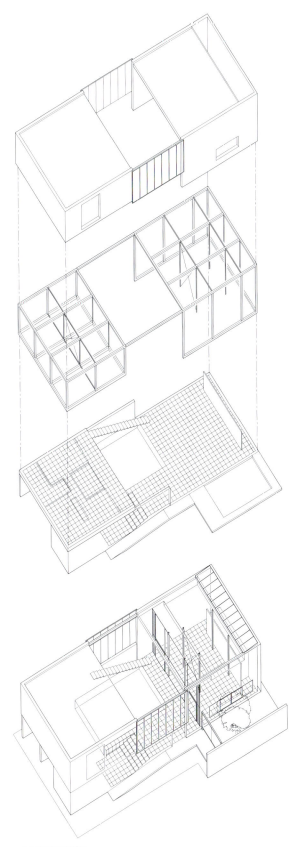

Axonometric Drawing

左/〈倉庫〉のような南側ファサード。
右/東側側面全景。ここから中庭へとアプローチする。
above / The warehouse-like south façade.
above right / General view of the east face. The courtyard is approached from this side.

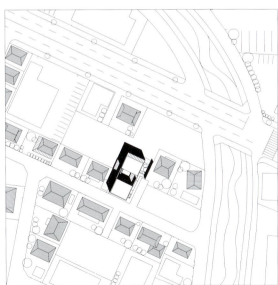

Site Plan 1 : 2000

堺の家
House in Sakai

2002, 大阪府堺市
Sakai, Osaka

大都市大阪の郊外、堺を通る私鉄沿線の住宅地に建つ夫婦2人の住宅である。奥に長い変形敷地の形状を生かしながら、その奥行き方向の長さを積極的に生かそうと考えていた。まず敷地の奥までアプローチを引き込み、もっとも奥にリビング・ダイニングを配置し、道路側に戻るほどにプライベートな空間である寝室を配するという全体計画である。一般的には表に近い所ほどパブリックな空間を配し、奥に行くほどプライベートな空間を置くというのが模範解であろうが、その真逆の計画とした。さらに外部に向けては開口を持たず、敷地東側の〈通り庭〉と西側の壁で閉じた〈中庭〉にのみ開口を持ち、あとはスカイライトからの採光が奥行き方向の長さをさらに強調するように計画した。

敷地の奥行き方向に平行に細長い直方体のヴォリュームを配置しているが、計画している最中にそれが敷地から数ブロック東の線路を走る車両を思い起こさせることに気付き、その電車と同色のダークブルーの外装色に決めたのだった。それは1990年代に自分が指向していた白く抽象的な建築からの意識的な乖離、精神的な距離の取り方であったことを今、改めて思い出させてくれた。内部空間も、スカイライトからの光が落ちる白い空間だけでは満足出来ず、その白く抽象的な空間の中、スティールで補強された木材の柱を意識的に表現したのも、同じ理由からだった。

This house for a couple is located in a residential neighborhood near a private railway line in Sakai, outside the great city of Osaka. I sought to make the most of the irregular shape and length of the deep lot. I drew the approach into the depths of the site, positioned the living/dining room at the very back, and put the bedroom by the street to set up an overall plan in which the spaces become more private towards the front. A model solution would have put the public spaces closer to the front and private spaces further towards the back, but I did the opposite. Moreover, I did not give the house any windows to the exterior. Instead, I gave it windows that look into the *tooriniwa* [passageway garden] on the east side and the *nakaniwa* [inner garden] bounded by the wall on the west side, and I also positioned a skylight in such a way that it further emphasizes the length of the site.

When I was developing the plans, I noticed that the long, narrow, boxy volume spanning the site in the long direction resembled the train cars on the railway just a few blocks to the east, and I chose to make the exterior color the same dark blue as the trains. I now recall that I did this to consciously depart from and to mentally keep a distance from the white abstract architecture that I had been fixated on in the 1990s. For the same reason, I was not going to be satisfied by simply making a white space with light shining in from the skylight, so I deliberately articulated the steel-reinforced wood columns within the white abstract interior.

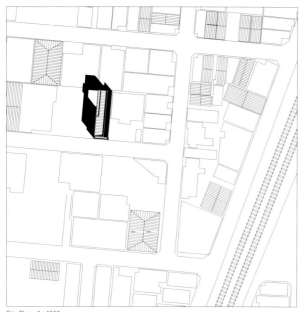

Site Plan 1 : 1500

右／大阪郊外の都市風景の中に建つ全景。
右頁／閉じた表情のファサード。
above / View of the house in the suburban Osakan landscape.
opposite / The closed façade.

左、右／東側のアプローチコート。
右頁／アプローチコートからリビングルーム越しに西側の中庭を見る。
above and right / Approach court on the east side.
opposite / View through the living court to the west courtyard from the approach court.

1 リビング・ダイニング　living/dining room
2 中庭　garden
3 納戸　storage
4 個室　bedroom
5 アプローチコート　approach

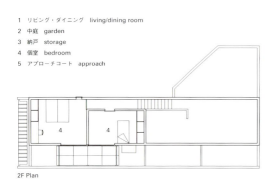

2F Plan

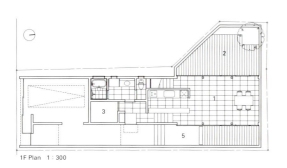

1F Plan　1:300

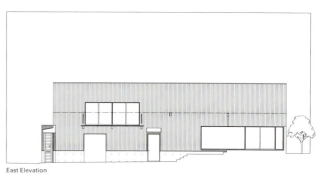

East Elevation

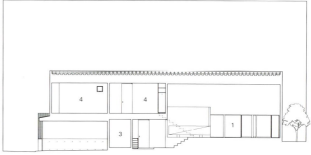

Section

● House in Sakai

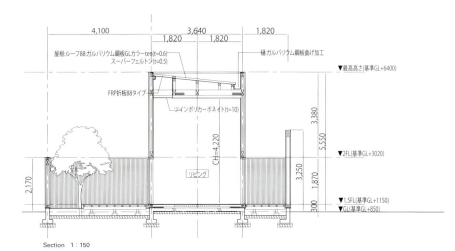

Section 1:150

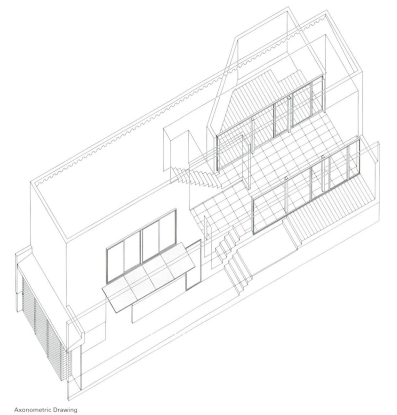

Axonometric Drawing

上／右にアプローチコート、左に中庭というふたつの屋外の空間を持つリビングルームを見る。
右頁下／リビングルーム見返し。

above / The living room has two outdoor spaces, with the courtyard on the left and approach court on the right.
opposite, bottom / View back into the living room.

左、右／スカイライトと階段の関係。
下、右頁／構造と意図的にずらした開口部と室内外の関係を見る。

left / Relationship between the skylight and stairs.
below and opposite / Relationship between the inside and outside through the openings that I intentionally shifted off from the structure.

● House in Sakai

和歌山の家
House in Wakayama

2002, 和歌山県和歌山市
Wakayama, Wakayama

何年も夢見続けていると実現することもある、ということを教えてくれたのがこの住宅だった。

バリ島での水との出会い。ウブドの近く、主要国道から緑溢れる谷に下りて行く。そこに出現する小さな寺院と沐浴するための静寂な水面。その中に建つ小さなお堂。周辺に溢れる緑の自然の中に出現する静謐な水平面。暴力的なほど力強い、それも不定形の緑の自然の中で、同じ自然の一要素でありながら、さながら人工的な幾何学の所産であるかのような水平面の形態を取る〈水〉という存在に魅せられた。建築と自然とを水が仲介する建築をつくりたい、と思うようになったきっかけは、その寺、ティルタ・エンプルだった。それからずっと、何年も〈水庭〉を創りたいと思い続けていた。それもティルタ・エンプルのように沐浴するための聖なる空間としての水庭ではなく、人間のための庭の空間なのに、そこに入ることが出来ない水の庭は出来ないだろうか、と夢見続けてきたのだ。

この住宅でそれを実現することが出来た。それには初めてバリ島でヒンズーの寺院と出会ってから10年以上の歳月を必要としたが、そんな破天荒な、建築家の極めて個人的な夢をクライアントと共有出来る機会と出会えたことは、どうしようもなく幸せだったと今、感じている。

This is the house that taught me that sometimes the things you keep dreaming about for years will come true.

I once had an encounter with water on the island of Bali. I descended into a lush valley off of a highway near Ubud. There appeared a small temple with a tranquil pool of water for performing ablutions. In it stood a small shrine. The sight of that serene horizontal plane emerging from the lush natural setting was powerful, almost violently so. I was fascinated by the *water* that assumed a form so flat that it seemed to be a manmade product of geometry, even though it was an element of nature no different from the irregularly shaped natural vegetation around. That temple, the Tirta Empul, was what brought me to want to create a building in which water mediated the architecture and nature. For years after that, I continued to dream about making a *water garden*. Specifically, I wanted to make one not as a sacred space for ritual bathing like at the Tirta Empul but as a space that would not be enterable despite being for humans.

I managed to realize that dream with this house. Although it took me over 10 years to do from when I first encountered the Hindu temple in Bali, I now feel unbelievably fortunate to have come across the opportunity to share my eccentric, utterly personal dream with a client.

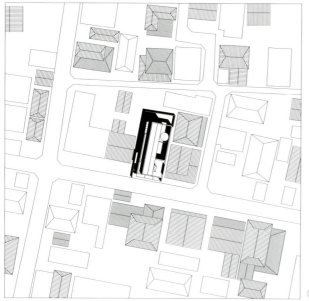

Site Plan 1:1500

左／配置図。敷地周辺の都市環境を示す。
右／バリ島のティルタ・エンプル。
右頁／水庭の奥行方向を見る。左側1階は寝室、2階は2層分の高さを持つリビング・ダイニングルーム。

left / Site plan showing the house's urban setting.
above / Tirta Empul in Bali.
opposite / View towards the back of the water garden. The bedroom is on the first floor on the left, and the double-height living/dining room is on the second floor.

ファサード。
Façade.

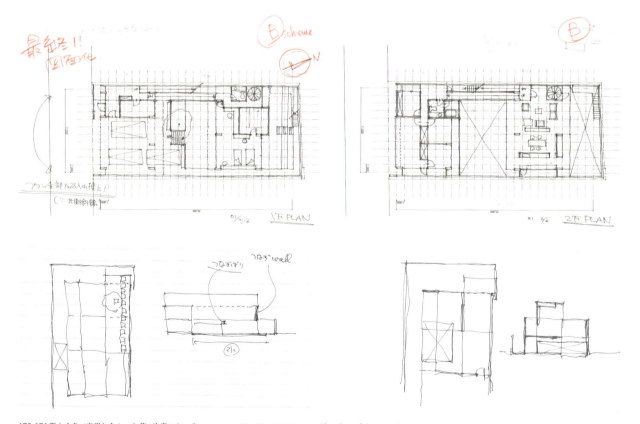

170-171頁上4点／実現しなかった第1次案スケッチ。
170-171頁下4点／実施案に向けての別案スケッチ。

pp. 170-171, middle row / Sketches of the unrealized initial scheme.
pp. 170-171, bottom row / Sketches of an alternative scheme that led to the built scheme.

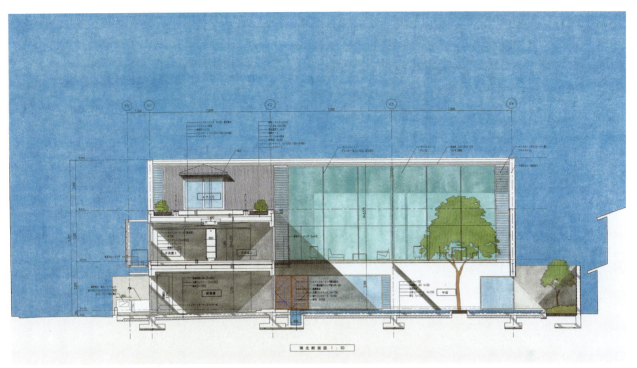
Section Drawing

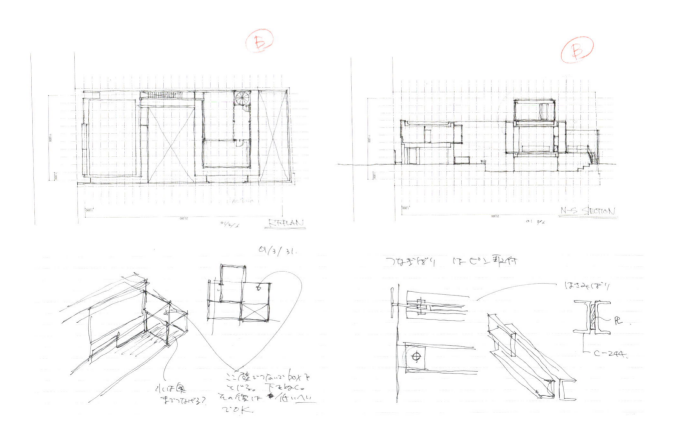

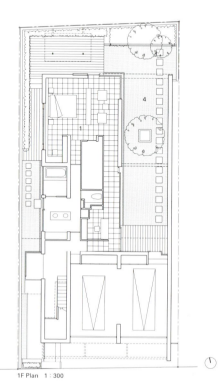

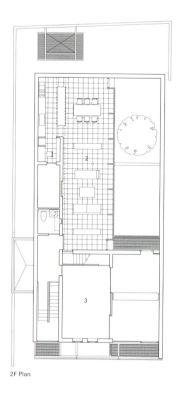

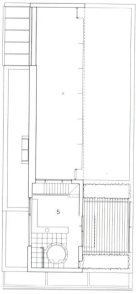

1　寝室　bedroom
2　LDK　living/dining/kitchen
3　個室　private room
4　水庭　water garden
5　スパ　spa

1F Plan　1：300

2F Plan

3F Plan

● House in Wakayama

172-173頁／水庭の夕景。水庭と寝室の関係を示す。
左頁、上／階を上がると明るく開放的な空間へと変化する様子を示す。

pp. 172-173 / Evening view of the water garden, showing its relationship to the bedroom.
opposite top and above / The transition into the brighter, more open spaces on the upper level.

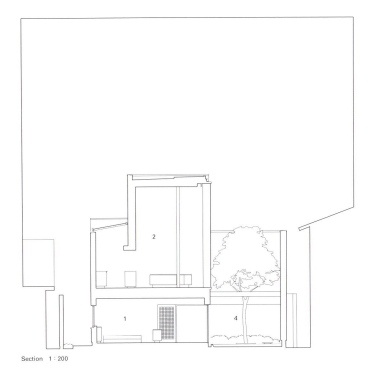

Section 1:200

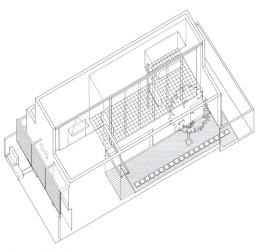

Axonometric Drawing

リビング・ダイニングルームと水庭との関係を示す。
Relationship between the living/dining room and water garden.

Hu-tong House

2002, 西日本
Western Japan

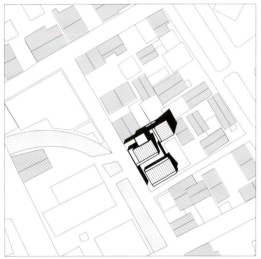

Site Plan 1:1500

北京の胡同〈Hu-tong〉。
A *Hu-tong* in Beijing.

現代美術の作家のアトリエ付き住宅である。
　この住宅では全体を〈個室群のブロック〉、〈リビング・ダイニングのブロック〉、そして〈アトリエのブロック〉の3つのブロックに分け、それぞれ、〈プライベートなアクティビティ〉、〈コミュニケーション主体のアクティビティ〉、〈1人になれる仕事場〉という、異なった機能に異なった場所が対応するという提案だった。結果としてひとつの敷地に3棟の建物が建つ構成となり、それらを繋ぐ外部空間の重要度が増し、個人住宅なのに都市的な様相を呈してくる。敷地外部に拡がるのは地方都市の瓦屋根の連続とその向こうに拡がる自然の山並みという風景であり、この3棟はその風景との連続性を考えて、片流れ屋根をそれぞれ異なった方向に架け、それらを繋ぐ屋外空間はさながら都市の街路空間の連続であるかのように設計した。
　その頃興味を持っていた北京の都市空間である〈Hu-tong〉。昼間はひっそりとした狭い街路である空間が、夜の訪れと共に様相を変え、屋外のリビングルームと化すような空間の存在に魅了されており、形式的な〈パブリック──プライベート〉という対位法的論理での空間理解に飽き飽きしていた自分にとっては、その〈Hu-tong〉の空間は刺激的だった。このプロジェクトを「Hu-tong House」と命名したのは、この住宅の中庭とも通路とも言えない屋外空間の彼方に、北京の〈Hu-tong〉を夢見ていたからだ。

This is a house and atelier for an artist of contemporary art.
　I proposed to separate the house into three blocks—bedroom block, living/dining block, and atelier block—and to have each one respond to a different function—private activities, communicative activities, and solitary work activities, respectively. The connective outdoor space of the resultant composition with three buildings on the single site took on increased importance, and the project assumed an urban character despite being a private residence. I gave the blocks shed roofs that each sloped in a different direction so that the house would have continuity with its surrounding provincial city landscape with an unending skyline of tiled rooftops and the nature of the mountains in the distance, and I also designed the outdoor space connecting the blocks to appear to be continuous with the spaces of the city's streets.
　At the time of this project, I held an interest in the urban spaces called the *Hu-tong* in Beijing. I was fascinated by how the narrow streets that were quiet during the day changed in character when night fell and turned into outdoor living rooms. The spaces of the *Hu-tong* were stimulating to me as one who had been tired of the customary "private-versus-public" dichotomous reading of space. The reason why I named this house the Hu-tong House was because I had been dreaming of Beijing's *Hu-tong* somewhere beyond the outdoor space of this house that was neither quite a courtyard nor a passage.

右頁／平面・断面ドローイング。
opposite / Plan and section drawings.

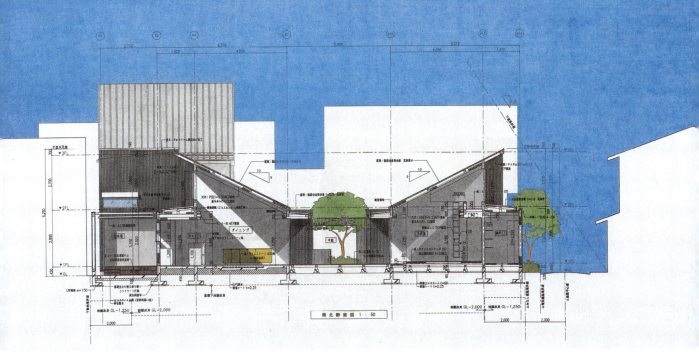

南北断面図 1:50

一階平面図 1:50

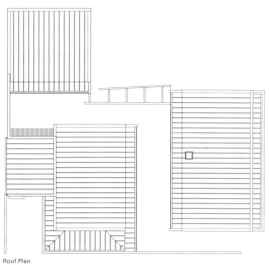

Roof Plan

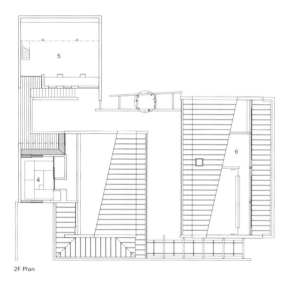

2F Plan

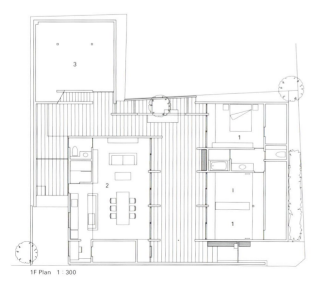

1F Plan 1:300

1 寝室　bedroom
2 リビング・ダイニング　living/dining room
3 倉庫　storage
4 和室　tatami room
5 アトリエ　studio
6 ロフト　loft

● Hu-tong House

上／全景。都市とスケールを合わせること。
下／都市に閉じたファサード。

above / General view. I matched the scale of the house to the scale of the city.
right / The façade is closed from the city.

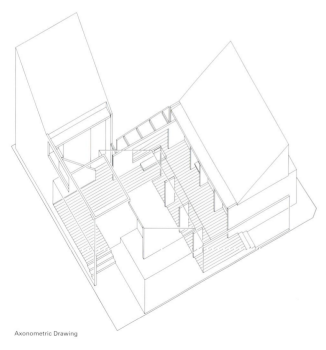

Axonometric Drawing

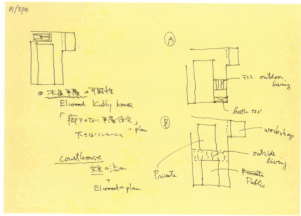

Conceptual Sketch

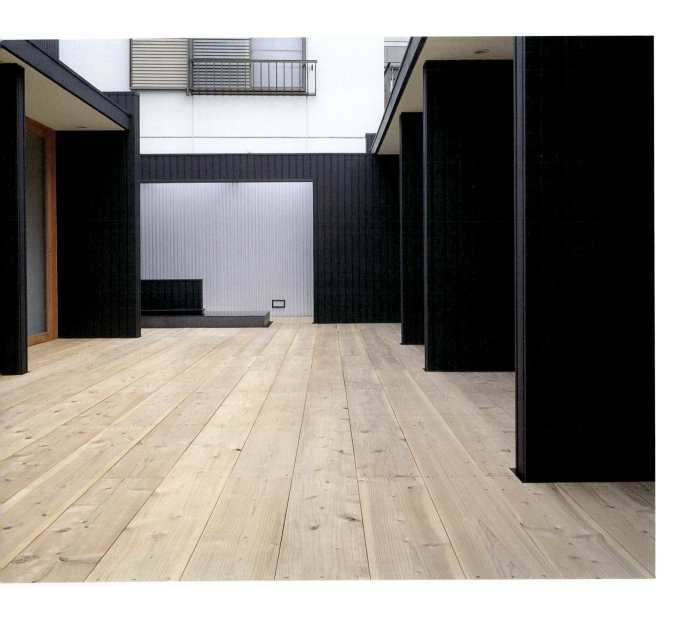

左頁／エントランス。
上／左がリビング・ダイニング棟、右が寝室棟。正面左奥からアトリエ棟へと繋がる。
下／〈Hu-tong〉見返し。

opposite, top left / Entrance.
above / The living/dining wing is on the left and the bedroom wing is on the right. The atelier wing is reached through the back at left center.
right / View into the "*Hu-tong*".

上／リビング・ダイニング棟内部。左上部が和室の開口部。
下／リビング・ダイニング棟から〈Hu-Tong〉越しに寝室棟を見る。
右頁／左がアトリエ棟、右がリビング・ダイニング棟、正面が寝室棟。

above / Living/dining wing interior. The opening at top left opens into the tatami room.
left / Bedroom wing as seen from the living/dining wing across the "*Hu-tong*".
opposite / The atelier wing is on the left, the living/dining room is on the right, and the bedroom wing is at back center.

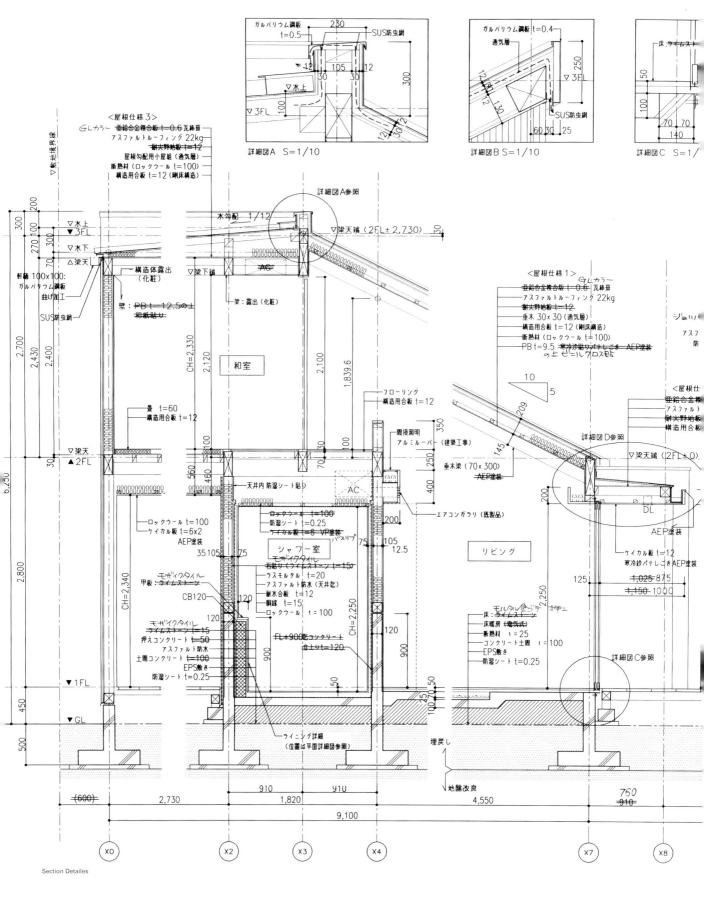

Section Detailes

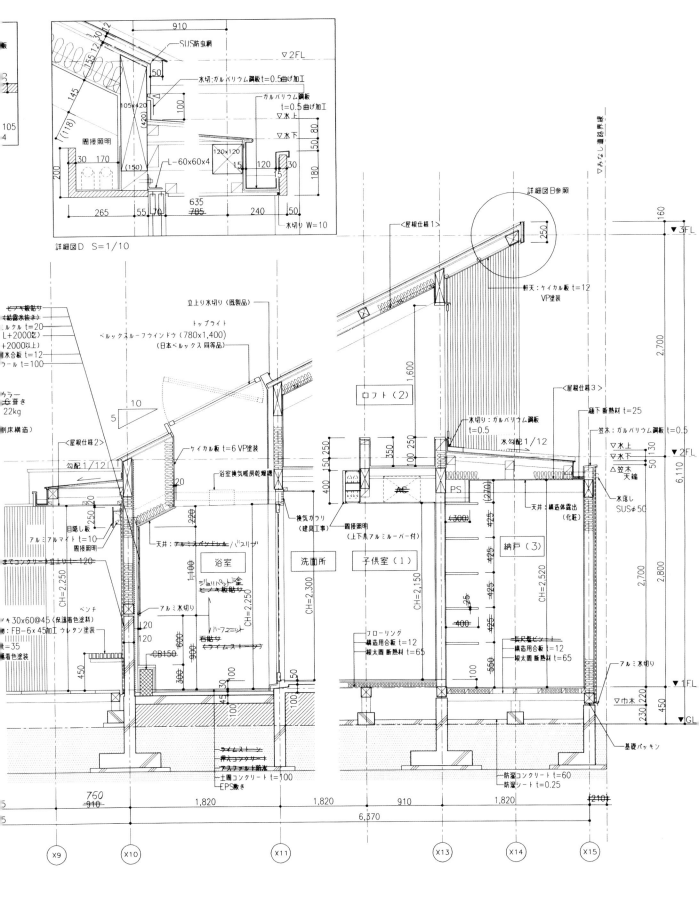

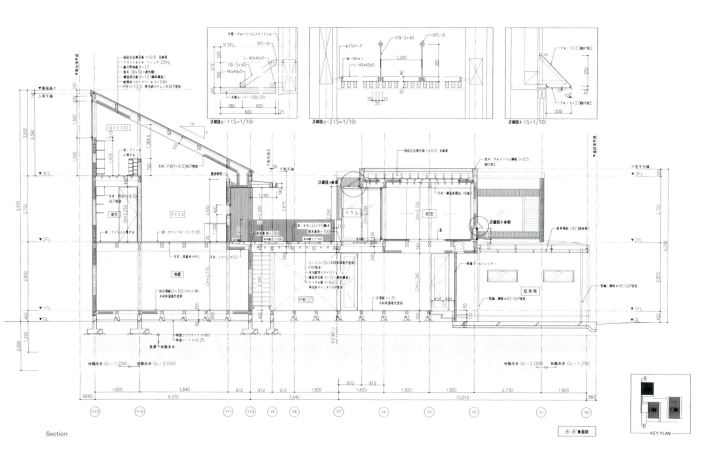

Section

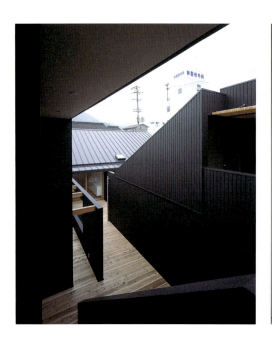

左／アトリエ棟2階から見下す。奥に家並、その向こうに山並が見える。
右／アトリエ棟2階から和室へと繋がるブリッジ。
右頁／光と影の空間。

far left / Looking down from the second floor of the atelier wing. Houses are visible in the back with mountains in the distance.
left / Bridge connecting the second floor of the atelier wing to the *tatami* room.
opposite / A space of light and shadows.

● Hu-tong House

子午線ライン 明石船客ターミナル
Akashi Meridian Line Ferry Terminal

2003, 兵庫県明石市
Akashi, Hyogo

明石と淡路島を結ぶフェリーのターミナルの計画であり、明石市の港に面して建つ。

明石が日本の子午線の街であるため、それの象徴としての時計台を備えること、それに旅立つ〈駅〉のイメージを担うものとして天井高の高いドーム状の天井が欲しいというのが、設計を始める時点の与件であった。機能的には切符売り場に待ち合いのホール、それに桟橋までの通路、というのが要求される機能の全てであり、時計台、それにドーム天井を持つことという要求にどう答えるのか、というのがもっとも重要なポイントだった。

子午線の街に建つということから考え始め、建物そのものを日時計とすることを提案した。屋根は薄い鋼板構造であり、それに日時計としての十字形をスカイライトとして刻み込む。その結果、屋根面が独立した4面に分かれるため、構造的に屋根面は4枚のキャンティバーとし、支えきれない大きな面にのみ、もっとも合理的に必要な場所に垂直荷重だけを支える柱を追加する。さらにその4面をひとつの薄いドーム形状とすることで、それぞれの鋼板面は球面の一部を切り取った形状となり剛性を確保する。

その結果、日時計の内部に居るかのような光の状態を実現することが出来た。

騒然とした都市風景からつかの間の〈旅〉である船への移動の間のバッファ空間として、時間の変化や光に象徴される自然とつかの間でいいから日時計という形で出会って欲しい、忙しい日常の中で船を待つ暫くの間くらい、時間や自然の流れにふと気付くような場所としたい、と考えていた。

This is a terminal building for a ferry that connects Akashi and Awaji Island. It stands facing the harbor in the city of Akashi.

The initial design brief called for the provision of a clock tower that would stand as a symbol for Akashi as a city located on the standard meridian of Japan, in addition to a high domed ceiling that would evoke the image of a *station* and a place for departure. The only required functions were a ticketing booth, waiting hall, and walkway to the pier, so the primary problem was to figure out how to answer to the requests for the clock tower and domed ceiling.

I started out by thinking about how the project was in a city on a meridian and came up with the idea to make the building itself as a sundial. I proposed to make the sundial by cutting a cruciform skylight into a thin steel plate roof. This meant that the roof surface would be divided into four independent pieces, so I structured each as a cantilever and added columns purely to bear vertical loads only at points where they were rationally necessary to support the larger pieces. I also made the steel pieces more structurally rigid by concaving them so that they would form a shallow domed shape together. As a result, I succeeded to create a quality of light that should make one feel like they are inside a sundial.

What I wanted to do was to create a buffer space for the transition between the noisy urban landscape and the short "journey" on the ferry. I wanted to make it a place where people would encounter nature even just briefly through the sundial that embodied the ever-changing time and light and take notice of the flow of time and nature for the short moments they spent waiting for the ferry during their busy everyday lives.

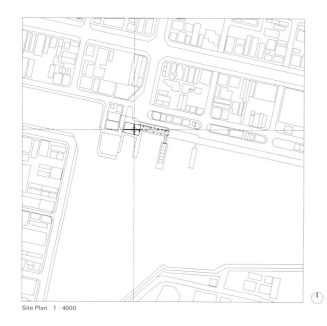

Site Plan 1 : 4000

右頁／待合ホールに落ちる光。日時計としての建築の内部空間。

opposite / Light shining into the waiting hall. The interior space of the building acts like a sundial.

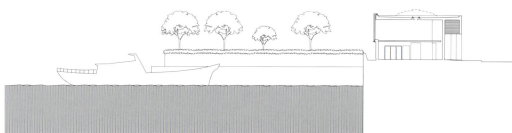

Section

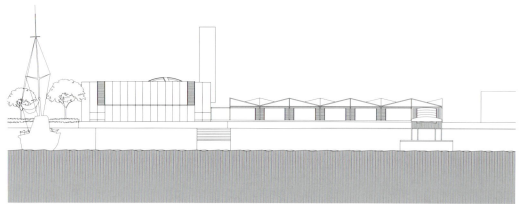

South Elevation 1 : 500

● Akashi Meridian Line Ferry Terminal

上／海側からの立面。さながら倉庫のようなそっけなさ。
下／街からのアプローチ。内部空間が想像出来ない外観。
above / Elevation on the sea side. It appears unassuming like a warehouse.
below right / Approach from the city. The exterior gives no hint of the space inside.

1　待合ホール　waiting hall
2　通路　passage

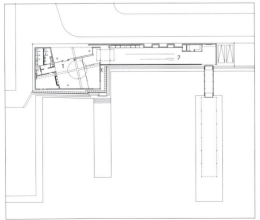

Plan　1 : 1000

待合ホールの日時計。屋根は鉄板構造でボックス状の外壁からのキャンティレバーでは支えきれない場所にのみ柱が建ち、垂直荷重を支える。

Sundial of the waiting hall. The columns stand only in places where the steel plate roof that cantilevers from the box-shaped outer wall needs supports to carry the vertical loads.

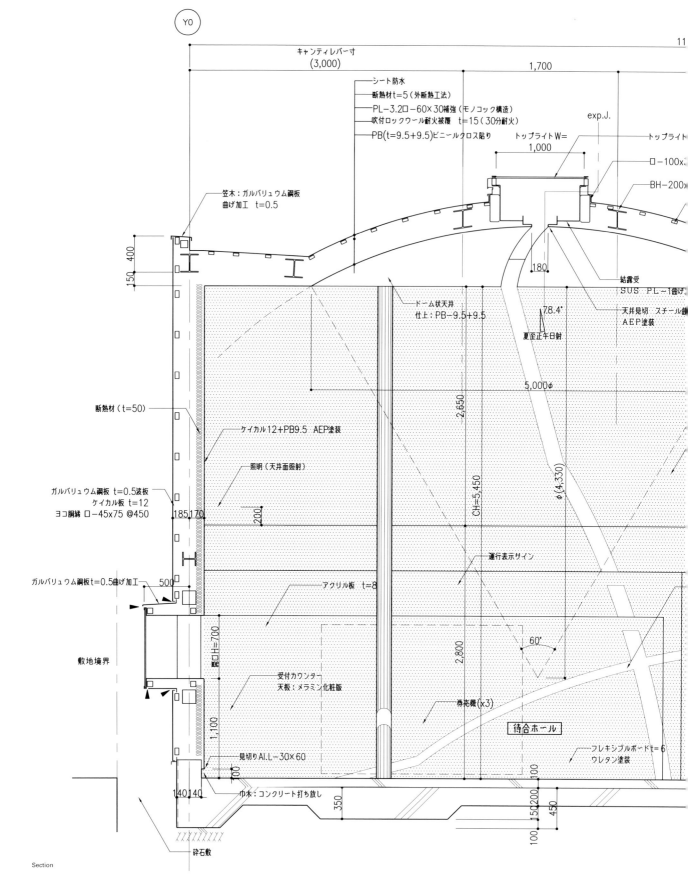

Section

Akashi Meridian Line Ferry Terminal

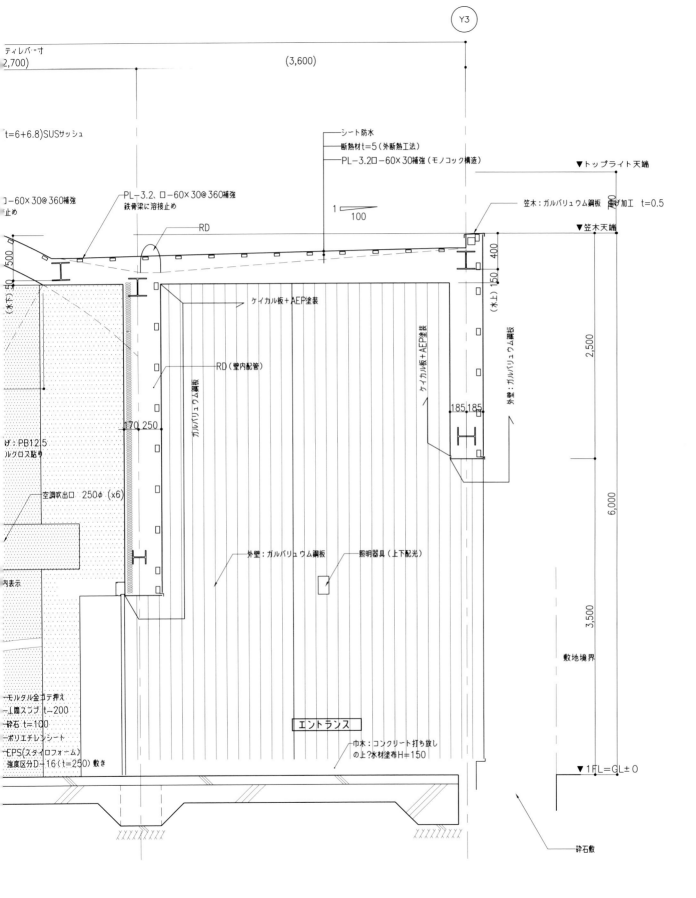

上／日時計としての待合ホールから出ると、工業製品だけで出来た連結路の先に船が待つ。
左下／全景。
右下／工業製品の組み合わせだけのディテール。
右頁／海からの全景。

above / Leaving the sundial hall, one reaches the waiting ferries via a walkway made entirely of industrial products.
below left / General view.
below right / Details made by assembling industrial products.
opposite / General view from the sea.

● Akashi Meridian Line Ferry Terminal

京都・小野
Zen Lounge I

2003, 京都市中京区
Nakagyo-ku, Kyoto

曹洞宗の仏具を扱うショールームである。

　寺院そのものに必要な仏具から僧侶の衣類、それに身辺の装飾品まで、曹洞宗の僧侶にとって必要なものを全て揃える店舗であり、予約のみで顧客と接客する場所であり、通常時は閉まっている。当初、その話を聞いただけではどんな使い方をするのか、どんな空間を設計すればいいのか、まるで見当が付かなかった。店主とコミュニケーションを重ねるうちに、商品はその顧客との会話の中でその僧侶に最適なものを店主が読み取り、在庫しているものであれば奥から出し、あるいはその僧侶に合わせて改めて制作するというものであり、具体的な商品を陳列する必要は無いこと、むしろ僧侶である顧客とのコミュニケーションのための空間をつくればいいことを理解した。

　その場所を2種類用意し、ひとつはテーブルでの会話、もうひとつは床面に座っての会話が可能な空間だけを用意した。僧侶と店主とのコミュニケーションの場として都市の喧噪から距離を感じる場所とするため、床面にはたたきや名栗といった寺院で使われている素材を現代的な文脈の中に置き、それの素材感を強調するように自然光が横からなめるように入るよう計画した。壁面には天井から吊るした黒錆鉄板や瓦を積層させた壁など、質感の在る面をつくり、それらの直交する面を構成的に配置しただけである。

　日本の伝統的な素材感を持つ材料で出来た床＝水平面や壁＝垂直面を、近代主義的な手法で〈構成〉すること、そうすることで現代の日本的な空間が出現するのではないか、と考えていたのだ。

This is a showroom that offers products related to Soto Zen Buddhism.

　The store offers everything Soto priests need, including altar fittings, garments, and accessories, but it only accepts clients by appointment, so its doors are normally closed. When I initially heard this, I had no idea how the building would be used or what kind of spaces I needed to design. As I continued my communications with the shopkeeper, I eventually came to understand that he would be offering products that he felt his clients needed based on their conversations. The products would either be brought out from the back if in stock or be newly made to suit the needs of each priest, so it was unnecessary to display any actual products. What I therefore needed to create were spaces for the shopkeeper to communicate with his clients.

　I set up two types of spaces for this: one for talking while sitting at a table and one for talking while sitting on the floor. In order to create a sense of distance between these spaces for communication and the noise of the city, I selected materials traditionally used in temples, such as *tataki* [tamped earth] and *naguri* [textured chestnut wood] floors, placed them within the modern context, and emphasized their textures by softly illuminating them with natural light brought in from the side. For the wall surfaces, I created textured planes, such as black rusted steel plates suspended from the ceiling and walls of stacked tiles, and simply arranged them in an orthogonal composition.

　I believed that I might be able to produce a modern Japanese space by making floors (horizontal surfaces) and walls (vertical surfaces) with traditional Japanese materials and *composing* them in Modernist fashion.

Axonometric Drawing

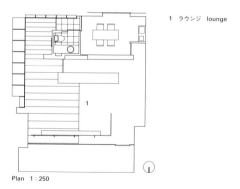

1　ラウンジ　lounge

Plan 1 : 250

右頁／名栗の仕上げを引き立たせるように水平方向に光を導入する。影をつくっているのは天井から吊るされた黒錆仕上げの鉄板。
opposite / The light drawn in horizontally emphasizes the *naguri* finish of the floor. The black rusted steel plate suspended from the ceiling creates a dark shadow.

上／瓦の積層仕上げの壁面。
下／名栗と黒錆鉄板を際立たせる光と影。
left / Wall finished with stacked tiles.
below left / The *naguri* finish and black rusted steel plates are articulated by the light and shadows.

上／全景。名栗と土のたたきの床、瓦の積層やシルク貼の壁にけやきの天板。光と影の中にそれらの素材が浮かび上がる。
右頁／ファサード。慎ましやかに都市に語りかける。
above / General view. The *naguri*-finished floor, earthen floor, tile walls, silk-covered walls, and zelkova tabletop float within the light and shadows.
opposite / The façade speaks to the city in a reserved manner.

熊野古道情報センター
Kumano-kodo Information Center project

2003, 三重県尾鷲市
Owase, Mie

コンペの提出案である。
　残念ながら、佳作だった。
　ここでは〈木〉の構造を主題として扱いながら、柱梁構造や伝統的な木構造といった、木を線材として扱うのではない構造形式はないだろうか、というのが最初の発想だった。結果として矩形断面の材木が直交して積み重ねられているような形態を構想し、その材木の森の中に導線や主空間を洞窟のように埋め込む。外皮はガラスのスキンとし、ポーラスな構造体の隙間を光や空気が抜けながら入って来る空間を考えた。線材や面材に代表されるソリッドな構造材料が力を受けるのではなく、むしろ隙間だらけのポーラスな素材が建築全体を支えるという構造、しかもどこが構造という1次部材でどこが2次部材かが判別不能な、全体として構造でもあり仕上げでもある、という建築を提案した。
　これまでにはない木構造であるため、木材の経年による部材寸法の変化をどう吸収するか、など解決すべき課題はたくさんあったが、挑戦的に提案した計画案である。

This is a proposal that I submitted to a competition.
It unfortunately only received an honorable mention.
I started out by wondering whether I could work with *wood* to create a structure in which the wood would not be treated as a linear component like in traditional post-and-beam timber structures. This led me to conceive a form composed of rectangular timber components stacked at right angles. I then embedded the circulation and main rooms into this forest of timber to create a cave-like space, and I made the envelope as a glass skin to allow light and air to flow through the gaps in the porous structure. What I essentially proposed was an architecture supported entirely by a porous mass of material instead of solid linear and planar load-bearing components. The whole building acted both as the structure and finish as there was no way of making a distinction between primary and secondary structural components.
This was a plan that I daringly proposed despite the many problems that needed to be resolved with the unprecedented timber structure—such as how to absorb the deformations that would occur in the timber components over time.

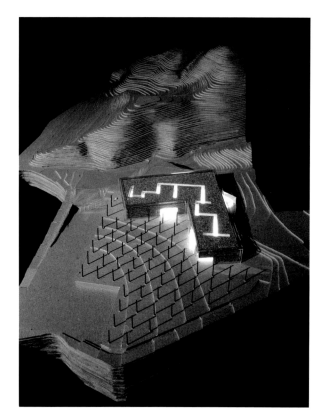

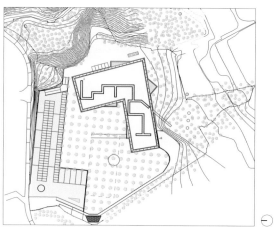

Site Plan　1 : 4000

左／模型全景。積層した材木による歪んだ矩形の建築とそれとは逆に厳格な幾何学グリッドに並んだ樹木列。そのふたつが自然と親和しながら対比を表現する。
右頁／積層する材木の中を散策する。深い森の中に落ちてくる光と深い闇のメタファー。

left / General view of model. The warped form of the architecture made with stacked timber and the trees arranged in a rigid geometric grid exhibit an affinity with nature while contrasting against each other.
opposite / Walking through the stacked timber. The space evokes a thick forest with light shining down into the deep shadows.

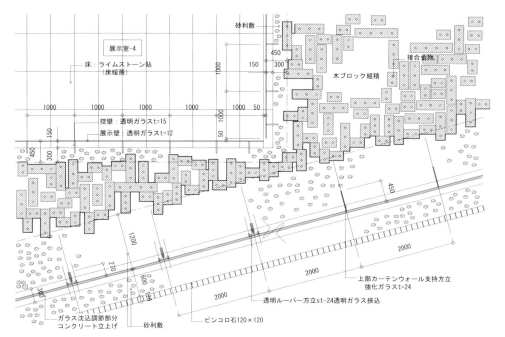

Wall Detail

柱―梁といった線状部材による木構造以外の可能性の追求。積み上げられた材木の山を見た時、その内部にどんな空間が拡がるのか想像した。その想像を現実へと変換する。

I sought to create a wooden structure that was not composed of linear components such as columns and beams. When I saw a pile of stacked timber, I imagined what kind of spaces could unfold within it. I then converted these visions into reality.

1 エントランス	entrance
2 カフェ	cafe
3 事務室	office
4 会議室	conference room
5 映像ホール	theater
6 体験工房	workshop
7 図書室	library
8 展示室	exhibition room
9 収蔵庫	storage

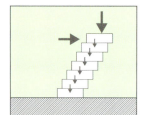

構造スケッチ Structural Diagram

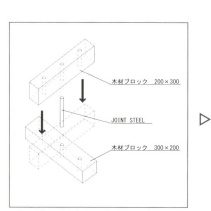

1F Plan 1:1600

小部材の木材ブロック
Small wood block component

1種類の金物での木材ブロックの接合
Blocks joined by single type of connector

木材を同じ金物で連結した構造体
Structure joined with universal connector

● Kumano-kodo Information Center project

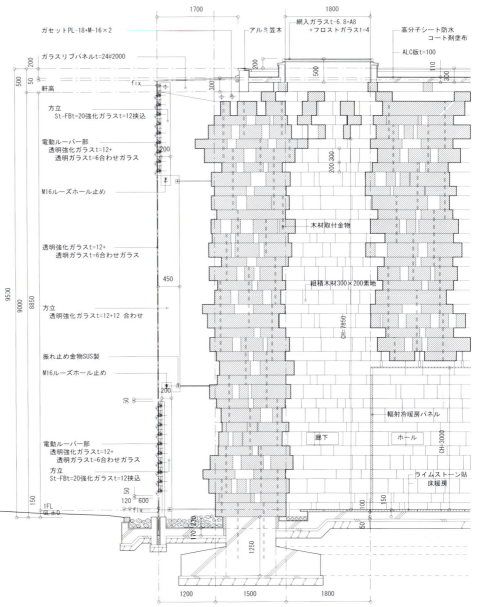

Wall Detail 1:80

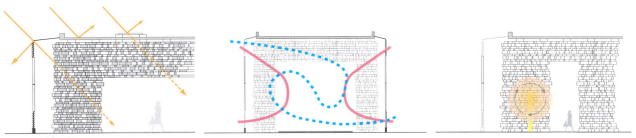

光と空気の流れ　Light and air flow

上／森を抜けると広場に出る。空から降ってくる光と突然水平方向に拡がる風景。
右頁／熊野の神話性を想い出させてくれるような風景を夢想していた。初めて設計しようと試みた〈闇〉の建築。

above / A clearing appears within the forest. One's field of view expands dramatically and light shines down from the sky.
opposite / I imagined a scene that would evoke the mythological quality of Kumano. This was my first attempt at designing an architecture of darkness.

1 カフェ cafe
2 事務室 office
3 映像ホール theater
4 収蔵庫 storage

Section

West Elevation 1：1200

● Kumano-kodo Information Center project

ライカ銀座店
Leica Ginza Showroom

2006, 東京都中央区
Chuo-ku, Tokyo

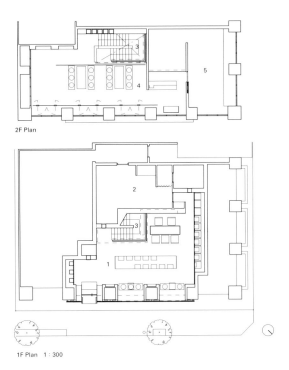

2F Plan

1F Plan 1:300

1　ショールーム　showroom
2　事務室　office
3　階段室　stairwell
4　サロン　salon
5　リペアルーム　repair room

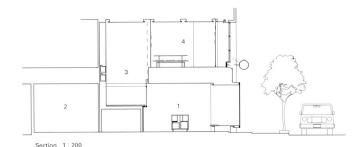

Section 1:200

1914年に世界で初めて35mmフィルムを使用するカメラを製造し、ガラス乾板を使用する大判カメラの写真の世界から飛び出し、新しい写真の世界を創造したのがライカ・カメラだった。もはや神話的な写真であるロバート・キャパのスペイン戦争の兵士の写真などの写真によるドキュメンタリーが可能になったのも、このいつでも持ち運べる、戦場にさえ持って行くことの出来るカメラのシステムが出現、ライカが創造した新しい写真の世界だった。一方、1990年代以降、安価なアナログ・カメラやデジタル・カメラの出現で、ライカは趣味人の愛玩の対象物へと変化していく。

そういう風潮の中でもう一度ライカ・カメラを日常の生活の中に普通に存在する道具としたい、ライカ・カメラ初のデジタル・カメラの発売に時期を揃えるかのように、東京銀座にドイツのライカの直営旗艦店としてのショップを設けることになったのには、そうした背景がある。

趣味人のための閉じた空間ではなく、女性でもブティックに立ち寄るのと同じ感覚で立ち寄れる空間としたいという意向を受け、我々が設計することとなった。

カメラを製造しているドイツサイド、出資に責任を持つフランスサイド、そして実際に運営する日本サイドのそれぞれの意見がぶつかり合い、背景の異なる多文化の衝突の中でひとつのものを創り上げるという経験は得難いものだった。

Leica Camera opened up a new world of photography in 1914 when they produced the first 35 mm film camera and leapt out of the world of photographs made with large-format cameras that used glass photographic plates. Documentary photographs such as Robert Capa's now mythical image of the soldier in the Spanish Civil War were only made possible because of this new world of photography that Leica created by coming out with a system of cameras that could be carried around anywhere, even to battlefields. However, the Leica came to be seen as more of a hobbyist's toy from the 1990s with the advent of inexpensive analog cameras and digital cameras.

This was the context that led the German company to open a directly operated flagship store in Ginza, Tokyo. This seemed to be timed with the release of the first digital camera offered by Leica Camera, which was eager to see the Leica become a common tool of everyday life once again in the face of the recent trends.

We were commissioned to design the shop with a request that it be made not as a closed space for hobbyists but as a space that even women would be able to walk into in the same manner as a boutique.

This project gave me the rare experience of putting together a single solution amidst the conflicting views and cultural differences of the German manufacturer, French investor, and Japanese management.

右頁／ファサード夕景。都市に語りかけるような表情。
opposite / Evening view of the façade. It appears to speak softly to the city.

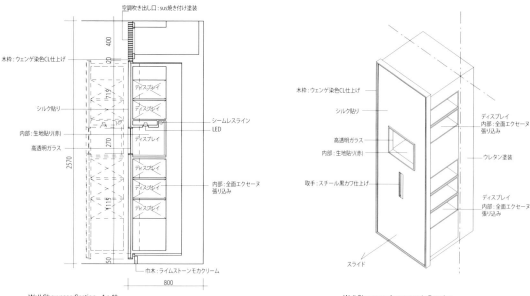

Wall Showcase Section 1:40

Wall Showcase Axonometric Drawing

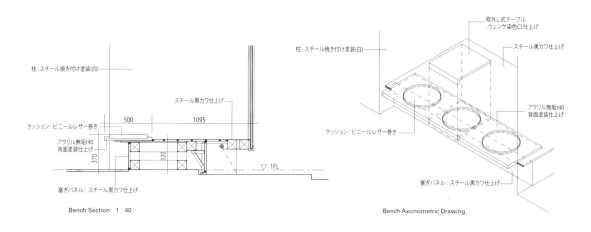

Bench Section 1:40

Bench Axonometric Drawing

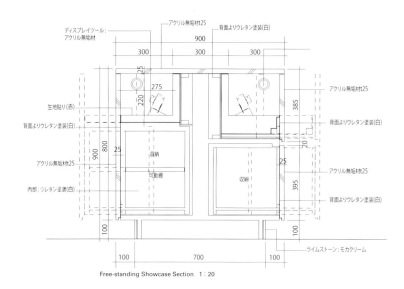

Free-standing Showcase Section 1:20

いつもの建築設計とは逆ベクトルの設計方法。まず家具をデザインし、それがインテリア・デザインを決め、最後にそのインテリア・デザインと都市とのインターフェイスを考えるとファサードが決まる。

I attempted to reverse my usual design approach. I started by designing the furniture, which informed the interior design, and then formulated the façade last as an interface between the interior and the city.

● Leica Ginza Showroom

右上／2階サロン。現実の銀座の風景をバックに写真と出会う。35mmライカ・カメラの持つドキュメンタリー性の表現。

右中／1階と2階の繋ぎの空間。染色されヘアライン掛けされたアルミやステンレス・メッシュ、それにシルクの布の壁など、異素材の出会い。

下／1階。最小限の数だけ展示されたカメラを鍵に店のスタッフとのコミュニケーションが始まる。

above right / Second-floor salon. Visitors behold the photographs against a backdrop of the real landscape of Ginza. I aimed to express the documentary quality associated with the 35 mm Leica camera.

right / Connection space between the first and second levels. Visitors encounter various materials, such as the tinted aluminum, stainless steel mesh, and silk walls.

below / First floor. Customers initiate communication with the store staff over the cameras that are displayed sparingly.

Suzhou Vanke Villa

2007, 蘇州市, 中国江蘇省
Suzhou, China

中国蘇州の大湖近く、中国の住宅デヴェロッパーであるVanke万科が開発したタウンハウス形式の住区で提案したモデルハウスである。高層のタワーを何本か建てる形式で展開されるのが中国の住区開発の通例なのだが、ここ蘇州で万科は中国では極めて珍しい形式——中庭を持つ3階建てのタウンハウス——が連続する低層集合住宅をつくることを決めた。そうした形式が日本では一般的であるため日本の建築家であるわたしと、中国の事情に通じている香港のデザイナーであり私の古い友人でもあるアラン・チャンとの2人のコラボレーションで、モデルハウスをつくることになった。

わたしが空間を設計した上でアランが備品や家具をコーディネートするという役割分担である。

蘇州を含む江南地方は運河が交通のインフラであった地方であり、その運河や大湖の存在を通じて、伝統的に水に近い生活が営まれてきた場所である。そこで中庭を水庭とし、これに面するリビングルームのサッシは上方に電動でスライド可能な形式、水庭を挟んで向かい側のダイニングルームは横方向にスライドする形式とし、どちらのサッシも開放すると壁の中に消え、リビングルーム、ダイニングルーム共に屋外空間である中庭＝水庭と一体化する計画とした。

従って1階の全ての床仕上げを中国の庭園に典型的な瓦仕上げとすることにより、より内外が一体的で連続性を感じられるような屋外的な空間とした。

伝統的な江南地方の住宅の雰囲気を感じさせながら、同時に現代的な空間でもあることが当初の目標だったが、ひとつの解答となったのではないか、と考えている。

This is a model home that I proposed for a townhouse development built near Lake Tai in Suzhou, China, by the Chinese residential real estate developer Vanke. Residential developments in China are typically built in a format consisting of several high-rise towers, but for this project in Suzhou, Vanke chose to build three-story townhouses with courtyards—a very rare format in China—to create a series of low-rise housing blocks. This was a common format in Japan, so I, being a Japanese architect, was brought in to design a model home. I worked in collaboration with Hong Kongese designer Alan Chan, who was an old friend of mine that was knowledgeable about matters in China.

We split up our roles so that I would design the spaces and Alan would coordinate the fixtures and furniture.

The Jiangnan region, where Suzhou is located, is an area where waterways have historically been used as transportation infrastructure, and it is a place where life has traditionally taken place nearby water because of the presence of its canals and Lake Tai. In light of this, I planned to make the courtyard as a water garden while equipping the living room and dining room that faced it with an electrically operable vertically sliding sash window and a horizontally sliding sash window, respectively. I then designed the sashes to disappear into the walls when opened so that the living room and dining room would become one with the outdoor courtyard/water garden.

Accordingly, I finished all of the floors of the ground floor with tiles typically used in Chinese gardens. This increased the sense of continuity between the inside and outside and created a space with an outdoor feel.

My initial goal was to create a contemporary space that would also give the feeling of the traditional houses of the Jiangnan region. I believe that I successfully managed to come up with one way of achieving this.

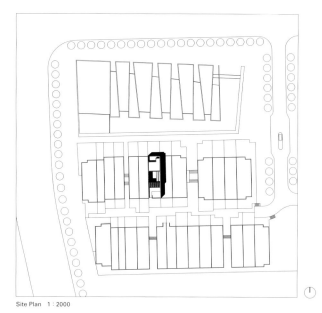

Site Plan 1 : 2000

右頁／集合住宅全景。水が公共導線を暗示する。
216-217頁／水の中庭越しにダイニングルームを見る。

opposite / General view of the housing development. The waterways suggest the public circulation routes.
pp. 216–217 / View of the dining room beyond the courtyard water garden.

左上／リビングルーム。
左下／ギャラリーとして使われる2階コリドール。
右上／書斎。
右下／書斎の壁面ディテール。
below / Living room.
bottom left / Second-floor corridor that doubles as a gallery.
below right / Study.
bottom right / Detail of a wall in the study.

●Suzhou Vanke Villa

上／ダイニングルームから水庭越しにリビングルームを見返す。正面のサッシは電動で上の垂れ壁の中に収納される。

above / View from the dining room back towards the living room beyond the water garden. The electrically operated window sash in the center can be stowed into the underhanging wall.

右頁／水庭を見下ろす。
opposite / View down into the water garden.

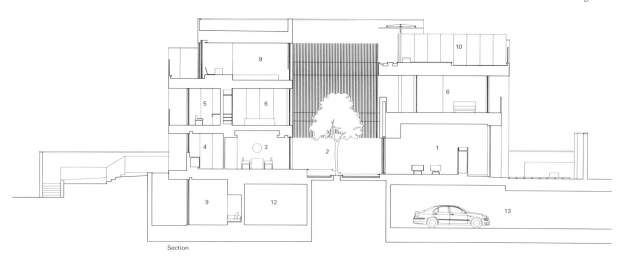

Section

1	リビング	living room
2	水庭	water garden
3	ダイニング	dining room
4	キッチン	kitchen
5	浴室	bathroom
6	寝室	bedroom
7	ギャラリー	gallery
8	クローゼット	closet
9	書斎	study
10	テラス	terrace
11	通路	passage
12	納戸	storage
13	ガレージ	garage

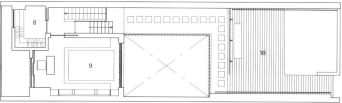

3F Plan

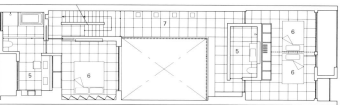

2F Plan

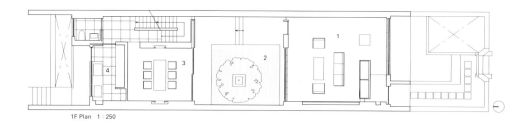

1F Plan　1：250

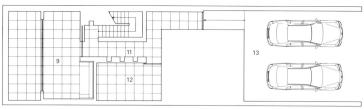

B1F Plan

● Suzhou Vanke Villa

紙屋HOUSE
Kamiya House

2009, 東京都渋谷区
Shibuya-ku, Tokyo

東京都渋谷区初台、山手通りから少し入った所にある170m²強の敷地に建つ集合住宅である。

全体の構成は単純で、最上階2層分がメゾネットのペントハウスであり、3階から5階までの3層が各階1ユニットのフラット住居、2階は歯科クリニック、1階はアプローチとエントランスホールである。各階を繋ぐエレベーターから降りると、そこは既に住戸のプライベートな屋外空間としてのテラスがあり、この構成は各階とも共通している。ここでは共有空間として用意されているのは1階のエントランスホールのみであり、2階から上の階は共有空間を排除し、住戸の独立性を高めた。集合住宅でありながら独立住宅のようなライフスタイルを可能にすること、というのが当初からの目標だったからだ。

都市の住居にとって、都市に対して閉じることだけが求められているわけではないだろう、とずっと考えてきた。住居が都市に対して閉じることの象徴でもあり、歴史や場所の違いを超えた普遍的な解答でもある〈中庭〉の代わりにプライバシーのない〈屋上庭園〉——近代という時代が提案した新しい概念——について考え始めたのは1990年代の初め、「日本橋の家」の頃からだった。20年以上の時が過ぎ、「日本橋の家」は「紙屋HOUSE」に姿を変えたのかもしれないと思う。実は、全体の断面構成や都市空間との関係の取り方は同じなのだから。

This is a condominium that sits on an approximately 170 m2 site just off the Yamate Street in the Hatsudai district of Shibuya, Tokyo.

The building has a simple overall composition with a maisonette penthouse on the top two floors, a living unit on each floor from the third to the fifth, a dental clinic on the second floor, and the approach and entrance hall on the first floor. On every floor, the elevator connecting all the floors opens up directly into a private outdoor terrace space that belongs to the unit on that floor. The entrance hall on the first floor is the only common space; I did not provide any common spaces above the first floor in order to make the living units more independent. This was because it was my aim from the start to make a condominium that provides the lifestyle of a detached house.

I have always believed that urban housing should not only be expected to be closed to the city. I have been thinking about the privacy-less *roof garden*—a new concept advanced in the modern era—as an alternative to the *courtyard*—a concept universal across time and place that symbolizes the very idea of closing houses off from the city—from around the time of the House in Nipponbashi in the early 1990s. I believe that the House in Nipponbashi may have transformed itself into the Kamiya House over the 20-plus years that passed between them. In point of fact, the projects share the same overall sectional composition and address the spaces of the city in the same way.

Site Plan 1:3000

Section 1:300

1 アプローチ approach
2 歯科医院 dental clinic
3 ユニットA1 unit A1
4 ユニットA2 unit A2
5 ユニットB unit B
6 ユニットC unit C

右頁／ファサード夕景。都市に開いた住居は可能かという、1990年代から考えていた自分の問い掛けへのケーススタディ。

opposite / Evening view of the façade. This was a case study on creating a house open to the city, which was a theme that I had been thinking about since the 1990s.

左／アプローチから階段と水庭を見る。
右／左から奥のエントランスホールにアプローチする。階段は2階のクリニックのためのアプローチ。
右頁／東側の垂直なヴォイドを見上げる。

above left / Stairs and water garden as seen from the approach.
above / The approach on the left leads to the entrance hall at the back. The stairs lead to the clinic on the second level.
opposite / View up through the vertical void on the east side.

1 アプローチ approach
2 エントランスホール entrance hall
3 機械室 machinery room
4 駐車場 parking
5 テラス terrace
6 待合室 waiting room
7 受付 reception
8 診察室 examination room
9 X線撮影室 X-ray room
10 準備室 preparation room
11 休憩室 resting room

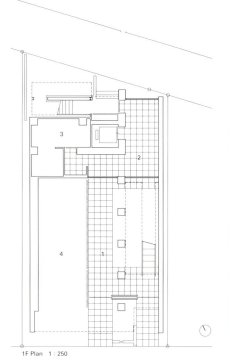

1F Plan 1:250

2F Plan

● Kamiya House

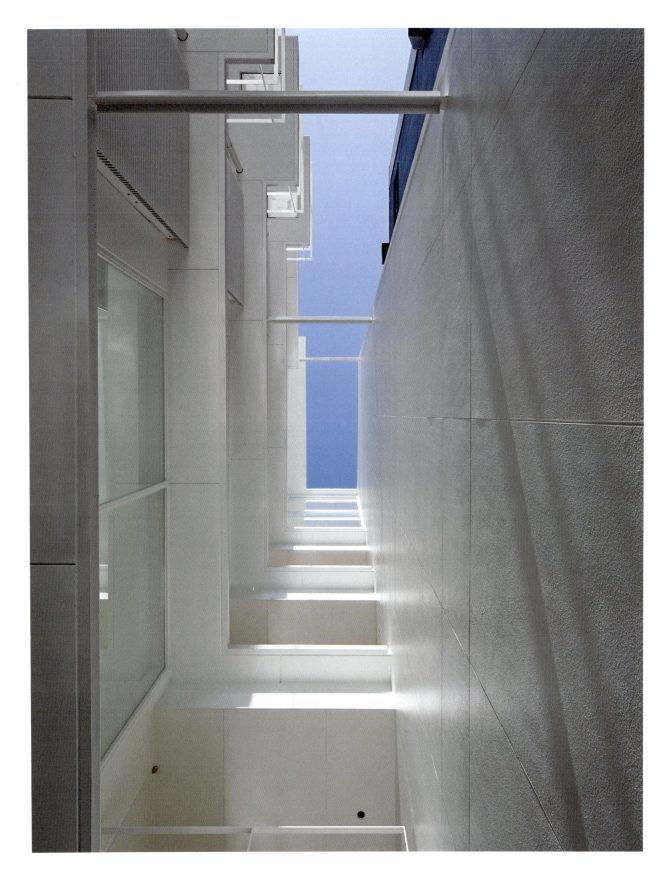

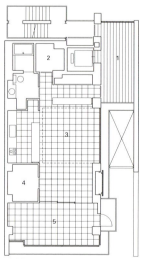

3F/4F Plan 1:250

5F Plan

1 テラス terrace
2 納戸 storage
3 LDK living/dining/kitchen
4 ウォークインクローゼット walk-in closet
5 寝室 bedroom

● Kamiya House

左／フルハイトの開口部で都市に開く空間。
上／障子による間仕切。
中、下／東側ヴォイドからの光。階による雰囲気の違い。

left / The space opens up to the city with its full-height openings.
below / *Shoji* screen partition.
below middle and bottom / The light from the void on the east side. Each floor has a different ambience.

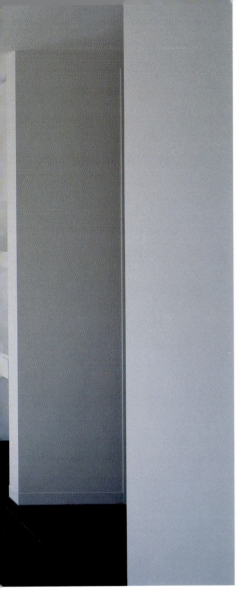

左上、右上／最上階メゾネットの階段と2層を繋ぐ吹き抜け。
下／和室。
右頁／最上階のリビングルーム。吹き抜けの光と影。

above left and above / The top-floor maisonette stairs and the double-height space that connects the two levels.
below / The *tatami* room.
opposite / The light and shadows of the double-height space of the top-floor living room.

1 キッチン kitchen
2 リビング・ダイニング living/dining room
3 納戸 storage
4 寝室 bedroom
5 和室 tatami room
6 テラス terrace

6F Plan 1:250　　7F Plan

● Kamiya House

上／最上部のペントハウス。モダン・デザインへの意識的回帰。
下／都市に開く個室空間。
右／個室が都市に開くのに対して、むしろ都市から閉じ、光と影と空を主題としたリビングルーム。

top / Penthouse at the top. I made a conscious return to modern design.
above / The bedroom opens up to the city.
right / Unlike the bedroom that opens up to the city, I closed off the living room from the city and put the focus on the light, shadows, and sky.

● Kamiya House

Tearoom project in the Center of Tokyo

2009, 東京都港区
Minato-ku, Tokyo

東京都心部、緑溢れる庭園の中に計画した茶室の計画である。

立礼、すなわち椅子とテーブルを使った茶席のための現代的な茶室空間を創るというプロジェクトだった。ライムストーンや版築の土の壁で構成され、庭に対して完全に開放することが可能な開口部を持つ茶席と、そこへのアプローチの空間のふたつが設計の主題だった。茶室の空間については、庭に開放した時の光のグラデーションが綺麗に拡がる天井面＝屋根形状としたいと考えた。屋根はスティール・シートにフラット・バーのリブで剛性を確保した鉄板のHPシェル構造とし、天井を張らずその構造を露出する。その結果少しずつ勾配を変化させるリブの連続に水平方向の光、それにライムストーンの床面からの反射光がミックスし、屋根の鉄板構造を浮かび上がらせる。それが眼の前に拡がる都市の中の自然の風景を強調するだろうと考えていた。

アプローチについては溢れる自然の風景から少しずつ距離を感じるようなシークエンスを考え、ライムトーンの壁と宙に浮かせたフロストガラスのスクリーンの間を抜ける導線とし、少しずつ自然から離れ、アプローチは進むと共に、徐々に内部空間化する。最後に180°振り返ると、そこで茶室の内部空間の向こうに改めて庭園の自然が顔を出し、再び対面することになる。その額縁となるのが自然光の逆光に浮かび上がるHPシェルの屋根というわけだ。

This is a tearoom that I planned in a lush garden in central Tokyo.

The project was to make a modern tearoom space for *ryurei*-style tea ceremonies—that is, tea ceremonies held using chairs and tables. The focus of the design was on the tea ceremony space—which I composed with limestone, rammed earth walls, and openings that fully open up to the garden—and on the approach spaces leading to it. I wanted to give the tearoom a ceiling/roof form that would create a beautiful gradation of light when the space was opened up to the garden. I thus made the roof as a hypar shell structure composed of steel sheets stiffened with flat bar ribs, and I exposed the structure by not installing a ceiling. As a result, the roof structure, with its series of ribs that follow a gradually changing gradient, would be lit up by a mixture of light entering from the side and light reflected off the limestone floor. I imagined that this would accentuate the natural landscape spread out before the tearoom within the city.

For the approach, I wanted to make a sequence that would give people the feeling of gradually moving away from the lush nature. I made the circulation so that people would pass between the limestone wall and floating frosted glass screen as they moved away from the nature, while the spaces would become more internalized as they moved further down the approach. Turning around 180° at the end, they would then reencounter the nature of the garden that would reappear beyond the tearoom. The hypar shell roof, backlit by the natural light, would serve as a frame for this moment.

上／外観。
左下／露地としてのアプローチ。
右下／自然に開く内部空間。HPシェルの屋根。
above left / View of exterior.
far left / Garden path approach.
left / The interior space under the hypar-shell roof opens to the nature.

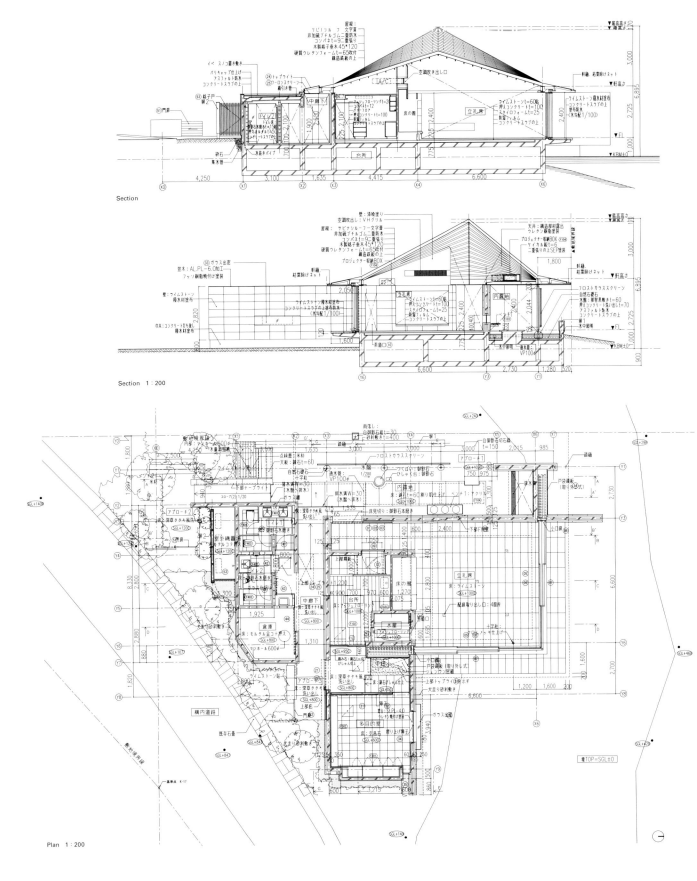

書院 / Penthouse
Zen Lounge II

2009, 西日本
Western Japan

曹洞宗の寺院、その寺院の屋根裏空間の再生である。

　曹洞宗の寺院が特別な機会に行う儀式、それに出席する猊下の宿所を準備することが必要になり、それをきっかけに恒久的には住職の書斎として使うことを目的に計画された。何年も使われていなかった屋根裏部屋を整備し、それに面していた屋上階を庭園として再生する。

　階下の主階には正式な書院の空間が用意されており、その書院の裏、一見するとそこに階段があるとは分からない扉を開けると、このペントハウスに繋がる階段が出現する。書斎というこの場所の機能を考え、主階の公式な書院と対になるように、私的な性格を持つ書院としてこのペントハウスを設計した。その外部には蓮の咲く水庭の屋上庭園を計画することで、ペントハウスへ続く階段はさながら天上へと至るかのような雰囲気を漂わせることになった。名栗の床、漆喰仕上げの白い空間に黒錆鉄板の壁パネルやヴェネチアン・スタッコの天井パネルが浮遊し、どこか非現実的な様相を漂わせる。

　下の主階の宗教空間からはむしろかけ離れた、どこか非現実的な、浮遊感のあるペントハウスの空間をつくろうというのが意図だった。ペントハウスという空間が本質的に持つ下階との精神的な距離の遠さ、隔絶感を積極的に捉えようとした試みである。

This is a renovation of an attic space in a Soto Zen temple.

　The project emerged when the need arose to prepare lodgings for the high priests who would be attending the rituals held at the temple on special occasions, but the space was then planned to be used in the long term as the priest's personal *shoin* [study]. This entailed refurbishing a long-unused attic and renovating the adjacent rooftop into a garden.

　On the main ground-floor level, there is an official *shoin*. Behind it, there is a door which at first glance does not seem like it would open into the stairway that leads to the penthouse. In view of its function, I have given the penthouse *shoin* a private character that contrasts to the official *shoin* below. Outside the space is a rooftop garden, which I designed as a water garden with flowering lotuses. Owing to this, the stairway to the penthouse now feels like it leads to the heavens. The penthouse itself presents somewhat of an otherworldly quality with its white stucco finish walls, *naguri* finish floors, floating black steel plate wall panels, and Venetian stucco ceiling panels.

　My aim was to create a penthouse that would somehow feel otherworldly and ethereal, contrasting from the religious space on the main floor below. I attempted to actively capture the sense of mental distance and isolation that the penthouse space naturally created in respect to the lower floor.

寺院全景。
General view of the temple.

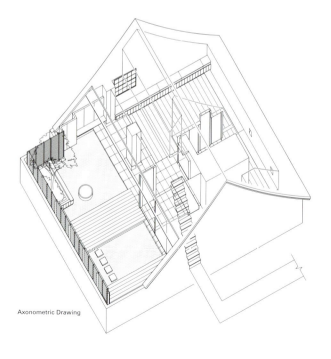

Axonometric Drawing

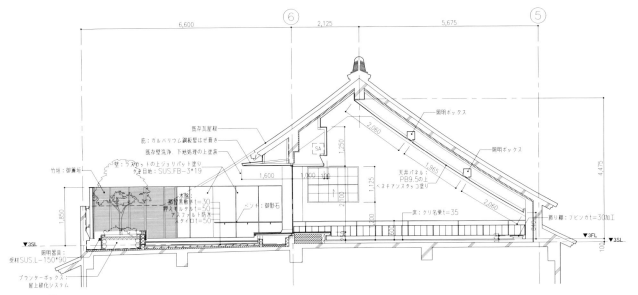

Section 1:120

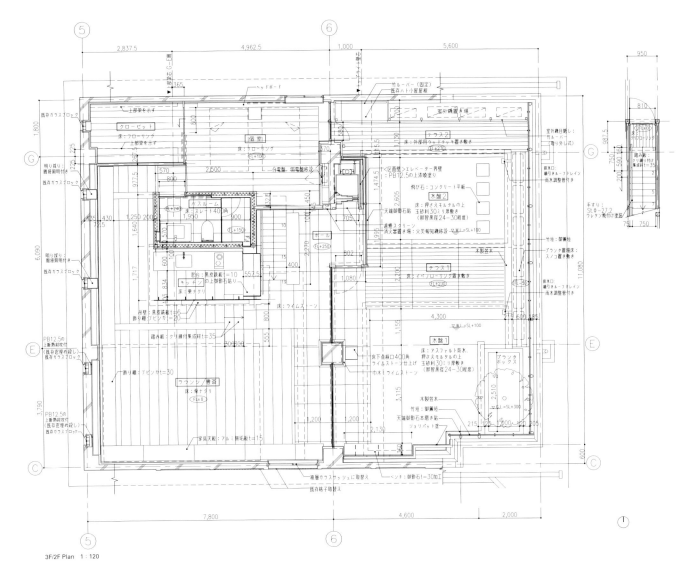

3F/2F Plan 1:120

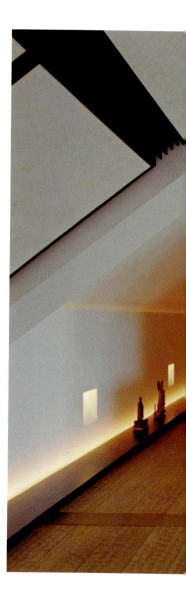

上／ヴェネチアン・スタッコ塗りの天井面に名栗の床。
左下／ペントハウスへの階段。
右下／仏様と出会う。

top / Venetian stucco-finish ceiling and *naguri*-finish floor.
above left / Stairs to the penthouse.
above / Encountering the Buddha.

上／全景。
下／蓮池に囲まれたペントハウス。
above / General view.
right / Penthouse bounded by the lotus pond.

書院 / Third-place
Zen Lounge III

2009, 東京都千代田区
Chiyoda-ku, Tokyo

東京都心に建つマンションの改装である。

大都市で暮らす人達にとっての日常的な、毎日の生活を過ごすための住宅を第1の住宅、週末や休日の時間を自然の中で過ごすためのいわゆる週末住宅を第2の住宅だと考えると、都心に居ながらも日常的ではない時間を過ごすための住宅を第3の住宅、ここではThird placeと呼ぶことにする。

この住宅はそうした都市に居住するクライアントにとってのThird place、仕事ではない時間を都市の中で過ごすための場所であり、ここでは立礼のお茶席とすることが求められ、茶会のための空間と家具を設計した。

立礼茶室としての空間はいわゆる壁、床、天井のインテリアデザインと、家具や、さらには備品のデザインまでもが等価で、しかも分かち難く在る。そこで行われる茶会の所作にとっては、それが家具と関わるものであれ、建築的要素と関わるものであれ、等価になる。そこで行われる人間の所作＝activityが空間の全ての要素を決定するというのが茶席の空間であり、それを設計する機会を得たことで、むしろ建築設計の原点、建築と人間との関係の在り方を再確認することが出来たと考えている。

This project is a renovation of a condominium in central Tokyo.

If a house where city dwellers spend their everyday lives is a first house, and if a so-called "weekend house" where they spend weekends and breaks amidst nature can be considered to be a second house, then a house where they can spend time outside of their everyday lives even while being in the city can be called a third house. This is what I am referring to as a "third place" here.

This house is a third place for the city-dwelling client. It is a place for spending non-working hours in the city. I was asked to prepare a setting for *ryurei*-style tea ceremonies, so I designed the space and furniture to be used for tea events.

In a space of a *ryurei* tearoom, everything from the interior designs of the walls, floor, and ceiling to the designs of even the furniture and appliances have equal weight and exist inseparably from each other. The activity of ceremonial tea-drinking that takes place there treats everything from the furniture to the architectural elements with equal value. A tearoom is a space in which every element is determined by the human activities conducted within it. I believe that the opportunity to design such a space allowed me to reconfirm the very fundaments of architectural design, which deals with defining the relationship between architecture and humans.

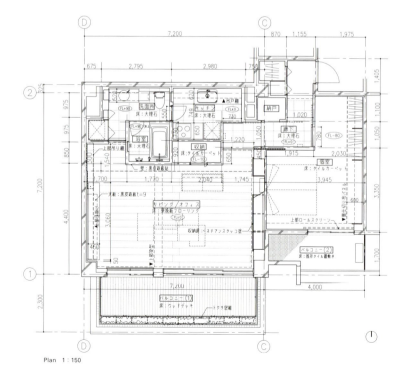

Plan 1 : 150

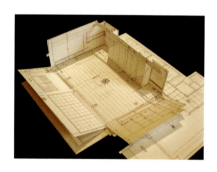

右／起こし絵。
右頁／リビング・ダイニング。

above / *Okoshi-ezu* [pop-up drawing].
opposite / Living/dining room.

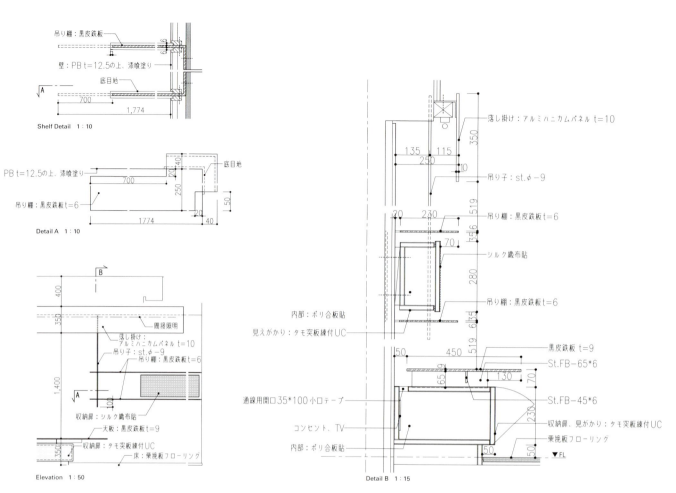

床(とこ)詳細図　Detail Drawing of "Toko"

この書院のためにデザインされたアルミと黒錆銀板の違い棚と手前の立礼卓。
The staggered shelves made of aluminum and black rusted silver plates and the *ryurei*-style tea ceremony table were designed for the study.

立礼卓は通常は長方形のテーブルとして使用し、お手前の時には一部を移動させると亭主のための場所が出来る。

The *ryurei*-style tea ceremony table can be used normally as a rectangular table, and it can be reconfigured to make a place for the tea host when holding ceremonies.

KIT HOUSE

2010, 京都市左京区
Sakyo-ku, Kyoto

京都工芸繊維大学の学生会館であり、1階にレストラン、2階にブックショップとコンビニエンス・ストアが入っている。

設計の第1のポイントは壁の素材を煉瓦としたことである。世界中、大学のキャンパスはネオ・ゴシックを基本とする煉瓦の建築を基本としており、このキャンパスも例外ではない。煉瓦タイル仕上げがキャンパス全体の基本的な外壁仕上げであったが、この小さな建物ではタイルではなく、むしろ煉瓦そのものを採用することとした。第2のポイントはこの建物は他の教室棟や研究室棟と異なり、学内全体の不特定多数の教員や学生が使用する、パブリックな機能を持つことである。そのことを考え、この建物の北側外壁は東西に揃っている他の建物の壁面線よりも5m、キャンティレバーで北側構内通路方向に飛び出しており、その場所に建物2階の外部空間へと繋がる緩やかな屋外階段を構内通路へと直接繋がるように配置した。

第3は屋根形状であり、この鋸状の屋根は同じ場所に過去に建っていた工房棟からの引用であり、卒業して時間の経ったOB諸氏にも新しい建物でありながらも、学生時代を思い出すきっかけとなるような建物としたいと考えたことの結果である。最後に4番目はキャンパス計画の系譜を受け継ぐことであり、すなわちこのキャンパスに建つ建物や外構計画に頻繁に見られる、北東に在る比叡山から京都という都市の中心方向である南西へと向かう斜めの方向性、京都の鬼門方向を暗示しているかのような斜方向性をこの建築にも導入することである。レストランの吹き抜けの斜め壁はその結果生まれた。

蛇足になるが、この建物は主階が2階に在る3層構造の建築であり、どこかでル・コルビュジエのサヴォア邸に捧げるオマージュとしたいと大胆にも考えていたこと、それを最後に告白しておきたいと思う。

This is the student union at the Kyoto Institute of Technology. It has a restaurant on the first level and a bookshop and convenience store on the second level.

The first key point of the design is the brick material of the walls. University campuses worldwide are made of neoclassical brick buildings, and this one is no exception. Brick tile is the basic cladding used on this campus, but I have instead used actual bricks for this small building. The second point is that this building, unlike the other classroom and laboratory blocks, contains public functions meant for all of the university's faculty and students. Taking this into account, I have pushed the north wall out 5 m beyond the walls of the other buildings aligned in the east-west direction, cantilevered the wall over the northern campus road, and positioned a gentle outdoor stairway in this space to link the road directly to the exterior spaces on the second level.

The third point is the roof form. The jagged roof makes a reference to the workshop block that used to occupy the same spot in the past. I did this with the hope of making the building feel new to the older alumni but also remind them of their student years. The fourth and last point is that it picks up on the overall plan of the campus. Specifically, I incorporated the same diagonal directionality seen throughout the campus' buildings and landscaping that aligns with the axis extending between Mount Hiei to the northeast and the city center of Kyoto to the southwest—an axis that suggests the direction of Kyoto's *kimon* [lit. "demon's gate"; refers to the northeast direction, where demons are considered to come from]. This is what gave rise to the diagonal wall of the restaurant atrium.

This may be superfluous, but I will end by confessing that I audaciously aimed to make this building which has a three-level structure with the principal floor on the second level as an homage to Le Corbusier's Villa Savoye.

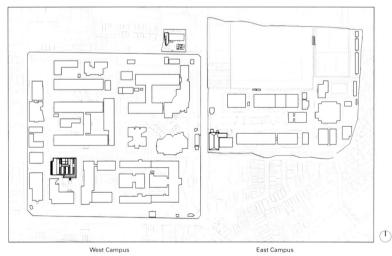

West Campus / East Campus

Site Plan 1 : 6000

右頁／北面2階へのアプローチ上部に飛び出して浮遊する2階煉瓦壁の重量感のあるヴォリュームと構造でもある鋸状の屋根。

244-245頁／浮遊する煉瓦壁に軽快に、そして半透明な面としての表現を導入する。重量感のある素材がその重さを失う瞬間。

opposite / The massive volume of the brick wall that floats above the approach to the second floor on the north side and the saw-shaped roof.
pp. 244–245 / I articulated a section of the floating brick wall as a light, translucent surface. The heavy material appears to lose its mass at this moment.

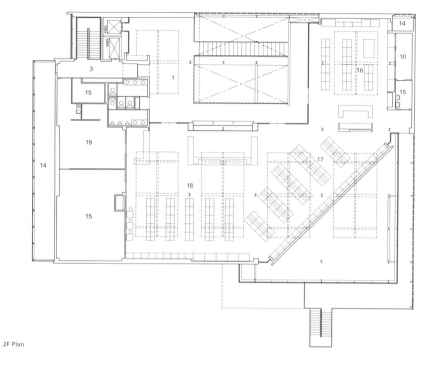

2F Plan

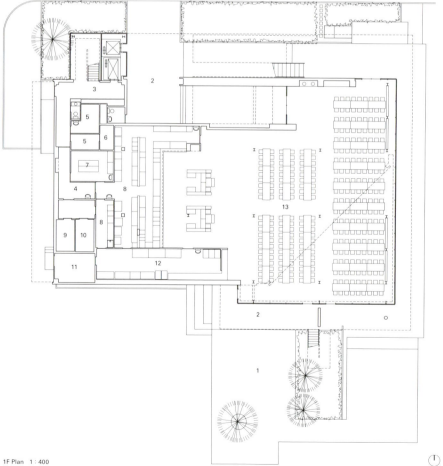

1F Plan 1:400

1 テラス　terrace
2 アプローチ　approach
3 廊下　corridor
4 前室　anteroom
5 更衣室　changing room
6 機械室　machine room
7 配膳室　pantry
8 厨房　kitchen
9 冷凍庫　freezer
10 冷蔵庫　refrigerator
11 ゴミ置場　trash room
12 洗浄室　dishwashing room
13 食堂　cafeteria
14 室外機置場　A/C condenser space
15 倉庫　storage
16 コンビニエンスストア　convenience store
17 ブックショップ　bookshop
18 購買　cooperative store
19 事務室　office

2階へと向かうアプローチと浮遊する煉瓦壁。
The approach to the second floor and the floating brick wall.

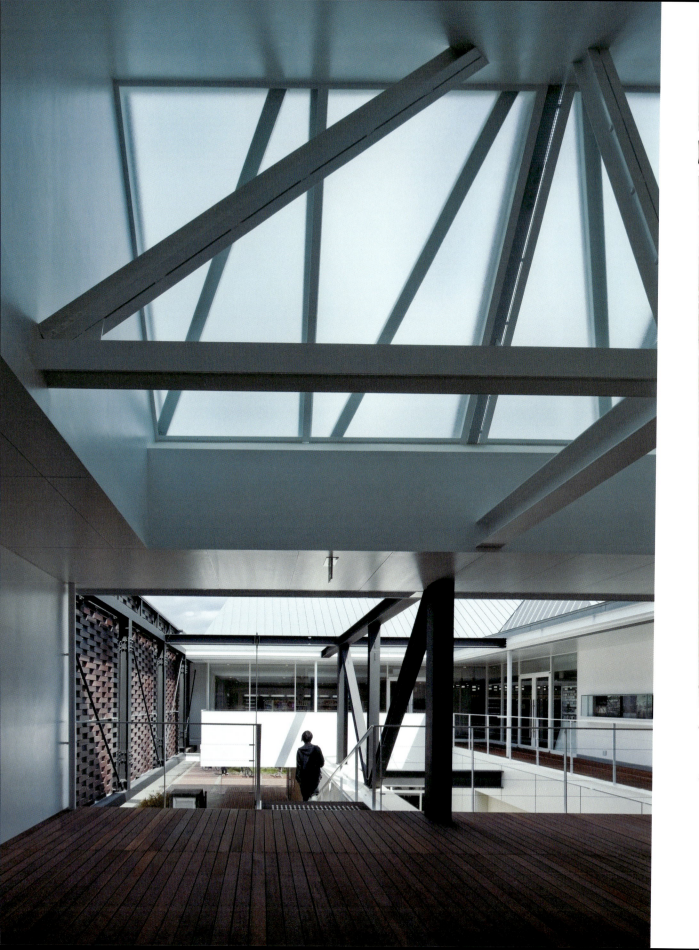

左頁／2階の屋外デッキと屋根。
上左／2階ブックショップ。
上中、上右／1階食堂吹き抜け部。
下／2階屋外通路。ブックショップから南側テラスへと至る。
250-251頁／1階食堂全景。2階壁面の写真は工事中の場所の記録。

opposite / Outdoor deck and roof on the second floor.
above / Second-floor bookshop.
above right / Atrium of the first-floor cafeteria.
right / Second-floor outdoor passage. It leads to the south terrace from the bookshop.
pp. 250–251 / General view of the first-floor cafeteria. The photographs on the second-floor wall are records of the site during construction.

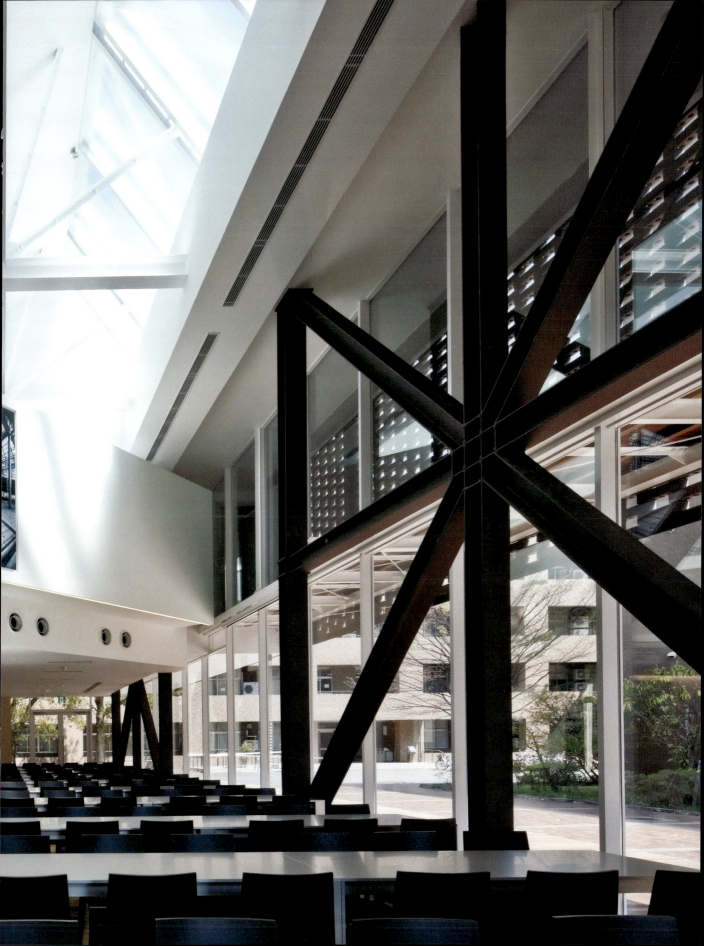

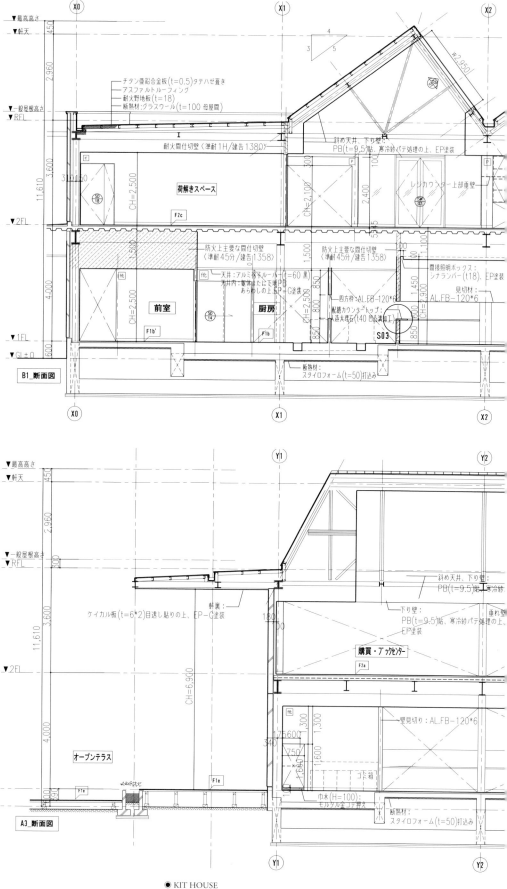

Section

● KIT HOUSE

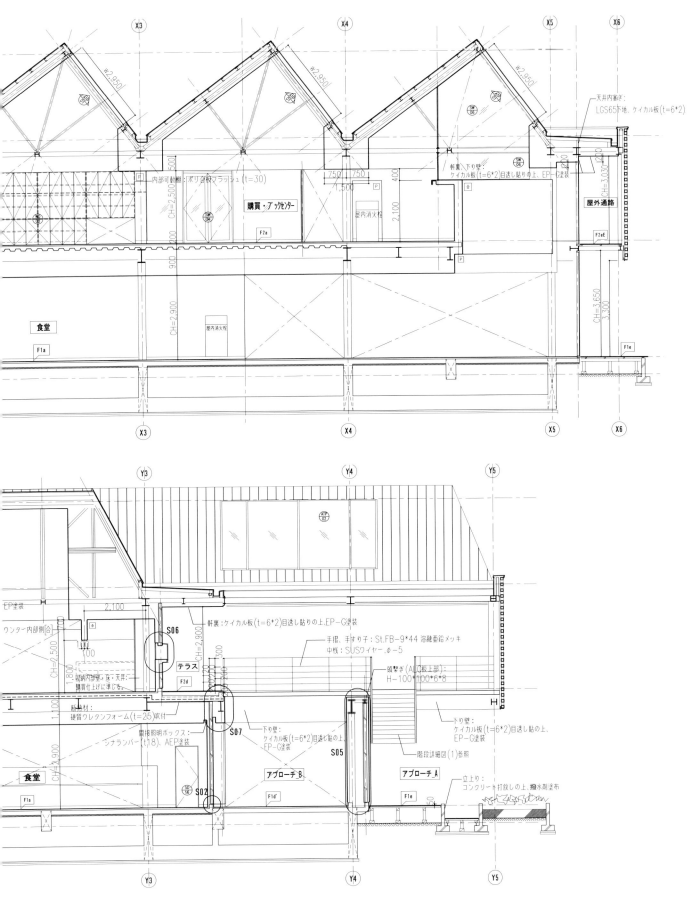

上／東南方向からの全景。
下／夕暮れの東側立面。
右／過去のイメージを残した屋根と南側テラス。テラスに立つ樹木も元からの位置にそのまま残したもの。
below / General view from the southeast.
bottom / East elevation at dusk.
right / The roof and south terrace preserve a memory of the site's past. The trees on the terrace also grow in their original positions.

御所西の家
House near Kyoto Gosho

2011, 京都市上京区
Kamigyo-ku, Kyoto

京都市中心部、御所の西に拡がる住宅街に建つ4人家族のための住宅である。

それぞれが個室の中に籠るのではなく、全体がひとつの大きな空間であるような住宅としたい、というところから設計が始まった。間口が狭く奥行きの長い、京都に典型的ないわゆる〈鰻の寝床〉の敷地であり、その長い奥行きに沿って、間口1.2m、奥行き5.3mの中庭を配し、残りの部分を前後に分け半階ずつずらしたスプリット・レベルの構成とした。従って全体は半階ずつずれながら上昇する、垂直に繋がった1室空間とした。

この場所は京都市の景観規制を受ける。ファサードの壁面線セットバックや仕上げ材料、それに指定勾配の屋根や軒の出寸法の指定などの規制を考慮し、屋根材は瓦以前の京都の町家の屋根に使われていた天然スレート葺きとしながらも、壁面は逆に現代の素材である金属パネルとした。過去から現在までの時代を横断的に捉え、〈伝統的なファサード〉なるものを改めて今日的にゼロから考え直したいという想いの発露であった。

This is a house for a family of four located in a residential district to the west of the Imperial Palace in central Kyoto.

I approached the design with the idea of making the house as a single large space rather than providing private rooms for the residents to seclude themselves in. The narrow, deep lot was one of Kyoto's typical "eel's nest" lots. I positioned a 1.2-m-wide, 5.3-m-long courtyard along its length and divided the remaining part into a front and back area to create split levels staggered by half a floor. This resulted in a single space that was connected vertically across the levels that rose upwards by half-floor increments.

The site was subjected to Kyoto's cityscape ordinance. I thus had to take into account things such as the façade set-back line, finish material restrictions, prescribed roof pitch, and allowable eave dimensions. I used natural slate for the roofing material—a material used on Kyoto's townhouses before roof tiles—but made the walls with modern metal panels. The design manifested my wish to rethink the notion of a "traditional façade" from scratch with a contemporary perspective that cuts across the ages, from the past to the present.

1 アプローチ／駐車スペース approach/garage
2 ゲストルーム guest room
3 ホール hall
4 リビング・ダイニング living/dining room
5 キッチン kitchen
6 プレイルーム playroom
7 寝室 bedroom
8 子供室 children's room

Section

Section 1:300

右頁／ファサード夕景。伝統的な素材と現代の素材との意識的な混在。

opposite / Evening view of the façade. I consciously mixed together the traditional and modern materials.

左、右／内法の有効寸法幅が1.2mしかない中庭。北側に配置することで十分な光が入ってくる。
右頁／2階のリビング・ダイニングを階段から見る。

far left, left / The courtyard measures only 1.2 m from wall to wall. It brings in plenty of light from where it is positioned on the north side.
opposite / Second-floor living/dining room as seen from the stairs.

1	アプローチ/駐車スペース　approach/garage	6	キッチン　kitchen
2	ゲストルーム　guest room	7	プレイルーム　playroom
3	ホール　hall	8	子供室　children's room
4	中庭　courtyard	9	寝室　bedroom
5	リビング・ダイニング　living/dining room		

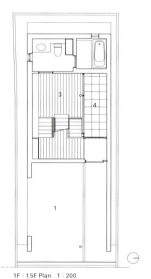

1F - 1.5F Plan　1 : 200

2F - 2.5F Plan　　3F - 3.5F Plan

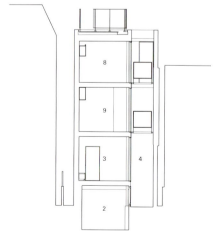

Section　1 : 200

● House near Kyoto Gosho

左頁左／中2階プレイルームから中庭方向を見る。
左頁右／2階リビング・ダイニングに中庭から入る光。

opposite, top left / View towards the courtyard from the playroom on the first-floor mezzanine.
opposite, top right / Light shining into the second-floor living/dining room from the courtyard.

左／2階リビングルームから中庭・階段方向を見る。
上／リビング・ダイニング2、3階の吹き抜け。
下／中3階子供室。左に中庭。

opposite, bottom / View towards the courtyard and stairs from the second-floor living/dining room.
top / Second and third floors of the double-height space beside the living/dining room.
above / Children's room on the second-floor mezzanine. The courtyard is on the left.

262-263頁／3階から奥行方向を見る。階が上になるほど、中庭からの光が増し、空が視野に入ってくる。

pp. 262–263 / View into the back of the third floor. As one climbs higher, the light from the courtyard grows stronger, and eventually one can see the sky.

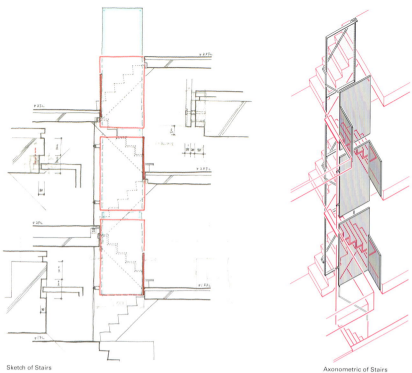

Sketch of Stairs

Axonometric of Stairs

Section 1 : 120

● House near Kyoto Gosho

階段のディテール。漆喰塗り、スティールのフラットバー・集成材パネル、スティール、パンチング・メタルなど、様々な素材が構造、視線の制御などそれぞれ最適な機能を担う。

Stair details. The various materials, such as the lacquer paint, steel flat bars, laminated wood panels, and perforated metal, each play an effective role by providing structure or regulating views.

上、中／最上階の光。
下、右上／鉄筋コンクリート構造の建築だが、垂直荷重のみを支える100㎜の無垢スティール柱をもっとも合理的な場所に配置した。

top left and above left / The light on the top floor.
left and above right/ This is a reinforced concrete building, but I added ø 100 mm exposed steel columns in the most rational positions to support only vertical loads.

● House near Kyoto Gosho

下／伝統的な景観に配慮したファサード。伝統と〈今日性〉のせめぎ合いの表現。

far right / I designed the façade with consideration for the traditional setting. It presents an expression that borders between tradition and "contemporariness".

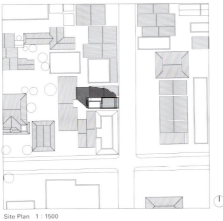

Site Plan 1：1500

日東薬品構内景観整備計画
NITTO PHARMA Landscaping project

2011, 京都府向日市
Muko, Kyoto

京都市郊外の住宅街の中にある製薬会社の構内に建つ工場棟の改装を手始めとする構内景観整備計画である。既に終了しているものは2棟であるが、現在も進行中のプロジェクトである。

最初の計画は工場棟改装であり、2階の実験機能を残しながら、1階を〈ホール／会議室棟〉へと機能変更することであった。製薬会社の建築であるため、外壁には様々な配管や機械が設置されている。それらは実験に必要な機能を担っている設備であるため、撤去や移設は難しい。内部の間仕切りや機能変更はさほど難しいものではないが、構内景観をどう整備するか、構内全体の景観整備に適用可能なルールと方法論をどうつくり上げるか、というのが一番大変な課題だった。結果として、既存建物の外部にバッファ・ゾーンをつくることを全体のルールとし、この〈ホール／会議室棟〉では2階の白い垂直ルーバー、1階では2辺方向に増設された庇や白煉瓦の壁、木製ルーバーやテントの可動日除け、それにウッドデッキなどで新しいバッファ空間をつくっていった。

2棟目はその向かいに建つ。これは1階を既存のまま構造補強をしつつも実験室としての機能を残しながら、2階を事務機能へと変更する計画だった。ここでは1棟目の〈ホール／会議室棟〉で決めたルール、外部のバッファ空間を新しく考えるというルールに従って、2階の全体を囲む白い垂直ルーバーとそれと絡む屋外階段による2階への直接のアプローチの新設、それに事務室へと変更することに依る2階への大きな開口部の新設など、〈ホール／会議室棟〉にはなかった新しいヴォキャブラリーも加えながら展開した。

これからも個別の建物のバッファ・ゾーンを過去のものとは少しずつ変化させながら展開し、その蓄積として本社構内の新しい全体景観計画を模索していきたいと考えている。

This is a project to redesign the premises of a pharmaceutical company located in a residential district in the outskirts of Kyoto. I have completed renovating two laboratory buildings so far in the ongoing project.

The first renovation entailed reprogramming the first level of a laboratory building into a hall and conference rooms while maintaining the laboratory functions on the second level. Because this was a pharmaceutical building, there were various ducts and machinery on the exterior walls. They could not be removed or moved as they served functions necessary for conducting laboratory experiments. It was not particularly difficult to rearrange the interior partitions and reprogram the spaces, but it was challenging to figure out how to rework the landscaping and to develop rules and a methodology for this that could be implemented on the premises as a whole. I ultimately established the general rule that buffer zones should be created around the existing buildings. I made the new buffer spaces of this hall/conference block by facing the second level with white vertical louvers and adding eaves, white brick walls, wooden louvers, operable tent screens, and a wooden deck on two sides of the first level.

The second building stands across from the first. It also was originally a laboratory building. The renovation entailed reinforcing the structure of the first level, which was to retain its laboratory functions, and turning the second level into an office. While adhering to the rule to create new perimeter buffer spaces that I established in the first renovation, I also added vocabulary elements not used in the hall/conference block—such as the direct approach to the second level, which I made by working external stairs into the white louvers that I wrapped around the entire second level; and the large opening in the second level, which I made in view of the floor's new function as an office.

I intend to continue to explore how to shape the new general landscaping plan for the company's premises as I develop the buffer zones of each building to be slightly different from the last.

Site Plan　1 : 4000

右頁上／〈ホール／会議室棟〉の全景。
右頁下／〈ホール／会議室棟〉東側立面。
opposite, top / General view of the hall/conference block.
opposite, bottom / East elevation of the hall/conference block.

ホール/会議室棟
Hall/Conference Division

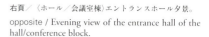
右頁／〈ホール／会議室棟〉エントランスホール夕景。
opposite / Evening view of the entrance hall of the hall/conference block.

改装前の〈ホール／会議室棟〉。
Hall/conference block before renovations.

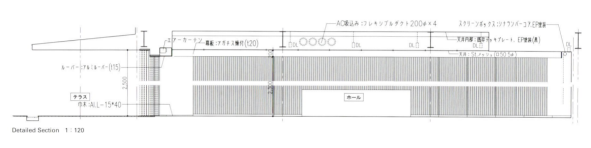
Detailed Section 1：120

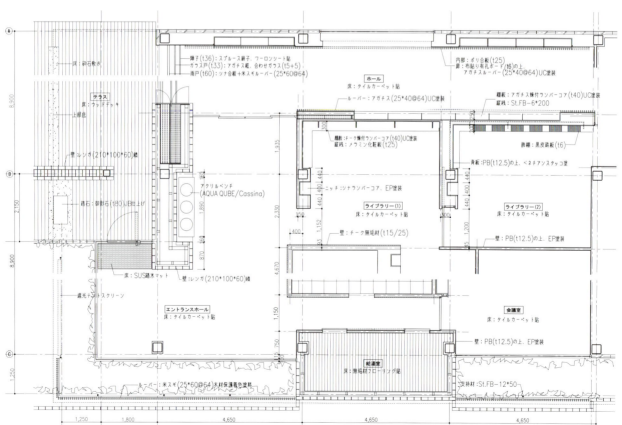
Detailed Plan 1：120

● NITTO PHARMA Landscaping project

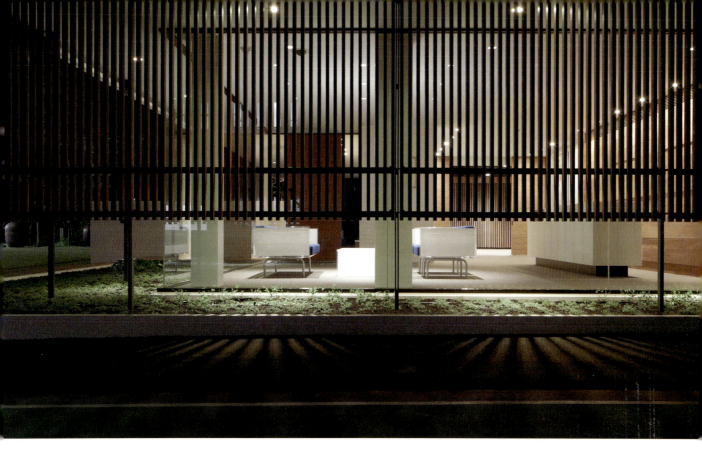

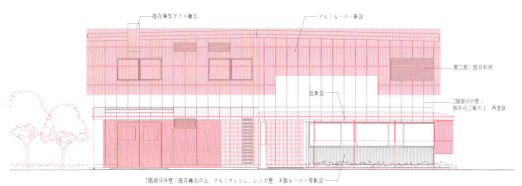

South Elevation (red : new alteration) 1 : 200

上2点／エントランスホール。
中2点／大会議室から南を見る。サッシュ、障子共に開放可能な開口部。
下2点／小会議室。
below, top row / Entrance hall.
below, center row / Southward view from the large conference room. The sashes and shoji screens are operable.
below, bottom row / Small meeting room.

実験室／事務室棟
Laboratory／Office Division

上／〈実験室／事務室棟〉全景。左の新設した屋外階段により2階の事務室へアクセスする。左に見えるのは〈ホール／会議室棟〉。
左／新設した屋外階段のディテール。
右／2階事務室に新設した開口。

top / General view of the laboratory/office block. The new exterior stairs on the left lead to the office on the second floor. The hall/conference block is visible on the left.
left / Details of the newly added exterior stairs.
above / New opening in the second-floor office.

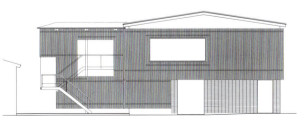

West Elevation　1：250

Wujiang New City Planning project, China

2008, 呉江市, 中国江蘇省
Wujiang, China

上海市の西、蘇州市中心部の南に呉江という都市がある。上海、蘇州という大都市に挟まれ、基本的には長江デルタの製造業、第2次産業地帯の中心に位置する呉江市が、太湖に面している干潟を整備し周辺を再開発することで人口150万人の新都心をつくるという計画である。

中国では計画の規模が基準を超えると、国際設計競技を経て、設計者を特定することになる。我々はその候補の1人に選ばれ、新都市計画を作成することになった。軸線を強調した変形グリッド状の都市が好まれるのは分かっているのだが、それをそのまま提案するつもりはなかった。ここでは太湖に向かう軸線部分をヴォイドの連続──広場や公園などの歩行空間が湖へと向かって延びる計画──とし、その湖の焦点に当たる場所、太湖の湖面の上に太湖水族館+自然史博物館を設けることを提案した。ウォーターフロントでの水際空間の整備も重要だが、水の中に延びていく桟橋とそこに計画された公共施設の姿こそが重要だと考えた。

例えば英国ロンドンからほど近い都市ブライトン、そのコンサートホールやアミューズメントなどを内包するちょっと異国情緒を感じさせる建物が海に浮いて見える桟橋（ブライトン・ピア）の風景、これがブライトンという都市の象徴的な風景であること、あるいはアメリカ西海岸の街サンタモニカの太平洋に飛び出した桟橋（サンタモニカ・ピア）の先にあるレストランや観覧車が印象的なアミューズメントパークの風景など、忘れられない都市の水際の象徴的な風景には、桟橋とそこにある公共的機能が重要だし、その都市の印象そのものさえも決定すると考えた故の提案である。

中国では主要な交通手段である自動車のための道路については、太湖に向かう軸線部分のヴォイドの両側に2本の主要幹線道路を通し、北側の幹線道路沿いにはこの新都心の東に位置するバスセンターと太湖湖岸を結ぶLRTを提案した。南北には湖岸沿い、中央部、開発区域の東端に3本の緑化帯を計画した。

この設計競技、幸か不幸か我々が勝ったのだが、それよりも建築家として興味深かったのは各社のプレゼンテーションだった。アメリカのチームはミニ・マンハッタン、オーストラリアのチームはミニ・シドニー、ドイツのチームはミニ・ベルリンのような提案だったからであり、呉江市都市計画局長が事前に、君達とは〈いとこ同士〉だから、と言ったことの意味が分かった。確かに我々の都市、京都は西安の写しだし、アメリカやオーストラリアの建築家の案と比べると、この提案は確かに〈中国的〉だったのかもしれない。

There is a district called Wujiang to the south of Suzhou's city center and to the west of Shanghai. This is a project to develop an area by Lake Tai's mud flats to create a new city center of 1.5 million people for Wujiang, which sits sandwiched between the major cities of Shanghai and Suzhou at the center of the belt of manufacturing industries based in the Yangtze River Delta. In China, when a project exceeds a certain scale, its architects are chosen through an international design competition. We were selected as one of the candidates for this project and had to produce plans for the new city. I knew that a city laid out on a warped grid with emphasized axes would be favored, but I had no intention of simply proposing such a plan. I instead proposed to make an axis as a series of voids extending towards Lake Tai—in the form of pedestrian spaces such as plazas and parks—and to build an aquarium and natural history museum themed on Lake Tai on the water at the focal point of this axis. While understanding the value of setting up waterfront spaces, I believed that the most important thing was the presentation of the pier extending into the lake and the public facilities built onto it.

This proposal came out of my belief that piers and public programs are vital for iconic waterfronts and can even define one's impression of a city. For example, the iconic view of the city of Brighton near London is the sight of the Brighton Pier, which gives off somewhat of an exotic feel with its concert hall and amusement park floating on the water, and the west-coast American city of Santa Monica is recognizable by the restaurants and iconic Ferris wheel built onto the end of its pier that extends into the Pacific Ocean.

The car is the primary means of transportation in China, so I proposed to put arterial roads on both sides of the void axis and to make an LRT line along the northern main road to connect the lakefront with the bus terminal to the east. I also planned three green belts running in the north-south direction along the lake, in the central area, and at the eastern edge of the development.

For better or worse, we came out as the winners of the competition. What interested me as an architect were the presentations given by each team. The American team proposed a mini-Manhattan, the Australian team proposed a mini-Sydney, and the German team proposed a mini-Berlin. I later understood what the director of Wujiang's urban planning bureau meant when he told me that we were "cousins". The layout of our home city, Kyoto, is based on that of Xi'an, so our scheme may certainly have been more "Chinese" compared to those of the Americans or Australians.

サンタモニカの桟橋。
Santa Monica Pier.

右頁上／新都市計画全景。
右頁下／太湖に飛び出した桟橋に計画した太湖自然史博物館と夕景時イベントの提案。

opposite, top / General view of the newly planned city.
opposite, bottom / The Lake Tai National History Museum that I designed on a pier extending out into the lake, and an idea for an evening event that I proposed.

広域分析図　Extended Site Analysis Diagram

鉄道交通システム計画図　Rail System Plan

周辺区域都市計画図　Urban Plan for Surrounding Area

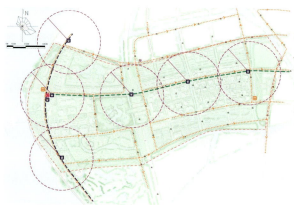

公共交通計画図　Public Transportation Plan

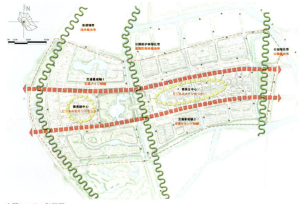

空間システム計画図　Spatial Strategy Plan

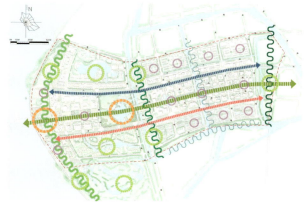

景観システム計画図　Landscaping Strategy Plan

● Wujiang New City Planning project, China

Section

Plan

上、右／太湖自然史博物館。
top, right / Lake Tai Natural History Museum.

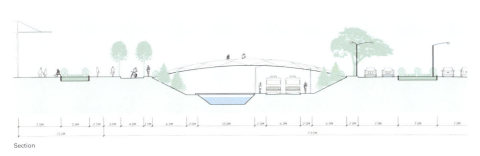

Section

LRTと水路による歩行者空間の提案。
Proposal for pedestrian spaces with LRT and waterways.

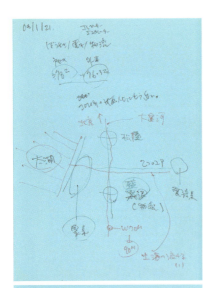
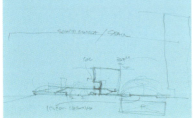

Conceptual Sketches

太湖から見た新都市の姿。
New city as seen from Lake Tai.

● Wujiang New City Planning project, China

象彦漆美術館
Zohiko Urushi Museum

2011, 京都市左京区
Sakyo-ku, Kyoto

江戸時代からの長い歴史を持つ京都の漆工芸の会社が、同社の伝統的な工芸品から現代の作品までを見せる新しい美術館を設立することになった。

本社ビルの1、2階を改装し、1階をレセプションと新しい漆の技術・技法の展示とコンサルティングの場所とし、同時に新設する庭園を横に見ながら2階へと上る階段を新しく設け、2階には美術館を配置する。漆がそうであるように、伝統的でありながら同時に現代的でもある空間をつくろうと考え、和紙、土、木材、畳といった伝統的な素材からアクリル、アルミ、黒錆鉄板といった現代的な素材までを組み合わせながら、それぞれの場所の求められる機能に合わせて空間をつくっていった。2層ある室内空間全体を支配する構成論理は単純で、水平・垂直の面、それも浮遊する面の構成で空間を分節化するという方法を採用した。構成的に空間をつくること、それは第一義的にはこの空間が近代主義的な論理でつくられていることの表現である。その上でそれとは相反するかのような、近代的な構成とは矛盾する光と影や素材感を導入する。面の仕上げとして採用した黒錆鉄板などの質感の在る素材と空間全体に導入した光と影の対比的な設計は、近代的で抽象的な構成に、素材感や光の陰影といった伝統的な要素を付け加えることで、前近代的な空間の持つ魅力を再現出来るのではないか、と考えている。

A lacquerware company in Kyoto with a long history going back to the Edo period had a plan to make a museum for its collection of traditional crafts and contemporary art.

The project entailed refurbishing the first and second floors of the company's headquarters. I made the first floor as a reception space, a space for showing new lacquer technologies and techniques, and a consultation space; installed a new staircase that ascends to the second floor beside a newly designed garden; and set up the museum on the second floor. I wanted to create spaces that were both traditional and contemporary, so I combined traditional materials such as *washi* paper, mud, wood, and *tatami* mats with modern materials such as acrylic, aluminum, and black rusted steel to shape the spaces to suit their required functions. The compositional logic behind the two-level interior is simple: The spaces are subdivided by a composition of floating horizontal and vertical planes. The use of this compositional approach signifies that the spaces have fundamentally been created with Modernist logic, but the elements such as light, shadow, and textures that I have introduced into the spaces contradict with Modernist composition. I believe that this contrastive design, with its planes of textured materials, such as the black rusted steel plates, and the light and shadow throughout its spaces, recreates the appeal of pre-modern space by adding the traditional elements of texture, light, and shadow to the abstract, Modernistic composition.

1 エントランス　entrance
2 打合せスペース　meeting space
3 坪庭　courtyard
4 展示室　exhibition room

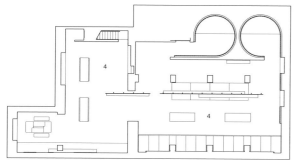

2F Plan

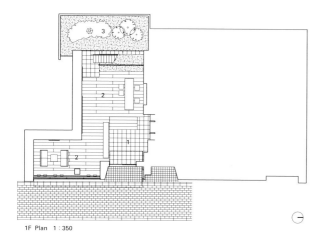

1F Plan　1:350

右頁／もっとも奥に配置した円形の展示室と和紙による〈光壁〉。その〈光壁〉に埋め込まれたディスプレイ棚。
282-283頁／1階エントランス全景。左はアクリルと漆で試作したパネル。〈日本的〉であることと同時に〈今日的〉でもあることという主題に向けてのケーススタディ。

opposite / The circular exhibition room at the very back and the "light wall" made of *washi* paper with built-in display cases.
pp. 282–283 / General view of the first-floor entrance. On the left are sample panels made with acrylic and lacquer. This was a case study to create something that would be both "Japanese" and "contemporary" at the same time.

スティールパネルで製作したファサードの庇。
The steel panel overhang on the façade.

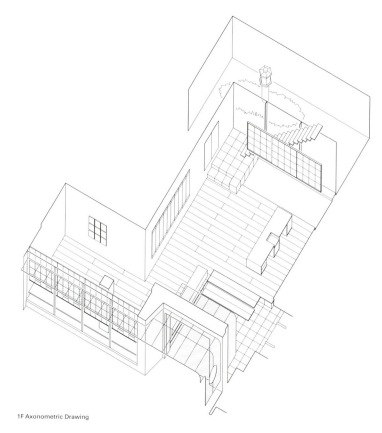

1F Axonometric Drawing

左、右／浮遊する障子スクリーンから飛び出したアクリル製の展示棚。アクリルのエッジから外部の自然光を内部に導く。
右頁／新しく整備した坪庭を横に見ながら2階に上る階段を配置した。障子越しに逆光のシルエットで人影が映る。

left, above / The acrylic display shelves extend out from the floating *shoji* screen. Daylight is drawn inside from the edge of the acrylic.
opposite / I positioned the stairs to offer a lateral view of the new pocket garden. Back-lit silhouettes are projected onto the *shoji* screen.

● Zohiko Urushi Museum

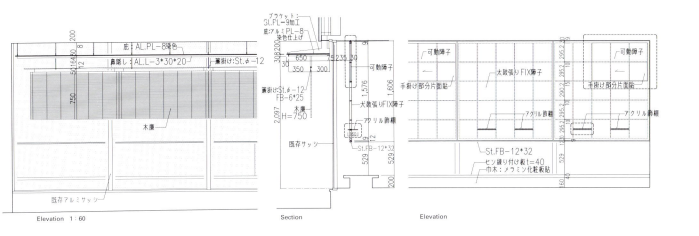

Elevation 1:60   Section   Elevation

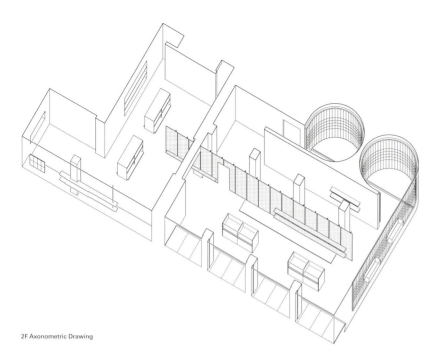

2F Axonometric Drawing

下／2階展示室全景。天井から吊るされた黒錆鉄板が空間を分節化する。

below / General view of the second-floor exhibition space. The black rusted steel plates suspended from the ceiling segments the space.

◉ Zohiko Urushi Museum

左、右／それぞれ異なる漆器の用途に合わせた展示空間を用意する。
下／もっとも貴重な漆器のための展示室。展示の邪魔をしない背景と光。

above / I prepared the exhibition spaces to suit the different uses of the lacquerware pieces.
below / Exhibition room for the most precious lacquerware pieces. I designed the backdrop and lighting to not interfere with the display.

Spiretec Office Headquarters project

2011, インド・デリー
Delhi, India

インドの建築の歴史や文化にはずっと興味があった。一度行きたいのだけれど、行く機会が無いなあと思っていたところ、設計競技に招待された。それは新しく開発中のリサーチパークの中、オフィスブロックの大まかな配置は決められているものの、オフィスやRandD部門、さらにここを訪ねて来る人のためのホテルに加えてコンベンションのための会議場を併設するなど、ひとつの小さな都市を設計するかのようなプロジェクトだった。行ったことは無いが、インドを勉強するにはいい機会だ、と考えて参加することにした。

高温で乾燥した気候、それに強い日差しといった、特徴的な環境での現代建築が求められている。そこでエアコンに頼っただけの現代建築ではなく、水の気化熱を導入することでの温度環境快適化やサンシェイドとしてのブリーズソレイユやアトリウムに架けられたテント屋根の提案など、この場所、この環境で有効な建築的装置を持つ現代建築を提案しようと考えた。

その後、全く違う機会を得てインドを訪ねることになった。そこで初めてインドの空気を実体験し、西海岸のヒンドゥー教の寺院や大航海時代の遺構を訪ねる機会を得る。その時訪ねたヒンドゥーの沐浴場、その床面、水面、それに水面ギリギリまで下げて架けられた屋根しかない沐浴場の空間に感動する。水の中を透過してきた方向性のない光が水面に架かる屋根裏の架構を浮かび上がらせる様は例えようも無く美しかった。建築家であれば誰もが訪ねるアーメダバードのル・コルビュジエやダッカのルイス・カーン、あるいはタージマハールやファテプルシークリ、それに階段井戸などを訪ねることは叶わない旅だったのだが、ケララ州トリシュールの沐浴場は自分にとっては、十二分に〈インド〉だった。これまで体験したことのない空間だったという意味で、だ。

I always had an interest in the history and culture of India's architecture. I had been hoping to visit someday, yet could not find an opportunity to do so—until I was invited to participate in this design competition. It was a project to design something of a small city within a new research park that was under development. The rough position of the office block was already set, but it needed to incorporate other facilities, such as offices, an R&D department, a hotel for visitors to the site, and a conference hall for holding conventions. Although I had never been to India, I figured that this would be a good opportunity to learn about the country and decided to participate.

The project called for a modern building adapted to the distinct environment with a hot, dry climate and a scorching sun. I was interested in making not a modern building dependant on air conditioning but a modern building equipped with architectural devices effective for the setting and environment. For instance, I proposed to create comfortable thermal environments by using water evaporation and sun-shading devices such as the *brise soleil* and the tent roof over the atrium.

I later went to India on a completely different occasion. That was when I really had my first first-hand experience of the Indian atmosphere, as I had the opportunity to visit Hindu temples and ruins from the Age of Discovery on the western coast. I was particularly moved by a Hindu ablution space that I visited at that time, which consisted only of a floor, the pool, and a roof that came right down to the water's surface. The sight of the scattered light from the water illuminating the understructure of the low-hanging roof was beautiful beyond words. On this trip I could not visit those sites that every architect visits—such as Le Corbusier in Ahmedabad, Louis Kahn in Dhaka, the Taj Mahal, Fatehpur Sikri, and the stepwells—but this ablution pool at Thrissur, Kerala, was thoroughly "Indian" for me. It was a space unlike anything I had ever experienced before.

南インド、トリシュールの沐浴場。水面すれすれまで下がった屋根だけが主役。水中を透過した光が内部空間を満たす。
Ablution space in Thrissur, India. The main feature is the roof that almost touches the water. The interior is filled with light filtering through the water.

右頁／会議場棟の中庭。太陽の光をどう制御するかを考えた結果としてのテント屋根と外壁ルーバー。ルーバーは場所により木材と石材を使用。
opposite / Courtyard of the meeting wing. The tent roofs and exterior louvers were solutions for regulating the sunlight. I used wood and stone for the louvers depending on their location.

上／どれだけ多様な外部空間を用意出来るかというのが主題だった。如何に直射光を避けた〈影〉の空間をつくるか、それらを繋ぐ要素としての〈水〉の導入、の2点が鍵だった。
右頁／オフィス・コンプレックス全景。オフィス、会議棟、商業施設、ホテルなどが入る。小さな〈都市〉の提案。

above / I aimed to create a diverse variety of exterior spaces. The two keys were to create spaces of *shade* sheltered from direct sunlight and to introduce *water* as an element for connecting these spaces.
opposite / General view of the office complex comprising offices, a conference wing, a commercial facility, and a hotel. It was a proposal to create a small city.

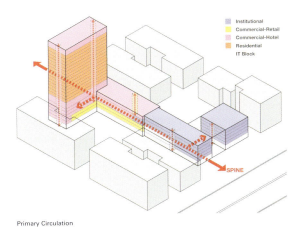

Primary Circulation

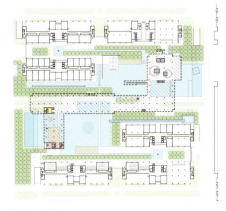

Site Plan 1 : 4500

曹洞宗 仏光山 喜音寺
Kionji Temple

2012, 兵庫県宝塚市
Takarazuka, Hyogo

曹洞宗の寺院の本堂と庫裏である。

　幾つか試みてみたいことがあった。ひとつはHPシェルの屋根である。以前実現出来なかった立礼茶室のプロジェクトでやろうとしたことでもあるのだが、直線を直線の上に載せていくと結果として曲面が出現するということ——3次元形態の曲面が2次元の直線の集合として出現する——そこには建築家の恣意性が介入する余地がない形態であることにずっと興味を持っていた。わたしは、カルテジアン・グリッドに載った四角い建築しかつくらない建築家、と呼ばれて久しい。自分の建築に恣意的な要素、たとえば曲線の導入を排除すると決めて久しいのだが、そこからそろそろ踏み出そうと考えた時に、HPシェルがあった。同時に現代的な宗教空間として、丹下健三の東京カテドラル聖マリア大聖堂のことが頭の片隅に在ったことは告白しておくべきだろう。

　もうひとつは仏様との出会いの空間とはどうあればいいのか、という設問だったが、その時頭に浮かんだのが、ニューヘヴンにあるベイネック稀覯本図書館の光が透過する石の壁だった。あの光る石の壁で仏様の光背を創れば、その光、逆光気味の光の中に仏様が浮かび上がることになるのではないか。本堂に設置される予定の仏様と対面しながら最初に考えたのは、そんなことだった。

　近隣と接する東側には可動木製ルーバーの外壁の庫裏を配し、逆の西側にある墓所との間に本堂を配置する。その前庭は版築の塀で囲まれた水庭とすることで東側の前面道路から本堂までの物理的な距離を確保すると同時に、日常的な風景から本堂へ、さらに墓所へと変化する風景を演出した。

　住職の住居である庫裏はもっとも日常的な風景である住宅地に面している。全周に配した可動木製ルーバーの内側には2階から3階に立体的に繋がるテラス空間や西の本堂側にもテラスを設け、住職の日常的な生活空間と近隣の住宅地や本堂との視覚的・精神的な距離を確保することを重点的に考えた。

　この俗から聖へのシークエンス、身近な日常から宗教的な場への精神的な距離の設計の試みが、この建築でやろうとしたことの3つ目である。

These are the main hall and priest's living quarters of a Soto Zen temple.

　There were several things that I always wanted to attempt doing. One was to make a hypar shell roof. I had attempted one earlier in the *ryurei*-style tearoom project, but it was never realized. I was interested in how the layering of straight lines produced a curved surface—a three-dimensional surface produced from a collection of two-dimensional straight lines—and in how this form left no room for the arbitrariness of an architect. I became interested in hypar shells when I was thinking about finally breaking a rule that I had set for myself long ago—to eliminate all arbitrary elements such as curves from my architecture—as it had been a while since I came to be known as an architect who only made orthogonal buildings based on Cartesian grids. I should probably also confess that Kenzo Tange's St. Mary's Cathedral of Tokyo always occupied a corner of my mind as a model for a modern religious space.

　Another thing that I wanted to attempt making was the wall of translucent stone of the Beinecke Rare Book & Manuscript Library in New Haven, which was what came to mind when I thought about what could be a suitable space for encountering the Buddha. When I encountered for the first time the Buddha that was to be housed in the main hall, I had the idea to place the luminous stone wall behind the Buddha to make the Buddha appear to be floating within a nimbus of light.

　I positioned the main hall between the cemetery on the west side and the priest's quarters by the neighboring houses on the east side. I made a forecourt as a water garden enclosed by rammed-earth walls to physically separate the main hall from the fronting road on the east side and to create a sense of transition between the everyday cityscape, main hall, and cemetery.

　The priest's quarters is where the priest lives, and it faces the everyday landscape of the neighboring residential district. I was particularly interested in providing a sense of both visual and spiritual separation between the priest's everyday living spaces, the surrounding neighborhood, and the main hall, so I made terrace spaces that extend from the west side of the second floor up to the third floor on the inside of the operable wooden louvers wrapped around the building.

　This sense of a transitional sequence, or spiritual separation, between the familiar everyday spaces and the sacred religious spaces was the third thing that I wanted to attempt to design through this project.

Section

Section　1:500

右頁／本堂内部。
294-295頁／本堂夕景。右側に庫裏が見える。

opposite / Interior of main hall.
pp. 294–295 / Evening view of the main hall. The priest's quarters is visible on the right.

Kionji Temple

1	外陣 main hall	8	和室 tatami room
2	内陣 inner sanctuary	9	個室 private room
3	開山堂 Kaizan-do hall	10	寝室 bedroom
4	水庭 water garden	11	書斎 study
5	墓所 cemetery	12	LDK living/dining/kitchen
6	玄関 entrance	13	テラス terrace
7	事務室 office		

右頁上／本堂前庭としての水庭越しに庫裏を見る。
右頁下／夕景全景。

opposite, top / The priest's quarters beside the water garden that serves as the forecourt of the main hall.
opposite, bottom / General view at evening.

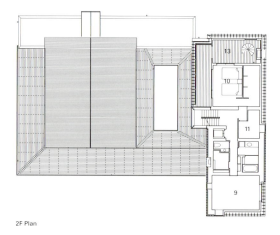

2F Plan

3F Plan

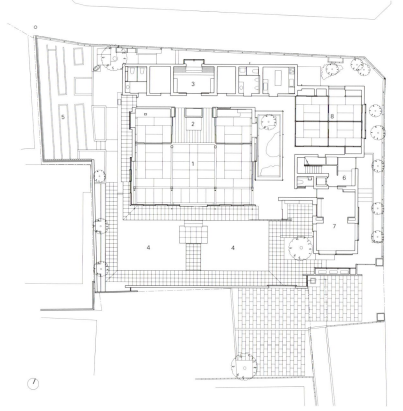

1F Plan 1:400

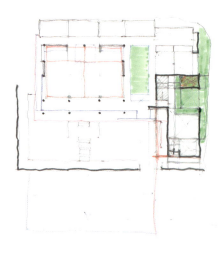

Conceptual Sketch

Kionji Temple

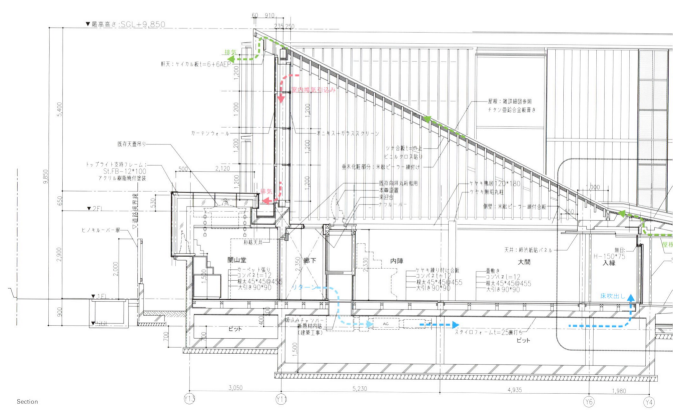

Section

● Kionji Temple

左頁／本堂内部を東側から見る。
上／本堂前庭方向の見返し。

opposite / View of the interior of the main hall from the east side.
above / View back towards the forecourt of the main hall.

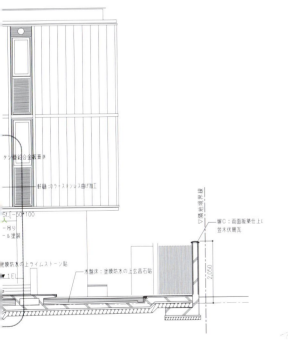

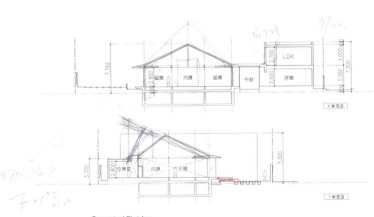

Conceptual Sketches

上／本堂アプローチのディテール。
下／本堂と和室を隔てる中庭。

top / Detail of the approach to the main hall.
above / Courtyard between the main hall and *tatami* room.

上／本堂の書院。
下／和室から中庭を見る。
right / *Shoin* of the main hall.
below / View towards the courtyard from the *tatami* room.

上／墓所から見た本堂。
下／右に庫裏、左に本堂を見る。
右頁／庫裏2階テラス。

top / Main hall as seen from the cemetery.
above / The priest's quarters is on the right and the main hall is on the left.
opposite / Second-floor terrace of the priest's quarters.

上／庫裏3階テラス。正面奥で2階テラスへと繋がる。
下／庫裏3階リビング・スペース。

above / Third-floor terrace of the priest's quarters. It connects to the second-floor terrace at the back.
left / Living room on the third floor of the priest's quarters.

下／北東方向からの全景。
below / General view from the northeast.

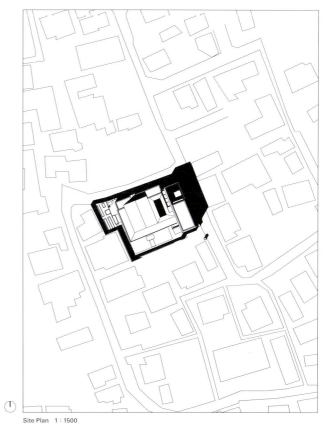

Site Plan 1：1500

GLA近畿会館
GLA Osaka Hall

2013, 大阪府吹田市
Suita, Osaka

宗教法人のための集会施設である。

敷地は大阪郊外にあり、南は交通量の多い主要国道、北は閑静な住宅街の細い道路に接し、この敷地の南と北はまるで異なる様相を見せる。結果として建物をふたつに分け、南側の国道に面しては鉄骨造6階建ての南棟、北側には鉄筋コンクリート造の1階に木造の架構を載せた2階建ての北棟を建てることとし、その中間をパーキングとして、車での来訪者と徒歩での来訪者の導線を分離することとした。

南棟には、2階に250人規模の講堂、最上階に聖堂を持ち、その他にはオフィス機能が入る。講堂、聖堂共に自然光の入る室内空間とし、しかもその自然光の採り入れ方をそれぞれの部屋で機能に応じて変え、講堂は日常的な自然光が壁面を明るくする形式、対照的に聖堂は象徴的な光の入る形式、いずれもスカイライトからの採光が主役となる室内空間を2種類用意することとした。それは、静謐で非日常的な空間が求められている講堂や聖堂の空間を南に拡がる騒然とした都市郊外の風景に直接繋げたくなかったためであり、講堂や聖堂と日常的な都市空間の中間にはバッファ空間としてのロビーを設け、来訪者が気分を切り替える助けとなる空間を準備することとした。

北棟はここで働いている人達のための建物であり、1階には談話室、2階には講演等の準備作業を行うための空間と小さな打合せ室を設けることとした。北棟を2階建てとし、木造の切妻屋根を架けた形式としたのは、近隣の住宅地の景観に配慮した故である。

南棟、北棟共に、それぞれの周辺環境に対して開放的な表情とすることを第一義と考えながら、南棟のプロフィリット・ガラスのダブルスキン・ファサードや北棟の波板ガラスのファサードを決定した。

This is a facility for a religious organization.

The site is located in the suburbs of Osaka. The two ends of the site have entirely different characters: There is an arterial road with heavy traffic on the south side and a narrow road of a quiet residential district on the north side. I thus divided the building into two parts: The south block beside the arterial road is a six-story steel building, and the north block on the residential side is a two-story building composed as a timber frame built atop a reinforced concrete base. I put a parking area between them to separate the circulation of visitors arriving by car and by foot.

The south block contains a 250-person auditorium on the second floor, a sanctuary on the top floor, and offices on the other floors. I designed both the auditorium and sanctuary spaces to be lit by natural light, but I changed how the light is brought inside according to each of their functions. I set up the auditorium so that a plain, everyday light illuminates one of the walls, and I set up the sanctuary so that it is lit by a symbolic light. I used skylights as the main source of light in the two different types of spaces. I did this because I did not want the tranquil, non-everyday spaces that the auditorium and sanctuary called for to be directly exposed to the noisy suburban landscape to the south. I also inserted buffer spaces between the auditorium and sanctuary and the everyday spaces of the city in the form of lobbies that help visitors shift their mood.

The north block is a building for the people who work for the organization. The first floor houses a lounge, and the second floor houses a space for preparing talks and a small meeting room. I designed the block as a two-story building with a timber gable roof in consideration of the appearance of the neighboring residential district.

I considered it of primary importance to give both the south block and north block an open appearance towards the surrounding environment. This is what led me to give the south block a double-skin façade of channel glass and the north block a façade of corrugated glass.

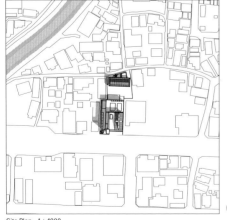

Site Plan 1 : 4000

右頁／南棟最上階に配置した聖堂の内部。屋根面から自然光を導入する。何度目かのHPシェルの試みで、ここでは4枚に分割している。

opposite / Interior of the sanctuary on the top floor of the south block. Daylight enters from the roof. I again attempted to use hypar shells, which I divided into four pieces here.

南棟
South Block

右頁上／南棟ファサード。交通量の多い国道に面する。
右頁下／都市とのインターフェイス空間としてのダブル・スキンの提案。
310-311頁／南棟エントランスホール。喧騒の都市から一歩入ると展開する静謐な、しかし自然光の溢れる空間。

opposite, top / Façade of the south block. It faces a national road with heavy traffic.
opposite, bottom / I proposed the double skin as an interface space to the city.
pp. 310–311 / Entrance hall of the south block. Natural light fills the quiet space that unfolds one step inside from the bustle of the city.

1　エントランスホール　entrance hall
2　受付　reception
3　打合せスペース　meeting space
4　ホワイエ　foyer
5　講堂　auditorium
6　研修室　meeting room
7　聖堂　sanctuary
8　聖堂前室　sanctuary anteroom
9　応接室　reception room
10　事務室　office
11　映像室　projection room
12　倉庫　storage
13　給湯室　pantry
14　控室　waiting room
15　機械室　machine room
16　駐車場　garage
17　車路　roadway

3F Plan

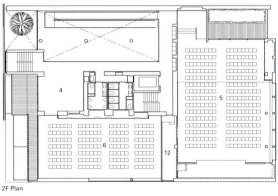

2F Plan

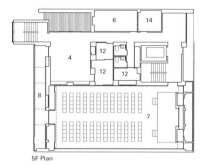

5F Plan

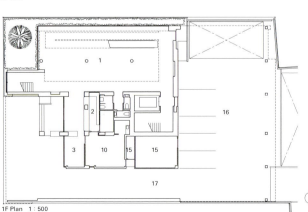

1F Plan　1 : 500

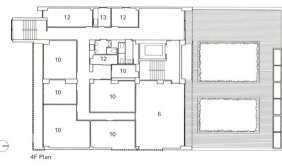

4F Plan

● GLA Osaka Hall

上／南棟最上階の聖堂全景。
右／全景。
右頁／南棟2階講堂の全景。
いずれも人々が集まる場所には自然光を導入することを
ルールとした。

above / General view of the top-floor sanctuary of the south block.
right / General view.
opposite, top / General view of the second-floor auditorium of the south block.
I made it a rule to bring natural light into the spaces where people would gather.

●GLA Osaka Hall

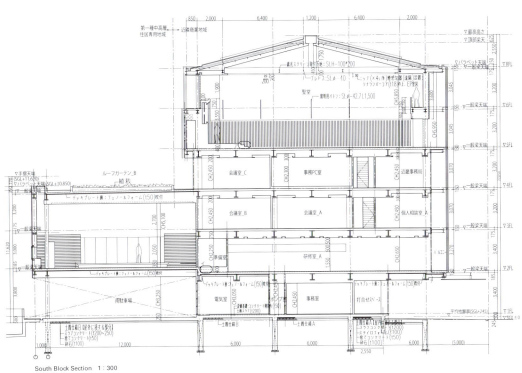

South Block Section 1:300

北棟
North Block

North Elevation

West Elevation

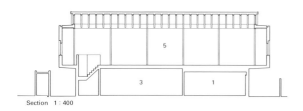
Section 1:400

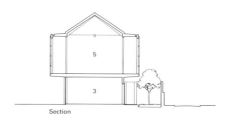
Section

1 談話室　lounge
2 給湯室　pantry
3 倉庫　　storage
4 事務室　office
5 研修室　meeting room

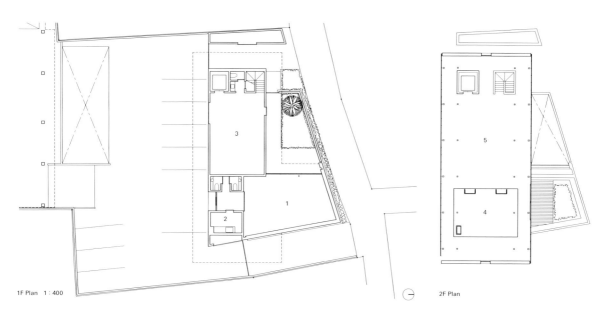
1F Plan 1:400　　　2F Plan

GLA Osaka Hall

左／北棟・中庭を見る。
右／北棟2階。1階の鉄筋コンクリート構造の上に載った2階は木構造と波板ガラスの外壁という簡素極りない構造とした。

above / Courtyard of the north block.
above right / Second floor of the north block. I made the second story that sits atop the reinforced concrete structure of the ground floor as a very simple structure composed of wood framing and exterior walls of corrugated glass.

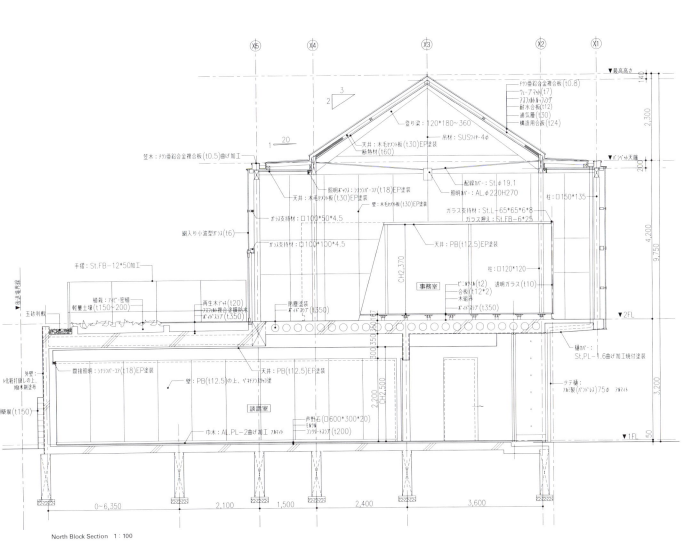

North Block Section   1 : 100

上／北棟2階全景。
下2点／2階の大空間の中にガラスボックスの執務空間。人間のスケールに落とされた内部空間を建築の〈内部〉に配置すること。

above / General view of the second floor of the north block.
below / The glass box of the office space sits inside the large space of the second story. I scaled the interior space down to a human scale and nested it inside the building.

GLA Osaka Hall

上／北棟を南棟から見る。
下／北側に拡がる住宅地側の立面。建築のスケールを住宅スケールに合わせること。

above / North block as seen from the south block.
right / Elevation facing the residential neighborhood on the north side. I scaled the building down to a residential scale.

京都大学北部グラウンド運動部部室棟
Kyoto University Student Clubhouse, north campus

2014, 京都市左京区
Sakyo-ku, Kyoto

いつも、なんでこんなにややこしいことばかり起きるのだろう、と思う。タイトルの通り、京都大学の北部構内、グラウンドに面した場所に建つ運動部部室棟の建て替えである。一見すると分かるように、リニアに延びる平面のままに鉄骨の構造が水平に延びる2階建ての単純な建築である。でもこの建築はそんなに簡単に実現したわけではない。まずこの場所には埋蔵文化財が埋まっている可能性があるため、建て替えに当たっては学内調査の必要のある場所だった。OB諸氏の寄附と学内予算の合算で動いている企画のため、限られた予算には埋蔵文化財調査に支出する余裕はない。調査を避けるためにはこれまで建っていた1972年に竣工した木造平屋建ての建物の、その基礎の深さと平面範囲の内側に新しい基礎を設けるしか手段はない。しかし同時に面積を可能な限り増やすためには、その基礎範囲よりも外部に構造を持ち出す必要がある。

さらにこの場所は京都市の景観規制を受けている。大学のキャンパスの内側なのに、京都市全体の規制を受けて勾配屋根を架けることを求められる。フラットルーフの校舎が建ち並ぶ構内に切り妻屋根という形式の妥当性をどう担保すればいいのか。

そんな様々な与条件の結果として現在の構造形式――浅い置き基礎にその基礎範囲から持ち出された構造体＝柱、それを引っ張り上げる構造要素としての屋根小屋梁――という奇妙な構造解答に至る。〈柱〉ととりあえずは呼んだものの、ダブルで並行に並ぶ同じ断面のH形鋼の一方は圧縮、一方は引っ張りを受けるという、正直ではない構造。これはせっかく与条件としての〈屋根〉が在るのだから、それを積極的に構造として生かしたい、単純なキャンティレバー構造にだけはしたくないという、意地の構造でもある。

出来上がった建築はそんな設計者の工夫、いや苦悩か、を垣間見せてくれはしない。たまに外周の柱が宙に浮いていることに気付き、疑問に思う人もいるが、それでも出来上がってしまえば切り妻平入の普通の建築だ。反語的な言い方になるが、でもこの場所で普通の建築が実現出来たこと、その事実にむしろ安心している自分がここにはいるのだ。

I always wonder why things need to be so complicated. Just as the title reads, this is an athletic clubhouse that faces a playing field on the North Campus of Kyoto University. And as one can see, it is a two-story building with a steel frame structure that simply extends horizontally along a linear floor plan. But it was not at all easy to realize. First of all, the site needed to be surveyed by the university in order for the new building to be built because there was a possibility that there were cultural artifacts buried underground. The project ran on a limited budget made up of alumni donations and university funds, however, so there was no money that could be spared for the survey. The only way to avoid the survey was to lay the new foundations to fit within the depth and width of the foundations of the existing single-story wooden building built in 1972. The new building thus needed to be extended out over the footprint of its foundations if the floor area was to be increased as much as possible.

The site was also subject to Kyoto's cityscape ordinance. Despite being within the university grounds, the building had to be given a gabled roof in respect of this ordinance for the city of Kyoto as a whole. But what could warrant the appropriateness of using a gabled roof in a campus lined with flat-roofed buildings?

These factors resulted in the peculiar solution for the structural system, which is composed of shallow slab-on-grade foundations, columns lifted out over the footprint of the foundations, and ceiling joists that pull these columns up from above. What I just referred to as columns are not actually honest structures: they are composed of two parallel steel H-sections with one member in compression and one member in tension. The structure reflects my determination to make use of the necessitated *roof* as part of the structure rather than making a simple cantilevered structure.

The completed building does not give any hint of these thoughtful efforts—troubles, rather—of its designer. Even though some people may take notice of the perimeter columns floating off the ground once in a while and wonder why they are that way, the realized building appears to be just an ordinary building with a gabled roof. This may be an ironic thing for me to say, but it is also true that I feel very relieved to have managed to realize an ordinary building on that site.

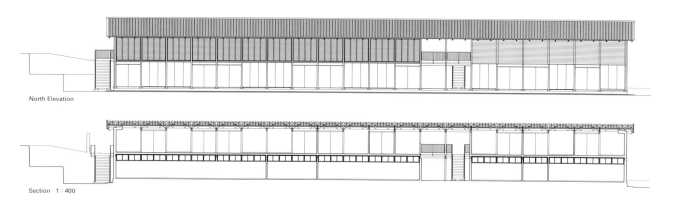

North Elevation

Section 1:400

319頁上／グラウンド側からの全景。
319頁下／型鋼、折板、角パイプ、型板ガラス・ジャロジーなど既製の工業製品の組み合わせで出来た建築。一番手前の柱板はRCスラブの端部に固定され接地しない。
左2点／工業製品の組み合わせだけで実現した〈即物的〉な空間。

p. 319 top / General view from the playing field side.
p. 319 bottom / An architecture made by assembling readymade industrial products, such as steel forms, folded steel plate, and textured-glass jalousie windows. The column plates in the foreground are fixed to the edge of the RC slab and do not touch the ground.
left / A "matter-of-fact" (*sachlichkeit*) space realized by simply assembling industrial products.

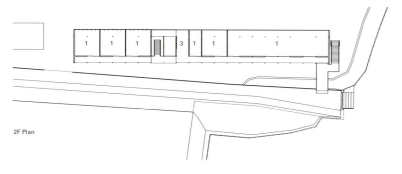

2F Plan

1 部室　clubroom
2 ホール　hall
3 テラス　terrace

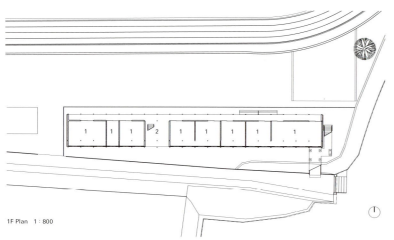

1F Plan　1：800

Kyoto University Student Clubhouse, north campus

2階部室全景。構造の軸と内部空間の軸線をずらすことで、左側グラウンド方向へと意識が向かう。

General view of the second-floor clubroom. One's focus slides towards the direction of the field on the left because the axis of the structure has been shifted off from the axis of the space.

1　部室　clubroom
2　ホール　hall

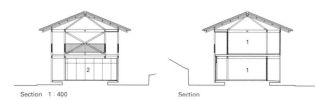

Section 1:400　　　　Section

山野井の家
House in Yamanoi

2014, 兵庫県姫路市
Himeji, Hyogo

子供達が既に独立した後の、夫婦2人のための住宅である。

お茶の趣味を持ち、友人達とのコミュニケーションを楽しまれる夫人のための茶室とその待ち合いを兼ねることも出来るリビングルーム、ヒストリック・カーのコレクションの趣味を持つ主人のための美術館のようなガレージの3つの空間が主役であり、それ以外には寝室と主人の書斎、それに仏間があるだけという住宅であり、夫婦2人共の開放的な性格を反映してか、住宅全体が小さな美術館のような様相を呈している。

歴史的な遺産である姫路城を毎日眺めながら生活したいという主人の意向を受け、2階にはガラスボックスのリビング・ダイニング・スペースがある以外は300m²を超える面積のテラスが拡がり、そのテラスは場所によって様々なアクティビティに対応出来ると共に、姫路城を眺めるための絶好の場所でもある。

設計時はその2階床面を想定地上面とし、それ以外は下階と考えて設計していた。実は1階を概念上の地階＝ルスティカ、2階が主階＝ピアノ・ノービレと考えながら、16世紀のルネッサンス・ヴィラのことを遠くに夢想していた。ガラスボックスの2階は緩勾配ではあるが〈屋根〉を持ち、鉄のソリッドな十字柱断面の列柱がその屋根を支える形式としたのは、それ故である。〈屋根〉と〈列柱〉を主階に持たないヴィラなど、あり得ないではないか。

21世紀にもなって、そんな古典主義的なタイポロジーに自らの立ち位置を求めること、それは圧倒的に懐古主義的に見えるかもしれない。しかし建築における進歩概念とはそんなに信頼出来るものなのだろうか。私にはローマも、ルネッサンスも、そして近代でさえ、そんなに異なる建築には見えないのだ。

This is a house for a couple whose children have already grown up and set out on their own.

There are three main spaces in this house: a tearoom for the wife to practice tea and socialize with her friends, a living room that doubles as the waiting room for the tearoom, and a museum-like garage for the husband's collection of historic cars. A bedroom, the husband's study, and an altar room are the only other rooms in the house. The house as a whole gives the feeling of a small museum, perhaps in reflection of the open personalities of the couple.

The husband wanted to be able to look out to the historic Himeji Castle every day, so I gave the second level a glass-box living/dining space and a terrace with an area of more than 300 m2. The terrace is not only a great place for viewing Himeji Castle but also can be used for various other activities.

When designing the house, I regarded the upper floor as the ground level and the lower floor as a basement. I had been dreaming about those distant 16th-century Renaissance villas as I treated the first level as a conceptual basement floor—*rustica*—and the second level as the principal floor—*piano noble*. This was also why I gave the glass box on the second level a gently sloping *roof* supported by a row of solid steel columns with cruciform sections. A villa would not be a villa without a *roof* or a *colonnade* on its *piano noble*.

It may seem utterly historicist of me to have grounded myself upon such a classicist typology in the 21st century. Yet, I question whether we can really be so sure about evolutionism in architecture. To me, Roman architecture, Renaissance architecture, and even Modern architecture do not seem to be all that different.

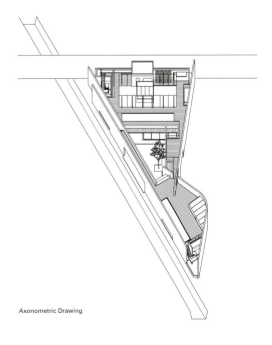

Axonometric Drawing

Site Plan 1 : 4000

右頁／全景。手前に用水路とインターフェイスとして植えた群植の竹。

opposite / General view. I planted the bamboo as an interface against the canal.

上／北側ファサード。2階をセットバックさせることでスケール感を落とす。
下／西側壁面。用水路と竹の植栽。
above / North façade. I set back the second level to bring down its sense of scale.
below / West wall by the canal and bamboo plantings.

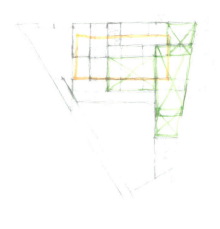

Conceptual Sketch

上／中庭から住居方向を見る。
下／中庭からガレージ方向を見る。

top / View towards the living spaces from the courtyard.
above / View towards the garage from the courtyard.

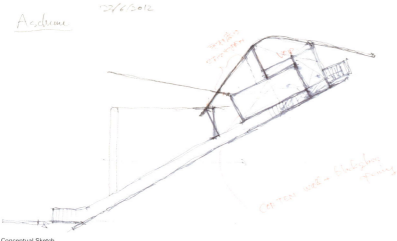
Conceptual Sketch

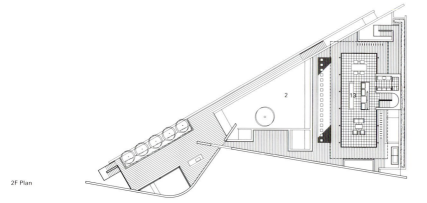
2F Plan

1	車路	roadway
2	中庭	courtyard
3	ガレージ	garage
4	玄関ホール	entrance hall
5	和室	tatami room
6	クローゼット	storage
7	浴室	bathroom
8	ライブラリー	library
9	寝室	bedroom
10	茶庭	tea garden
11	茶室	tearoom
12	水屋	preparation room
13	リビング・ダイニング	living/dining room

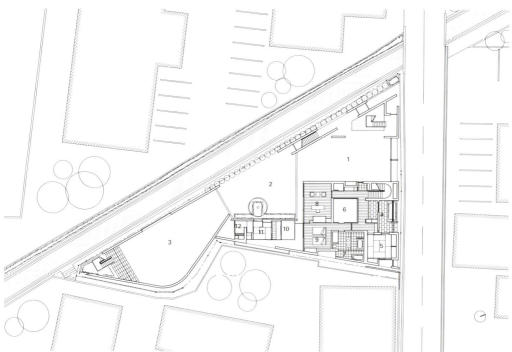
1F Plan 1 : 600

● House in Yamanoi

自然光の入るガレージ。日常的に使用する車は置かず、ここに置かれるのはクラシック・カーのコレクションだけである。クラシック・カーのための小さな美術館である。
The naturally lit garage. It is not used for parking the everyday car; it is reserved for housing the client's classic car collection. It is a small museum for classic cars.

茶室と露地。
Tearoom and garden path.

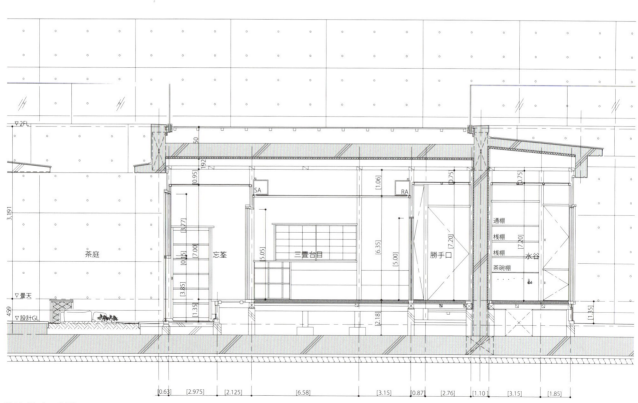

Detailed Section 1 : 70

上／茶室から庭を見る。
左／手前座の奥に中庭の植栽が見える。
右中／庭と茶室のインターフェイス。大徳寺孤篷庵（1793）から学んだこと。何度目かのケーススタディ。
右下／庭側からの内観。右奥に手前座。

top / Tearoom as seen from the garden.
above / The courtyard plantings are visible beyond the tea host's seat.
above right / The interface between the garden and tearoom. Based on what I learned from the Daitokuji Kohoan (1793). This was another case study.
right / Interior view from the garden side. The tea host's seat is at back right.

上／寝室から茶室を見る。
下／書斎から中庭を見る。奥にガレージ。
右頁／2階リビング・ダイニングルームを中庭越しに見る。
332-333頁／南からの夕景全景。

top / Tearoom as seen from the bedroom.
above / Courtyard as seen from the study. The garage is in the back.
opposite / Second-floor living/dining room as seen from across the courtyard.
pp. 332–333 / General view from the south in the evening.

2階リビング・ダイニングルームから南を見る。構造のリズムと意識的にずらしたサッシのリズム。

Southward view from the second-floor living/dining room. I intentionally did not align the rhythm of the sashes with the rhythm of the structure.

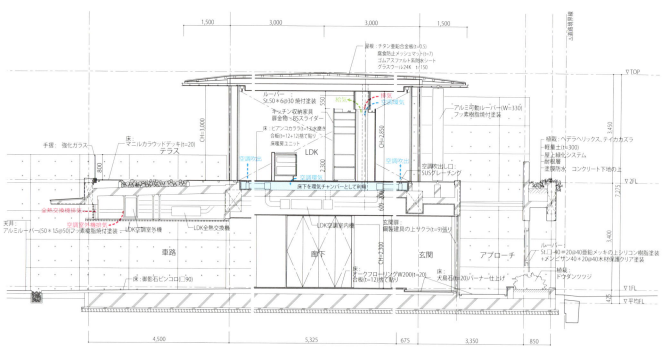

Section 1:120

● House in Yamanoi

上／2階キッチン越しに東を見る。
左／回転する金属ルーバーによる光の変化。
右／金属ルーバー、十字柱、そしてガラスの外壁。

above / Eastward view from the second-floor kitchen.
right / The changes in the light created by the rotating metal louvers.
far right / The metal louvers, cruciform column, and glass exterior wall.

上／2階テラスよりリビングルームを見る。可能な限り薄く表現した屋根。
下／ガレージ奥の階段。2階テラスへと繋がる。

above / Living room as seen from the second-floor terrace. I made the roof appear as thin as possible.
left / Stairs at the back of the garage. It leads to the second-floor terrace.

● House in Yamanoi

上／西側からの全景。遠くに姫路城が見える。
下／南側からの全景。
below / General view from the west side. Himeji Castle is visible in the distance.
bottom / General view from the south side.

白鳳堂京都本店
Hakuhodo

2014, 京都市中京区
Nakagyo-ku, Kyoto

日本の筆は文字を書くための伝統的な書き筆から女性のための化粧筆まで、その用途は幅広い。これはそうした様々な用途のための筆をつくる会社の京都本店ショールームの計画である。

鉄筋コンクリート造2階建ての小さな建築は、京都のお茶屋さんや骨董屋さんの多い、寺町通りに面する。この場所は京都市の景観規制を受けており、伝統的な表情を持つことが求められるが、それはこの会社の製品の性格上むしろ歓迎される要素であり、問題はそこにどれだけ現代的な表現を導入出来るか、という点にある。行政との度重なる打ち合わせの結果、本実型枠使用白コンクリート打ち放し仕上げの壁、木製ルーバーを用いた開口部格子と水平庇の表現、などについて、我々が意図したことは十全に理解され、実現することが出来た。

内部空間は空へと抜ける光の井戸として計画した入口近くの大きなスカイライトと、同じ大きさでそれと対応する店舗奥の黒い水庭としての中庭、それに3つ目は、奥行き方向を積極的に強調し、同時に白コンクリートの壁の質感を見せる北側の壁沿いに2層吹き抜けて走るスリット状のスカイライトという3カ所の自然光採光が、この室内空間に室内とも室外ともつかない光の状態と閉じた箱であるにもかかわらず開放的な雰囲気をもたらしてくれる。

ここでは陰影のある日本的な空間ではなく、むしろ自然光に溢れた室内空間を実現しようと考えた。それは化粧筆を実際に試用してみることがここでは重要であり、そのための光の状態を実現したいと考えたことがひとつ。もうひとつはこの筆という商品は現在では既に国際的に評価を得ており、ここを頻繁に訪れる外国のバイヤーにとって、もはや筆は国籍を超えたインターナショナルな商品であることを明るく、しかもどこか日本的にも感じられる空間で伝えたい、と考えたことに依る。

In Japan, there are brushes for a wide range of purposes, from traditional calligraphy brushes to makeup brushes for women. This project is the main showroom of a company in Kyoto that makes such brushes.

The small two-story reinforced concrete building faces Kyoto's Teramachi Street, which is known for its many tea shops and antique stores. The site was subject to Kyoto's cityscape ordinance, so the building needed to present a traditional look. If anything, however, this was a welcome factor considering the nature of the company's products. The issue was how to work modern expressions into the design. After holding numerous meetings with the city administration, however, I managed to gain their understanding for everything that I intended to realize, such as the white exposed concrete walls cast in tongue-and-groove jointed wood formwork and the wooden louver screens of the openings and flat eaves.

There are three sources of daylight in the interior: a large skylight nearby the entrance that takes the form of a light well extending to the sky; a courtyard garden at the back, designed with a black water garden that responds to the same-sized skylight; and a slit skylight that extends through the two levels along the north wall of white concrete while accentuating the depth of the space and the texture of the wall. They produce a quality of light that makes the interior spaces feel like they could be inside or outside, and they give the spaces an airy ambience even within the closed box.

What I wanted to create were not typical Japanese spaces characterized by shadows but spaces filled with natural light. One reason for this was that I wanted to provide a quality of light suitable for the makeup brushes to be tested inside. Another reason was that I wanted to convey to the foreign buyers expected to frequent the store that the brushes—which were already held in high regard around the world—were international products that transcended nationality by creating spaces that were bright and yet somehow felt Japanese.

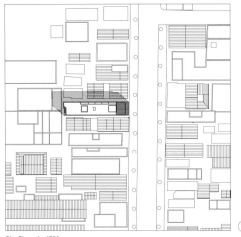

Site Plan 1 : 1500

右頁／ファサード夕景。
opposite / Evening view of the façade.

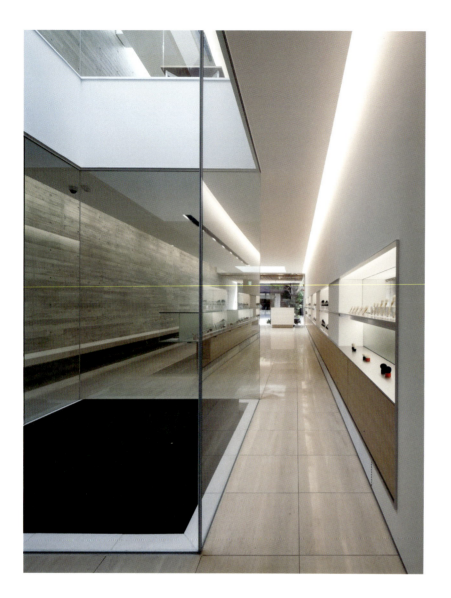

340-341頁／1階のショールーム全景。手前の天井開口は2階屋根面まで抜けるスカイライト、奥に水庭としての中庭。右は本実型枠による白コンクリート打ち放し。
左／ショールーム奥から道路方向を見る。手前に黒い水庭。
右／キャンティレバーで浮遊するガラスとアルミの展示棚。

pp. 340–341 / General view of the first-floor showroom. The opening in the ceiling extends to a skylight in the roof above the second floor. The courtyard water garden is at the back. The white exposed concrete wall on the right was cast in tongue-and-groove jointed wood formwork.
above / View towards the street from the back of the showroom. The black water garden is in the foreground.
above right / Cantilevered display case made of glass and aluminum.

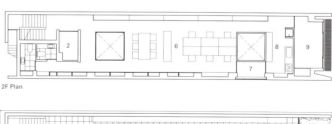

2F Plan

1F Plan 1 : 300

● Hakuhodo

1 打合せ室　meeting room
2 納戸　storage
3 機械室　machine room
4 水庭　water garden
5 ショールーム　showroom
6 事務所　office
7 更衣室　changing room
8 キッチン　kitchen
9 役員室　executive room

Section　1:300

Section

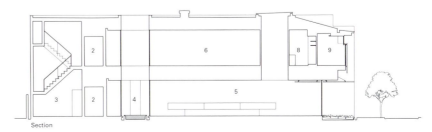
Section

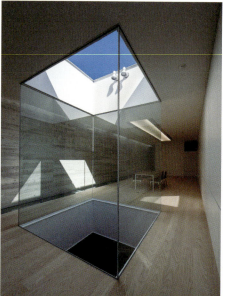

上2点／2階中庭上部の光と影。
左下／白コンクリート打ち放しの壁とスリット状のスカイライトからの光。
右下／1階ショールームのスカイライトと壁。
右頁／北側の白コンクリート打ち放し壁とスリットから落ちる自然光。2階床面を越えて1階まで光は落ちる。

left / The light and shadows on the second floor by the upper part of the courtyard.
below, far left / The white exposed concrete wall under the light from the slit skylight.
below left / Skylight and wall of the first-floor showroom.
opposite / The white exposed concrete wall on the north side and daylight shining inside from the slit. The light shines down to the first level through the floor of the second level.

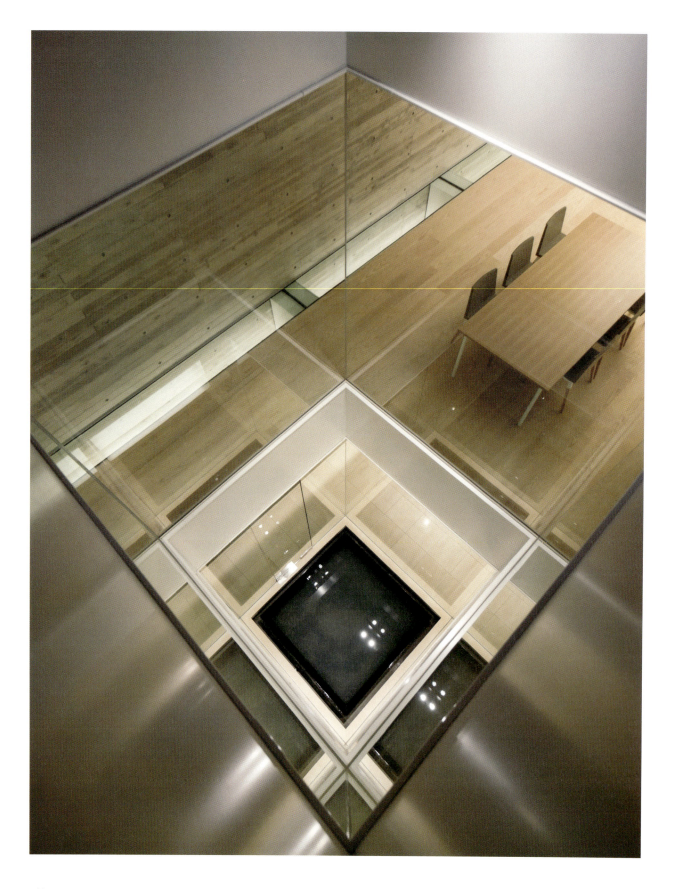
Hakuhodo

右頁／中庭を見下ろす。底に見えるのは1階の水庭。
opposite / View down into the courtyard. The water garden on the first floor can be seen at the bottom.

East Elevation 1：200

左／道路からセットバックした入り口。
右／寺町通りの街並とファサード。
above / The entrance is set back from the street.
right / Façade within the streetscape of Teramachi Street.

Warehouse Renovation at Minsheng-road

中国 上海
Shanghai, China

上海市の外灘〈Bund〉の向かい側、浦東地区の港に残る歴史的な倉庫群の改装計画である。これは設計競技として始まり、当初は海沿いの大きな倉庫の建て替えに加え、それに並ぶふたつの煉瓦造倉庫の改装と合わせて3棟のオフィス・コンプレックスとするという計画で、我々の案が採用された。

中国での計画の例に漏れず、この計画も上海市の意向に従い二転三転し、海沿いのオフィスビル計画はとりあえず置いたままで、煉瓦造倉庫2棟のオフィス空間への再生を先行させるということになった。この地域のランドスケープデザインの方針も変更になり、この煉瓦造倉庫2棟と新しいオフィスビルを繋ぐように計画していたガラスのアーケードも不可能になったため、この煉瓦造倉庫2棟を一体化し、独立したオフィスの計画として考えることとなった。2棟の中間にブリッジや階段、エレベーターなどの上下導線を計画し、2階建ての倉庫の上には鉄骨造の3階オフィスを増築し、さらにその屋上をレストランやカフェなどの商業空間とするというものである。

中国での計画はいつもそうだが、その時点ごとの変更要求、それも日本では想像も付かないような変更にそれぞれの時点で誠実に対応していると、いつの間にか竣工を迎えるというのがこれまでの経験だった。少し思索的な言い方をすれば、それぞれの時点での〈微分〉的対応の集積がいつのまにか〈積分〉した結果として竣工している、というのがこれまでの中国でのプロジェクトの正直な感想だが、このプロジェクトも2016年時点の現在でも、上海市の歴史建築保存の考え方の変化に伴い、さらに変化し続けていることは言うまでもない。

This is a renovation project of a group of historic warehouses situated in a port in the Pudong district across from the Shanghai Bund. It started as a competition that we won with our initial scheme to create a three-block office complex by replacing a large seaside warehouse and refurbishing two brick warehouses beside it.

As with every project in China, this project underwent several changes following decisions made by the Shanghai municipality. Ultimately, the plan for the seaside office building was put on hold, and we were told to first go ahead with renovating the brick warehouses into offices. The program for the landscaping of the site was also revised, however, and it became impossible to build the glass arcade that we had planned as a connection between the brick warehouses and new office building. We thus decided to merge the two brick warehouses and to think of them together as an independent office project. For this we planned to insert vertical circulation such as bridges, stairs, and elevators between the two buildings; build steel frame blocks with offices on top of the two-story warehouses; and create commercial spaces with a restaurant and café on the new rooftops.

Whenever I work on a project in China, it seems that I will be diligently responding to every new change made to the brief—changes unimaginable in Japan—and, before I know it, the project will be done. Or to put it slightly more speculatively, when I realize it, the projects will be built as an "integral" sum of the accumulated solutions that I make in response to each change in a "differential" manner. It goes without saying that this project is also still continuing to change even now in 2016 as the municipality has changed how it thinks about architectural preservation.

New Elevation 1 : 1000

Existing Elevation 1 : 1000

Site Plan

左上／提案した計画の立面。
左中／着工前の全景。3階への増築は撤去した後、新しい増築を行う。
左下／オリジナルの立面。
右頁／夜景全景。対岸の上海・外灘〈Bund〉を遠くに望む。

top left / Elevation of proposed scheme.
above center / General view before construction. The addition on the third floor will be replaced.
left / Original elevation.
opposite / General view at night. The Shanghai Bund is visible on the far shore.

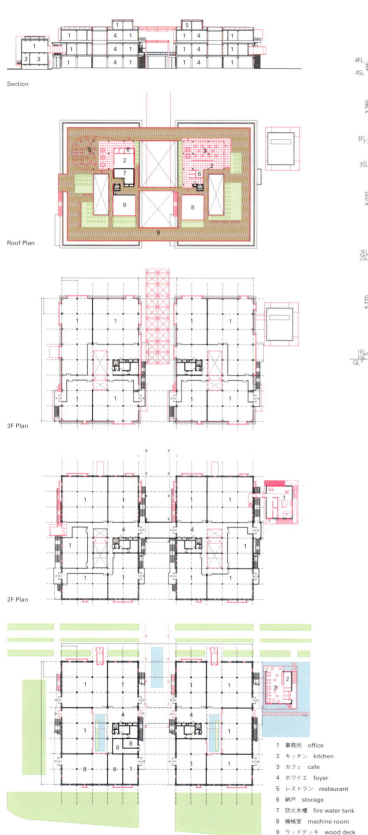
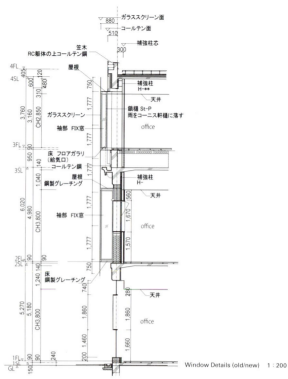
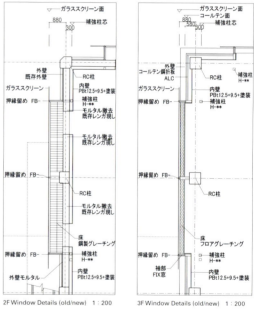

1 事務所 office
2 キッチン kitchen
3 カフェ cafe
4 ホワイエ foyer
5 レストラン restaurant
6 納戸 storage
7 防火水槽 fire water tank
8 機械室 machine room
9 ウッドデッキ wood deck

1F Plan (red : new alteration) 1 : 1500

左／新しく手を加える部分を赤色で示す。中央に中庭をつくるのが大きな変更部。
右／新旧、すなわち新しい開口、古い煉瓦の壁面、モルタル塗りの外壁などがガラス面の後ろで出会う場となるダブル・スキンの開口部の計画。

left column / New parts are indicated in red. The biggest change is the new central courtyard.
right column / Openings in the double skin, where the new meets the old—that is, where the new openings, old brick walls, and existing mortar finished walls meet behind the glass surfaces.

● Warehouse Renovation at Minsheng-road

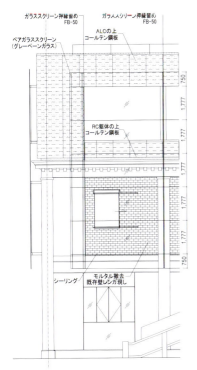

Window Details (old/new) 1:200

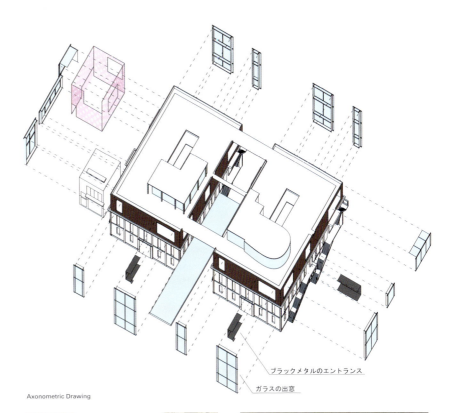

Axonometric Drawing

モルタルをはがし、煉瓦を確認する。
The bricks were checked by removing the mortar.

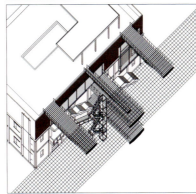

上／2棟の中間に残る古い導線。
下／オリジナルの導線に新しくブリッジ、階段、エレベーターを追加する。
top / The existing circulation between the two blocks.
above / New bridges, stairs, and elevators will be added to the original circulation.

上／中央に新しく穿たれた中庭のヴォイド。
下／中庭部の新しい表情の提案。
top / New void opened into the central courtyard.
above / Proposal for the courtyard with a new look.

South Panoramic Elevation

East Elevation

West Elevation

North Panoramic Elevation   1 : 1000

● Warehouse Renovation at Minsheng-road

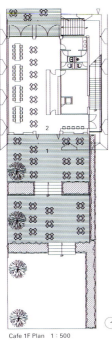

Cafe 1F Plan 1:500

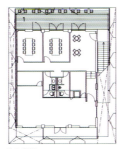

Cafe 2F Plan

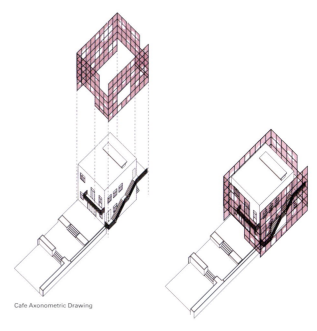

Cafe Axonometric Drawing

1 テラス terrace
2 カフェ cafe

上／付随する変電所のカフェへのコンバージョン。既存の躯体の外側に新しくガラススクリーンを回すことで新旧の立面が重層する表情をつくる。
下／全景。北側の通りより見る。

above / The adjoining substation to be converted into a café. A new glass screen will be wrapped around the existing structure so that the new elevations appear to be layered onto the old elevations.
below / General view from the road on the north side.

京都市美術館新館計画案
Kyoto City Museum Annex project

京都市左京区
Sakyo-ku, Kyoto

京都市美術館は京都市岡崎地区、長い歴史を持つ敷地に建つ。11世紀には円勝寺がこの場所に建っており、その後岡崎地区が第4回内国勧業博覧会の場所となった直後の時代には武田五一設計の京都市商品陳列所が建ち、それと同時に今も残る小川治兵衛作庭の庭園が造られた。そののちに大礼記念京都美術館として現在の京都市美術館の建物に建て替えられ、東側には川崎清設計の収蔵庫が増設された。現在は美術館本館、京都市商品陳列所時代の配置を残す門柱群、東側には同時期に建設された事務所棟のほか少々変更されたものの、その小川治兵衛の池泉回遊式庭園と収蔵庫が残る。

本館を現代の美術館として機能的に充実したものにすると同時に、現代芸術にも対応可能な新館を本館前広場の地下に設けるというのが、今回の計画である。

本館の前に建つ新館の設計についてはそれを建築だとは考えず、ランドスケープのデザインこそが重要だと考え、本館の前庭を新たに整備すると共に、岡崎地区全体のためのレストランやショップを設けるというのが提案であり、フロントコートと名付けた彫刻庭園はパブリックな広場としても機能する。このフロントコートは東側の池泉回遊式の日本庭園へのオマージュとして、回廊の廻った広場とした。また、象徴的な入り口ポーチを持つ本館のファサードを尊重して新しい美術館コンプレックス全体へのエントランスをこの本館ポーチからとし、誰にでも分かりやすいアプローチとした。地下の新館へは、本館中央の旧大陳列室に設ける地下へと繋がるエスカレーターで向かうこととした。本館へのアプローチ右側、つまりフロントコート南側には水庭と空へと開く地階テラスを設け、北端のライトコートや地下から地上へと繋がるランプも外光を取り入れる断面形とし、様々な場所で地下階へ光と自然を導入する。

本計画は東京駅丸の内駅舎で近代建築の保存の経験を持つ田原幸夫、地下建築の美術館展示方法について経験の深い日本設計との協働設計であり、それぞれの長所を生かしたチームであったと、自画自賛している。

Kyoto City Museum Annex project

The Kyoto Municipal Museum of Art stands on a site in Kyoto's Okazaki district that has a long history. It is where Enshoji Temple stood in the 11th century and where the Goichi Takeda-designed Kyoto Commercial Goods Museum later stood in the period immediately after the 4th National Industrial Exhibition was held in Okazaki. This was also when Jihei Ogawa made the garden that still exists on the site today. The current museum building was later built as the Tairei Memorial Art Museum of Kyoto, and a repository designed by Kiyoshi Kawasaki was also added to its east side. Currently, the museum's main wing, the gateposts marking the position of the Kyoto Commercial Goods Museum, an administration wing built onto the east side at around the time of the repository, the stroll garden by Jihei Ogawa, and the repository still exist with some modifications.

This project entailed enriching the functions of the main wing as a modern museum while also creating a subterranean annex suitable for showing contemporary art beneath the plaza in front of the main building.

When we designed the annex in front of the main wing, we did not think of it as a building and instead believed that the design of the landscape was what was important. We thus proposed to redesign the main wing's forecourt and also made a restaurant and shop to serve the Okazaki district at large. The sculpture garden, which we named the Front Court, was also to function as a public plaza, and we designed it as an open space ringed by a perimeter walkway in homage to the Japanese stroll garden on the east side. Respecting the main wing's façade with its iconic porch, we utilized this porch to make a simple, easily identifiable entry approach to the new art complex as a whole. An escalator was installed in the center of the main wing's former Grand Exhibition Room to provide access to the annex below. We then introduced light and nature into various parts of the subterranean level by creating a sunken open-air terrace on the right side of the approach to the main wing (i.e. the south side of the Front Court) and by shaping the sections of the light court at the northern end and the ramp connecting the basement and ground levels to draw daylight inside.

I made this proposal together with Yukio Tahara, who was experienced with modern architectural preservation through his work on the Marunouchi Station Building of Tokyo Station, and with Nihon Sekkei, which was experienced with how to exhibit artwork in subterranean buildings. If I may say so myself, I think we made a good team that capitalized on each of our strengths.

左／平安神宮方向からの全景。手前が新しく提案した前庭と回廊。その手前が地下へと降りるスロープ。
右上／奥に平安神宮。本館前庭南側の水庭が見える。
右下／地下の新館へと繋がる前庭水庭の空間。

far left / General view from the direction of the Heian Shrine. The newly proposed courtyard and covered walkway are in the foreground. The slope in the front descends to the subterranean level.
above left / View with the Heian Shrine at the back. The water garden is visible on the south side of the main wing.
left / The water garden space that leads to the new subterranean annex.

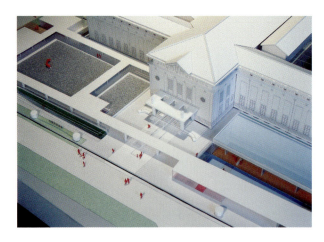

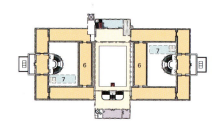

2F Plan

1F Plan 1:2500

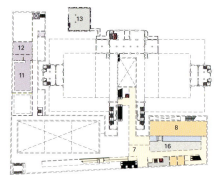

MB1F Plan

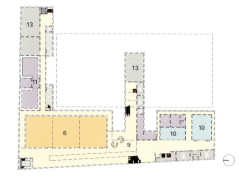

B1F Plan

上／本館と前庭。
中／回廊部と前庭。
下／地下の新館と本館へのアプローチ。

top / Main wing and forecourt.
center / Covered walkway and forecourt.
above / Approach to the subterranean annex and main hall.

● Kyoto City Museum Annex project

1 エントランス／コリドー　entrance/corridor
2 ショップ／レストラン　shop/restaurant
3 観光案内所　tourist information center
4 大展示室　main exhibition room
5 常設展示室　permanent exhibition room
6 展示室　exhibition room
7 ラウンジ／休憩室　lounge
8 ギャラリー　gallery
9 新館ロビー　annex lobby
10 講演室　lecture room
11 収蔵庫　storage
12 調査研究室　research laboratory
13 機械室　machine room
14 石庭　rock garden
15 水庭　water garden
16 サンクンガーデン　sunken garden
17 日本庭園　Japanese garden
18 神宮道　Jingu-michi
19 疎水　canal
20 二条通　Nijo-street

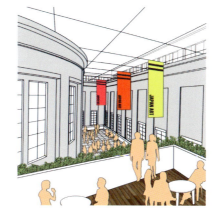

様々な部分空間の提案。
Proposals for various spaces.

本館、前庭、地下の新館の3者の関係を示す。
Relationship between the main hall, forecourt, and subterranean annex.

南泉禅寺再建計画
Nanquan Temple project

中国安徽省
Anhui, China

安徽省池州市南西の山林地区に、唐代の西暦795年に創建された南泉禅寺という禅宗寺院が1960年代に文化大革命で破壊されるまで存在していた。本プロジェクトはその再建のマスタープランである。我々は中国の村落や寺院において自然環境が多様な形で取り込まれていることに注目し、〈小さな村落のような建築群〉というメインコンセプトの下、4つのエリアを構想した。

第1の〈本殿エリア〉は南泉禅寺の名の由来である南泉が湧き出ると共に、大雄宝殿の遺構が発見された場所でもある。背後の山と大樹が形成する南北軸を計画の主軸とする形式性の高い構成とし、本殿は日本の唐招提寺に倣った寄棟の屋根の採用で本プロジェクトの中でもっとも格式の高い意匠とし、自然に比肩する建築を目指した。

第2の〈禅院エリア〉は座禅し黙想する場所であり、自然の風景が映り込む水盤と対峙することで、訪問者は自己を見つめる機会を持つ。ここでは周辺の自然と水盤だけが主役であり、屋根も光を通すテント構造とし、簡素な構造と意匠の建築とすることで対比的に自然を際立たせる。

第3の〈塔院エリア〉は当寺院コンプレックス全体へのレセプションエリアとして機能する。現存する石塔と新しくつくる木造の仏舎利塔がこの場所の主役であり、その木塔には中国には残存する歴史的な先行事例はない。ここでは日本の正倉院に残る玉虫厨子を基に復元した。

第4の〈ヒルサイドエリア〉は前3者とは性格を異にする。この敷地は採石場跡地であり、人間の手によって剥き出しにされた岩肌がそれを見る我々に人間の無思慮さを思い知らせてくれる。それを癒すこと、ここでは痛めつけられた自然を治癒することが求められていると感じた。機能的には来訪者のための宿房となる建物は幾何学的な形態と錆びたコールテン鋼の外壁を持ち、人間と自然との対峙を剥き出しにされた岩肌とは異なった形で表現する。逆に人間によって剥き出しにされた岩肌には植樹を提案し、長い時間の中で自然を癒すことを提案した。数十年も経てば、コールテン鋼の建築はむしろ岩肌に近くなり、また剥き出しだった岩肌は緑に覆われ、どちらも中国の自然の中にそれぞれの居場所を見つけてくれるのではないだろうか。

There used to be a Zen Buddhist temple called the Nanquan Temple in the city of Chizhou in Anhui Province. It was built in AD 795 at the time of the Tang Dynasty but was destroyed in the Cultural Revolution of the 1960s. This project is a master plan for its reconstruction. We proposed to create four areas with the concept of making a small village-like array of buildings while looking at how Chinese villages and temples incorporate nature in diverse ways.

The Main Area is where the spring that gave the temple its name welled up, and it is also where the ruins of the main hall were discovered. I set up a formal composition with a principal north-south axis informed by the mountains in the back and a great tree, and I designed the hall using the most formal language in the project by giving it a hip roof design based on that of the Toshodaiji in Japan. I aimed to make a building that would stand on par with nature.

The Zen Area is a place for meditation and reflection. It invites visitors to look inside themselves before a plane of water that reflects the natural landscape. The water and nature are the main subjects here, so I made the roof as a translucent tent with the aim of emphasizing the nature through contrast with a simple structure and design.

The Tower Area serves as a reception area for the complex. The existing stone pagoda and new wooden pagoda are its main features. There was no existing historical precedent for the wooden tower in China, so I designed it based on the Tamamushi Shrine held at the Shosoin in Japan.

The Hillside Area has a different character from the other areas. It used to be a stone quarry, and the bare rock surfaces exposed by human hands remind us of the thoughtlessness of man. I felt like I had to heal the damaged nature. I gave the building that serves as the lodging quarters for visitors a geometric form with walls of rusted steel, which express the opposition between man and nature in a different way from the rock surfaces. Meanwhile, I proposed to plant the rock surfaces with trees to heal the nature over a long time. Perhaps in several decades, the architecture of rusted steel will resemble the rock and the rock will be covered in nature when they are settled into China's natural landscape.

Site Plan 1 : 17500

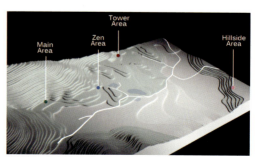

敷地模型。山に囲まれた谷＝盆地での計画。
Site model. A project in a valley/basin surrounded by mountains.

本殿エリア
Main Area

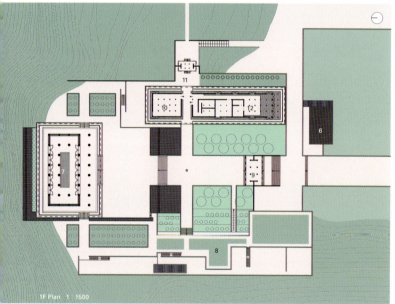

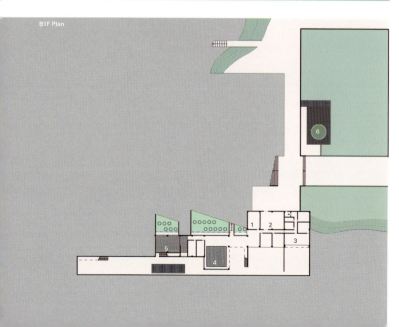

1	事務所	office
2	機械室	machine room
3	主人室	master's room
4	イベントホール	event hall
5	客室	guest room
6	シンボルツリー	symbol tree
7	メインホール	main hall
8	レセプション	reception house
9	メインゲート	main gate
10	展示室	exhibition
11	サブゲート	sub gate
12	休憩室	rest hall
13	案内所	visitor center

359頁上／本堂正面。中に自然をバックに御本尊が見える。
359頁下／南北の山を結ぶ軸線に乗り、今も残る泉を右下に見る本堂の計画。
右頁左上／メインエリアイメージモデル。軸線、水と泉、シンボルとして残る樹木と本堂の関係。
右頁右上／レセプションから前庭越しに付属棟を見る。
右頁左下／自然を背景とする御本尊の配置。
右頁右下／レセプションの外部空間。

p. 359 top / Front view of the main hall. The Buddha is visible inside against the backdrop of nature.
p. 359 bottom / The main hall sits on the axis linking the mountains to the north and south and overlooks the extant spring.
opposite, top row left / Conceptual model of the Main Area. Relationship between the axis, water, spring, symbolic tree, and main hall.
opposite, top row right / Auxiliary buildings beyond the forecourt as seen from the Reception Area.
opposite, bottom row left / The Buddha is positioned against a backdrop of nature.
opposite, bottom row right / Exterior spaces of the Reception Area.

Section

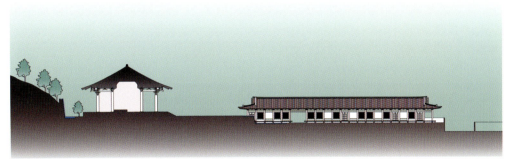
Section 1:1000

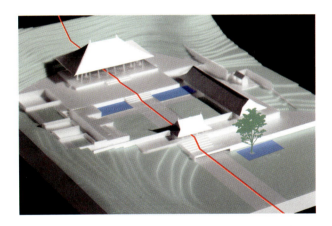

禅院エリア
Zen Area

Section

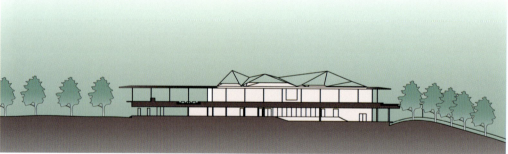
Section 1:1000

● Nanquan Temple project

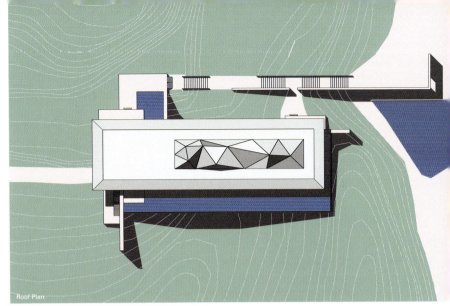

Roof Plan

1 図書館ホール　library hall
2 機械室　machine room
3 キッチン　kitchen
4 事務室　office
5 講堂　lecture hall
6 水槽　water tank
7 トイレ／ランドリー　washroom/laundry
8 禅スペース　Zen hall
9 テラス　terrace
10 池　pond

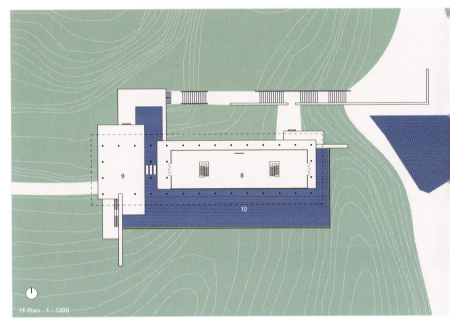

1F Plan　1:1200

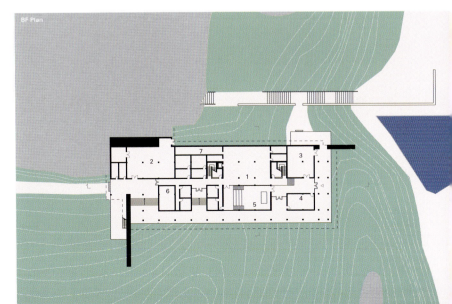

BF Plan

上／〈禅院エリア〉全景。水面の上に浮かぶ水平の屋根と不整形のテント屋根。
左頁下／自然とそれを映し込む水面。不整形のテント屋根からのやわらかな間接光が静かな室内に満ちる。

top / General view of the Zen Area. The flat roof and irregularly shaped tent roof float on the water.
opposite, bottom / The natural landscape and its reflection in the water. The soft indirect light from the irregularly shaped tent roof fills the tranquil interior.

塔院エリア
Tower Area

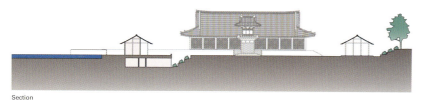

Section

Section 1:1200

上／〈塔院エリア〉全景。本堂の前に木塔が建つ。
中／本堂内部。スチール・ロッドを使用する張弦梁の屋根構造とし、その棟中央から光を導入する。自然の中で仏様と出会う本院とは対照的に象徴的な光の中で仏様と出会う。
左下／〈塔院エリア〉鳥観。
右頁中／本堂と地階回廊。
右頁下／石塔を池の中央に配置する。

top / General view of the Tower Area. A wooden tower stands in front of the main hall.
above / Interior of main hall. The roof structure of tensioned beams with steel rods draws light inside from the center. Unlike the main hall, where one encounters the Buddha within nature, here one encounters the Buddha under a symbolic light.
left / Bird's-eye view of the Tower Area.
opposite, left center / Main hall and basement corridor.
opposite, bottom left / The stone pagoda is positioned in the center of the pond.

● Nanquan Temple project

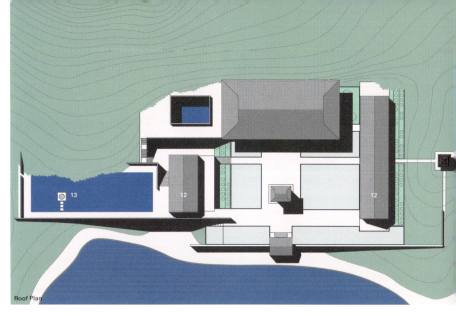

Roof Plan

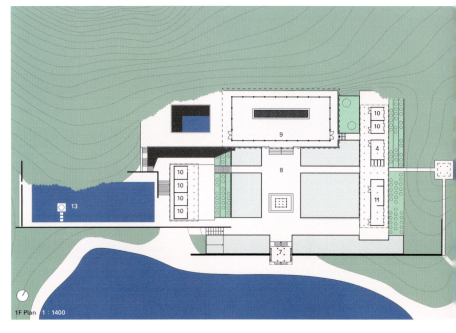

1F Plan 1:1400

B1F Plan

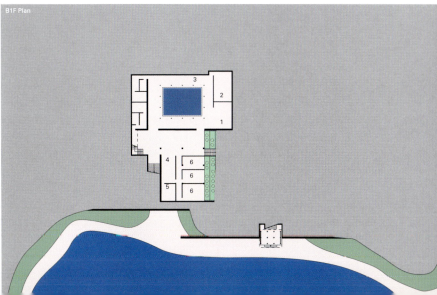

1	展示室 exhibition room	8	木塔 wooden tower
2	機械室 machine room	9	メインホール main hall
3	コリドール corridor	10	客室 guest room
4	事務室 office	11	キッチン kitchen
5	倉庫 storage	12	ビジターセンター visitor center
6	寝室 bedroom	13	石塔 stone tower
7	メインゲート main gate		

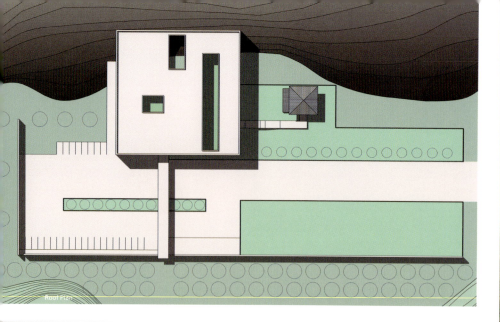

Roof Plan

ヒルサイドエリア
Hillside Area

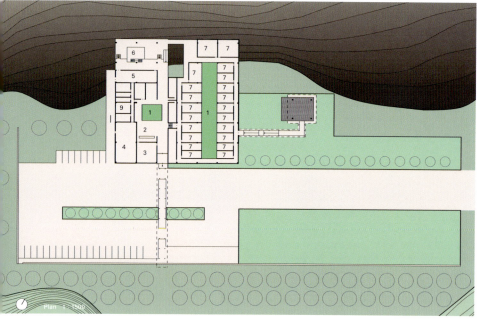

Plan 1:1500

1 中庭　courtyard
2 レセプション　reception
3 事務室　office
4 機械室　machine room
5 キッチン　kitchen
6 レストラン　restaurant
7 客室　guest room
8 瞑想室　meditation room
9 休憩室　resting room

Section

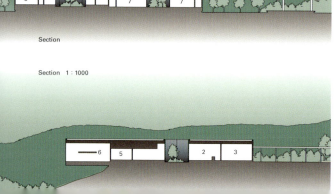

Section 1:1000

上／〈ヒルサイドエリア〉(宿坊)の全景。破壊された自然を建築で癒すこと。
左頁下／切り崩された山肌を治癒するための建築。
下／谷全体を見下しながら明日の修業を想うための場所。

above / General view of the lodging quarters. I sought to heal the damaged natural landscape with architecture.
opposite, bottom right / The architecture heals the razed slopes of the mountain.
below / A place for one to prepare their minds for the next day's training while looking out over the entire valley.

歴史の中の岸和郎

髙橋康夫
京都大学名誉教授／花園大学文学部文化遺産学科教授

岸和郎が日本的な洗練された美やユークリッド幾何学の端正さ・明晰さを特徴とする抽象的な建築作品を創出し、国内外から高い評価を得た建築家であることは言うまでもない。数世代遅れのモダニストである岸は、モダニズムの精髄に古典主義、水・自然、京都・日本さらにアジアや西欧の風土・歴史・文化などの情趣も添えているが、何よりも合理性や秩序の追求を徹底する知的な姿勢から、まさに真正のモダニストと呼ぶのが適切であろう。

I

1968年のパリ5月革命が日本に及ぼした大きな影響は、岸にも直接的に到達した。1969年、大学闘争の時代の最中、東京大学の入学試験が中止され、岸は京都大学工学部電気工学科に入学し、小さな歴史都市京都で下宿生活を送ることになった。4年後の1973年、電気工学科を卒業すると同時に建築学科に学士編入学したのは、下宿時代の交友、また京大生の生活圏の狭さがもたらした思わぬ結果であろう。

1975年、岸は建築学専攻修士課程に入学、建築史研究室に所属し、様々な地域と時代の建築史を研究する院生の中で建築家へのスタートを切った。建築家岸の思考に特徴的な歴史家的な視点はこの院生時代に自ずと身に付いたのであろう。

本書冒頭は、建築家岸の成り立ちや設計の背景が垣間見える、ある種の自伝であるが、その中で大切な建築に劣らず強い口調で語られたひとつの〈場所〉が興味深い。建築学教室本館図書室の書庫である。〈日本の戦前にこんな抽象的な建築が存在していたことに驚愕〉し、〈同時にその頃心酔していたコーリン・ロウやピーター・アイゼンマンの建築形態の読解や形態分析の延長上に土浦亀城の建築を分析するというアイデアを思い付いて興奮していた〉場所、〈どんなに反時代的であろうと、自分自身がモダニズムを継承しようと決心した〉場所。この書庫で、岸はモダニズムを古典として〈発見〉し、さらにそのモダニズムを継承する建築家となることを決意する。1970年代、世界では社会的価値観が大きく変化し、近代主義建築への批判、ポストモダニズムが勢いづく時代であったにもかかわらず。

岸の関心は確かにモダニズムに集中していたが、京都に住み、また建築史の研究室にいたので日常的に日本の歴史と文化に接し、時には伝統建築を体感する機会も少なからずあったはずである。昭和大修理が行われていた桂離宮の古書院で半日過ごした経験は、そのひとつに過ぎない。

1978年4月、岸は9年間を過ごした京都を離れ、東京の建築設計事務所に就職するが、東京生活はわずか3年という短期間で終わる。しかし、建築設計のみならずインテリア装飾やプロダクト・デザインなどの知識と経験も身に付けた岸は、縁あって京都造形短期大学（京都造形芸術大学）に職を得て、京都に帰ることになった。モダニスト岸和郎と歴史都市京都とのかかわりが再び始まるが、自分自身の決心によるものではない帰京や仕事が無い焦り、京都という場所、歴史と文化の重さ、時間の流れの遅さなどが、彼を苦しめたようである。

ともあれ、1981年4月から京都を拠点とする1人のプロフェッサー・アーキテクト岸の建築活動が始まった。1981年から1990年代前半にかけての岸は、70年代から変わることなく幾何学と光、秩序、抽象性を追求するモダニスト、あるいは古典主義者であるモダニスト（ル・コルビュジエやミース・ファン・デル・ローエのように）であり、また自身を〈日

本的〉であるとは意識せず、京都や日本、伝統に対して距離を置こうとしていた。これは当時の状況を眺めると、かなり風変わりな、というよりも天邪鬼な立ち位置であった。何故なら、1980年代末頃にはポストモダニズムの終焉が明白になり、代わって様々なモダニズムやポスト・ポストモダニズム、脱構築主義、ミニマリズム、ハイテクなどの動きの一方で、日本の伝統、すなわち歴史イメージや美意識、アイデンティティ、場所性などにも視線が注がれていたからである。建築固有の価値に執着する岸は、変わることなくモダニストとして終始一貫していた。

II
ところで、バブル経済の崩壊など大きな社会的変化が進行していた1990年代初め、岸和郎にとっても小さからぬ出来事があった。彼の意表を突くふたつの国際的な評価があらわれたのである。ひとつはアメリカ人ジェフリー・キプニスによる〈ダイハード・モダニスト〉、もうひとつはスペイン人による〈日本的〉、という評価である。

　岸は〈ダイハード・モダニスト〉という言葉を〈ようやく生き残ったモダニスト〉と解し、キプニスの言葉のニュアンスについて、モダニズムが置かれた現代社会の状況を全て承知の上で、あえて意図的・意識的にモダニズムの流れの中に身を投じている、と説明する。しかし、この明快な説明と〈ようやく生き残ったモダニスト〉とのあいだにはやや違和感がある。

　モダニズム批判の最中にモダニズムを選び取った岸は、当然ながら〈ようやく生き残った〉絶滅危惧種ではないし、1988年公開の映画〈ダイ・ハード〉の〈不死身〉というような意味もふさわしくない。"die hard"にはもともと〈（古い習慣、信仰などが）なかなか滅びない〉とか、〈最後まで抵抗する（頑張る）人〉、〈頑固な保守主義者〉といった意味があるので、キプニスは〈ダイハード・モダニスト〉=〈最後まで頑張る頑固な保守主義のモダニスト〉と言ったのではないか。ともかくも、〈ダイハード・モダニスト〉は時代の動向や流行に左右されない岸和郎の性格をよく捉えており、彼もまたキプニスの評価を受け入れたようである。

　一方、スペインの仕事の中で〈日本的〉と指摘されるまで、岸は自分を京都の建築家と捉えていなかったし、〈日本的〉であろうと思ったこともなく、また日本の伝統的な建築や都市が自分のもの、自分に関係あるものと思ったこともないという。むしろ彼は、意識して日本と伝統建築を避けてきた。にもかかわらず、自分の作品には〈日本的〉な特徴が明らかに内在している。この事実を、岸は外国人の眼によってはっきりと自覚させられた。既に自分が〈京都〉の建築家であり、〈日本的〉であり、日本の伝統建築が自分に関係がある、という確かな事実を納得するほかなかった。

　これを大きな転機として自身の身体・心・精神の中に〈日本的〉なものがあることを認め、岸は積極的に自分のものとして〈日本〉というテーマを抱え込む。ついに岸と京都との関係の不整合性——京都に住むにもかかわらず、京都から距離を置く——が解消され、伝統都市〈京都〉の建築家であるという覚悟のもと、京都はもちろん日本の伝統と文化を意識しつつ、西欧の文脈から日本の建築、特に古典主義的建築を考えるようになった。東京や世界の動向に対して時間と空間に〈ゆとり〉のある現代都市京都もまた、冷静で批判的な眼差しや設計活動の在り方のほかにも、小さくない影響を与え

たであろう。

　こうして岸は〈日本的〉な古典主義とヨーロッパ的な〈ダイハード・モダニズム〉を基盤として新たな段階へ進む。この岸和郎をネオモダニストと言ってもよいのであるが、1990年半ば頃彼自身が繰り返した偽悪的な方便を借りて〈モダニズムを偽装する〉建築家とするのが、心情的にも信条的にも彼にとってよりふさわしいのかも知れない。

　国内外において広く岸和郎の名前と作品が知られ、受注する建物の規模やクライアントの要求が変わると、それに応じて日本やアジアなどのリージョナルな香りや、歴史の建築、現代の都市などへのレファレンスを感じさせる建築作品を創り出し、近年はいわゆる商業建築やインテリア・デザイン、さらに都市プロジェクトなどにも手を拡げているが、その根底に古典主義的なモダニズムがあるのは変わらない。

　1993年に岸は京都工芸繊維大学へ異動し、その後、2010年4月に京都大学大学院教授となる。プロフェッサーで在り続けた岸が、歴史と現代への広い視野のもと、豊富な設計経験や明快な作品分析、西洋と日本の建築についての該博な知識を生かして建築設計教育を担当していたことは、『建築を旅する』(2003、共立出版)、『重奏する建築──文化／歴史／自然のかなたに建築を想う』(2012、TOTO出版)などからもうかがえる。この2冊は建築家岸の設計の根拠を、仕事の舞台裏や自身の大切な記憶などとともに語る本でありながら、近代建築史の参考書としても分かりやすく読みやすい。

Ⅲ

分析的な眼差しと直感的な建築理解、そして論理的・知的な操作によって近・現代の建築のみならず歴史上の建築をも解き明かす岸は、批評家かつ歴史家の見方と精緻な分析手法を併せ持った希少な建築家の1人である。その岸が一貫して課題としてきたのは改めて言うまでもなくモダニズム、特に建築のモダニズムであった。現代が依然として近代の文脈上に在るという歴史観のもと、モダニズムの意味とその受容の在り方を問い直す作業を続けている。これに関連して岸と日本の伝統とのかかわりを眺めてみよう。

　本書冒頭において岸が挙げた日本の伝統建築は、光と明確な論理性の大徳寺孤篷庵忘筌(その忘筌に対極的な〈官能的で感性的な空間〉大徳寺真珠庵庭玉軒)と、若い頃より強い関心を持ち続けていた〈列柱空間〉、〈どこかひ弱な「構築性」〉を持つ西本願寺対面所・白書院である。前者から日本建築の二面性──ラショナリズム(クラシシズム)とロマンティシズム──を知り、後者は寝殿から書院、茶室への史的展開という日本建築史の〈極めて個人的な理解〉のもと、論理的な思考によって日本建築、とりわけ書院の在り様を探究する端緒となった。岸にとって極めて大切なこれらの日本の名建築がいずれも近世の建築であることは偶然ではない。日本近世は、実は合理主義の時代であった。

　単なる私見に過ぎないが、日本近世の建築は、西洋の文脈を参照しつつ概括すると、古典主義を重要な基層として、その上にマニエリスム──古典主義の延長、古典主義の拡張・多様化、反古典主義──が広汎に展開したと考えられる。日本の文脈に言い換えると、和様や禅宗様などの古典主義とその組み合わせ(折衷主義)、そして古代以来の〈数寄〉(マニエリスム)が分化・純化した〈綺麗(はなやかな洗練された美しさ)〉と〈侘び(もの静かで簡素な風趣、世俗的な秩序や価値

観の否定、それらからの自由)〉を基調とする空間志向の大流行、と理解することが出来る。

　ところで、〈綺麗〉と〈侘び〉には前述の際立った相異点のほかにも、黒木の〈侘び〉と白木の〈綺麗〉、また〈侘び〉は過去、〈綺麗〉は未来を指向するという鮮烈な対比がある。さらに〈侘び〉を千利休の言葉を借りて簡潔に〈黒は古き心なり〉というなら、〈綺麗〉は〈白は新しき心〉である。しかし、極めて対照的な〈綺麗〉と〈侘び〉の真に大切な核心は、共に古典や伝統を尊重・継承しつつ、それらを否定、破壊し、新規なまた革新的なものと相互作用して新しい古典と伝統を創り出すところにある。敷衍すると、〈数寄〉とその動的な構造が〈伝統的なもの〉はもちろん、〈日本的なもの〉と等価であること、また外国文化受容期における〈近代化〉の在り方とも相似的であることはおのずから明らかであろう。〈数寄〉や〈伝統的〉＝〈日本的〉＝〈和風〉は、飛鳥・奈良時代から幾度も繰り返されてきた、ダイナミックな文化的な営みであり、その所産であると言ってよい。

　こうした〈数寄〉によって明確に特徴づけられる建築こそ、16世紀に成立した書院と茶室である。まず茶室についてみると、千利休による〈侘び〉の茶室を古典として、17世紀以降様々な創意溢れる工夫が試みられるが、それは端的に言ってマニエリスム、とりわけ反古典主義的な傾向（〈綺麗〉な、あるいは書院風の茶室など）を明瞭に認めることが出来る。他方、書院については、近世という時代を切り拓いた豊臣秀吉が首都京都に建設した大城郭、聚楽第の大広間（よく似た遺構が二条城二の丸御殿大広間）を古典、規範とする。その典型的な変形として古典的・正統的な西本願寺対面所・白書院、〈綺麗〉な桂離宮の書院、そして〈綺麗〉と〈侘び〉の融和した書院（大徳寺孤篷庵忘筌）、〈侘び〉の書院などがある。

　岸和郎の源泉となった日本の近世建築は、合理的でいて、しかも〈古典－反古典〉と「綺麗」－「侘び」のふたつの両義性を併せ持つ、まさに〈日本的〉な建築である。彼の作品における〈日本的〉なもの、その中核は、当然、これらの〈伝統的〉建築に由来していよう。彼は日本の〈伝統的〉建築を、初めは意識することなく、のちには意図的に受け入れ、西洋と日本の無意識かつ自然な混合・融合からさらにそれらの意識的な統合へ向かった。この意味で、建築家岸和郎はまさに〈日本的〉な〈近代化〉の一典型であると言えよう。

IV
岸和郎にとって近代運動は、残念ながら心奪われる同時代の動向ではなく、すでに高い評価を獲得した歴史的な出来事であった。彼はル・コルビュジエやミースのモダニズムを古典主義の作品として、さらに言えばそれらをギリシャやローマ、ルネサンスなどの古典主義建築の延長にあるものとして受け継ぐ一方、7世紀以来の伝統を内包する〈日本的〉古典主義建築をも自らのものとした。

　ギリシャと日本、すなわち文明の周縁において育まれたふたつの古典主義を継承するモダニストとして、彼は歴史の中に稀な、そして重要な位置を占めるに違いない。

Waro Kishi_within the context of History

Yasuo Takahashi
Professor Emeritus, Kyoto University /Professor, Department of Cultural Heritage, Faculty of Letters, Hanazono University

I do not need to explain that Waro Kishi is as an architect who has received international acclaim through making abstract architecture characterized by a refined Japanese aesthetic and Euclidean geometries articulated with clarity and decorum. Kishi, who adds touches of classicism, water/nature, Kyoto/Japan, and qualities of Asian and Western climates, histories, and cultures to the essences of Modernism, is a Modernist several generations behind his time. Yet, considering the intellectual stance with which he rigorously pursues rationality and order, he correctly should be called a true Modernist.

I.
The 1968 May Revolution in Paris had a great impact on Japan and a direct effect on Kishi as well. In 1969, when the University of Tokyo's entrance exams were suspended amidst student protests, he entered the electrical engineering department at Kyoto University and began living in a dormitory in the historical city of Kyoto. His friendships in the dormitory and the restricted habitat of the university's students in general were presumably what led him to take an unlikely turn four years later in 1973, when he switched into the undergraduate architecture program upon graduating from the electrical engineering department.

In 1975, Kishi entered the architecture department's master's program, joined a research laboratory specialized in architectural history, and made a start on his path to becoming an architect in the company of graduate students who researched the histories of architecture of various places and times. It was no doubt during these years when Kishi acquired the historian-like perspective that would become a characteristic trait of his thinking as an architect.

Kishi's text at the start of this book reads as an autobiography that provides glimpses into the architect's formative moments and the background of his work. Particularly interesting is that one certain place he speaks about with the same ardor as when he speaks about the architectural works that hold special meaning to him: the library stacks in the architecture department building. That was where he was surprised by the abstract architecture that existed in prewar Japan; excited by his idea to analyze the Kameki Tsuchiura Residence using the approaches of formal analysis employed by his idols Colin Rowe and Peter Eisenman; and resolved to commit himself to Modernism even if it was out of step with the times. Those stacks were where Kishi "discovered" Modernism as a classical mode of architecture and decided to become a Modernist architect—despite the fact that the 1970s was a time when social values were changing worldwide, Modernist architecture was under fire, and Postmodernism was gaining momentum.

Regardless of his interest in Modernism, however, Kishi should have regularly been exposed to Japan's history, culture, and traditional architecture by living in Kyoto and studying in an architectural history laboratory. His experience of spending a day at the Katsura Villa when it was undergoing extensive repairs was just one such instance.

In April 1978, Kishi left Kyoto, the city where he had lived for nine years, and joined an architectural firm in Tokyo. However, his life in Tokyo only lasted for three short years. After having gained knowledge and experience about not only architectural design but also interior decorating and product design, Kishi happened to be offered a position at the Kyoto College of Art (now Kyoto University of Art and Design) and wound up back in Kyoto. And so resumed the relationship between the Modernist and the historical city. Yet, there he struggled to come to terms with the unplanned return to Kyoto, the anxiety of having no projects, the weight of the history and culture of the place called Kyoto, and the slow pace of the city.

At any rate, he started his architectural activities as a professor/architect based in Kyoto from April 1981. From 1981 to the early 1990s, Kishi continued to explore geometry, light, order, and abstraction as a Modernist—or a classicist Modernist (like Le Corbusier and Mies)—as he had been doing since the '70s. He did not consciously think of himself as being "Japanese", and he tried to distance himself from Kyoto, Japan, and tradition. This stance he took was quite queer, or rather perverse, considering the circumstances of that time: As Postmodernism's end became palpable by the late 1980s, architects turned to various movements such as Modernism, Post-Postmodernism, Deconstructivism, Minimalism, and High-Tech and also reexamined Japanese tradition—namely, its historical image, aesthetics, identity, and sense of place. Kishi, who instead remained fixated on architecture's inherent values, never changed and persisted as a Modernist.

II.
In the early 1990s, when great societal changes such as the bubble collapse were unfolding, Kishi was also faced with an incident of great significance: two unexpected evaluations of his work arose overseas. First, Jeffrey Kipnis, an American, called him a "die-hard Modernist"; second, a Spaniard described him as "Japanese".

Kishi has interpreted "die-hard Modernist" as "a Modernist who managed to survive", which he explains means that he is deliberately putting himself in the lineage of Modernism even while being fully aware of its status in today's society. However, it seems to me that there is an incongruity between Kipnis' description and Kishi's lucid explanation of it.

Kishi picked out Modernism while it was being criticized, so he obviously is not any sort of endangered species that "managed to survive". The term "die hard" was not used to describe an "immortal" in the sense of the 1988 film Die Hard either. The term was originally used to describe "things (old customs, faiths, etc.) that do not readily perish", "people who put up resistance (do not give up) until the end", and "stubborn conservatives", so Kipnis probably said "die-hard Modernist" to mean "a conservative Modernist who will not give up until the end". In any case, "die-hard Modernist" captures very well the character of Kishi, who does not sway with the trends of the times, and he too seems to have accepted Kipnis' evaluation of him.

Meanwhile, Kishi never saw himself as a Kyoto architect or "Japanese" architect before being told so while working on a Spanish project. He claims that he did not think that Japan's traditional architecture and cities were a part of him or were related to him in any way. If anything, he consciously avoided Japan and its traditional architecture. Despite of this, there are clearly "Japanese" qualities in his work. Kishi was only made fully aware of this fact through the eyes of a foreigner. He had no choice but to accept the truth that he had become a "Kyoto" architect, his work was "Japanese", and Japan's traditional architecture did have something to do with him.

This was the major turning point where Kishi recognized that there was something "Japanese" in his body, mind, and spirit, and he began to actively engage "Japan" as a personal theme. Having finally resolved the dissonance in his relationship with Kyoto—which he had tried to keep his distance from despite living in it—and having made up his mind to be an architect of Kyoto, a city of tradition, Kishi started to think about Japanese architecture (particularly classicist architecture) through a Western context while being mindful of the traditions and cultures of not only Kyoto but also Japan. The "ease" that the modern city of Kyoto offered him both in terms of time and space when compared to Tokyo most likely also had an influence on shaping his cool, critical eye and the mode of his practice.

In this way, Kishi advanced into a new phase founded on "Japanese" classicism and European "die-hard"

Modernism. We could call Kishi at this point a Neo-Modernist, but perhaps he would find it to be more fitting to say that he was just "assuming the guise of Modernism"—borrowing the words that he repeatedly used in the mid-1990s.

As Kishi and his works came to be known internationally, and as the scale of his buildings and the demands of his clients changed, he started producing works that reflected regional qualities of Japan and Asia and that made references to historical architecture and modern cities. In recent years, he has been working on commercial architecture and interior designs, and he even has been trying his hand at urban projects. However, the fact that a classicist sense of Modernism lies at the foundation of his work remains the unchanged.

Kishi relocated to the Kyoto Institute of Technology in 1993 and became a professor of the university's graduate school in April 2014. His books such as Kenchiku wo tabi suru [Journey Through Architecture] (2003, Kyoritsu Shuppan) and Juso suru kenchiku—Bunka/rekishi/shizen no kanata ni kenchiku wo omou [Architecture in Ensemble—Thinking of Architecture Through Culture, History, and Nature] (2012, TOTO Publishing) give us a sense of how Kishi, who has always been a professor, teaches architectural design while drawing on his experience with architectural design, his clear analyses of architecture, and his extensive knowledge of Western and Japanese architecture that he has gained through his wide field of view across history. In these two books, Kishi speaks about his basis for designing while sharing behind-the-scenes anecdotes from his projects and his special memories, but they can also be read as very comprehensive and legible reference books on the history of Modern architecture.

III.
Kishi, who interprets the architectures of not only the present and recent times but also historical periods with his analytical gaze, intuitive understanding for architecture, and logical/intelligent operations, is one of those rare architects that has both the eye and meticulous analytical method of a critic and historian. There is no need to restate that modernism—specifically, Modernism in architecture—has consistently been the project of this architect. He continually questions the meaning of Modernism and how it should be accepted while maintaining a view of history that sees the present as still being part of the same context as the Modern period. With this in mind, let us examine Kishi's relationship with Japan's traditions.

The traditional Japanese architecture that Kishi discusses at the start of this book are the Daitokuji's Bosen tearoom, which has a distinctive light and clear logicality (he also mentions, as its antithesis, the "sensual, visceral spaces" of the Teigyokuken tearoom), and the Nishi Honganji's Taimensho and Shiroshoin, which respectively possess a "colonnade space" that has been an object of interest from his youth and a "delicate nature of construction". The former has taught him about the two-sided character of Japanese architecture—i.e. rationalism (classicism) vs. romanticism—and the latter has led him to apply logical reasoning to explore Japanese architecture—namely shoin-style architecture—based on a "very personal reading" of the historical development of Japanese architecture from shinden- to shoin- to chashitsu-style architecture. It is no coincidence that these Japanese masterpieces that hold special meaning for Kishi are works from Japan's Early Modern period, which was very much an age of rationalism.

This is nothing but a personal opinion, but if one should sum up Japan's Early Modern architecture using Western contextual references, one can say that it had a significant classicist foundation upon which a wide variety of mannerisms unfolded (e.g. classicism extended, classicism expanded/diversified, and anti-classicism).

Using Japanese contextual references, one can say that there was a great trend of spaces based on the classicist styles of wayo [Japanese style] and zenshuyo [Zen style], a mix of these styles (eclecticism), and refined/distilled forms of the age-0ld suki (mannerism) such as the kirei (brilliant, refined beauty) and wabi (quiet, plain taste; the rejection of and freedom from secular order and values).

There are other marked contrasts between kirei and wabi than those noted above, such as the use of kuroki ["black wood"] with wabi vs. shiroki ["white wood"] with kirei and the past-oriented character of wabi vs. the future-oriented character of kirei. If one should borrow the words of Sen no Rikyu and describe wabi simply as "black is the heart of the old", then kirei can be described as "white is the heart of the new". The true heart of the contrastive kirei and wabi, however, lies in how they both respect/inherit classical models and traditions even while denying them, breaking them, and meshing them with fresh things to create new classical models and traditions. From this it should be clear that suki and its dynamic system are equivalent to the things considered to be "traditional" or "Japanese" and similar in nature to the "modernization" that took place in the period when foreign cultures were introduced into Japan. The notion that the suki and "traditional" = "Japanese" = wafu [Japan-esque] is a product of a dynamic cultural cycle that has been repeated innumerable times since the Asuka/Nara periods.

The shoin and chashitsu architecture born in the 16th century are clearly characterized by suki. Rikyu's wabi tearoom represents the classical model of chashitsu architecture. Many creative variants have been made from the 17th century onwards, but, if put bluntly, they clearly exhibit mannerisms, namely a tendency towards anti-classicism (e.g. kirei, shoin-esque tearooms). The Ohiroma of the Jurakudai—the castle of Hideyoshi Toyotomi, who opened the doors to the Early Modern period—represents the classical model of the shoin (the Ohiroma of the Ninomaru Palace of Nijo Castle has a similar layout). Typical variants of this include the classical/orthodox shoin of the Taimensho and Shiroshoin, the kirei shoin of Katsura Villa, shoin that fuse kirei and wabi (e.g. Bosen), and wabi shoin.

The Early Modern works that became sources of inspiration for Kishi are very much "Japanese": they are rational and also embody both sides of the classical vs. anti-classical and kirei vs. wabi dichotomies. The "Japanese-ness" in his work naturally stems from this traditional architecture. He initially ignored Japan's traditional architecture, then deliberately incorporated it, then unconsciously and naturally mixed/fused it with Western ideas, and then deliberately synthesized them. In this sense, it can be said that Kishi represents an architect model that is "Japanese" and that has been "modernized".

IV.
For Kishi, the Modernism unfortunately was not a gripping real-time movement but a historical event that had already earned its honors. On one hand, he inherited Corbusian and Miesian Modernism—which he saw on the same continuum as the classicist architecture of Greece, Rome, and the Renaissance. On the other hand, he also made the "Japanese" classicist architecture that embodied traditions from the seventh century onwards his own.

As a Modernist who has inherited these strains of classicism nurtured in Greece and Japan—that is, two peripheral civilizations—Kishi undoubtedly holds a rare and important place in history.

作品データ
Project Data

凡例　legend

作品名
Project Name
1 : Location
2 : Function
3 : Site Area (m²)
4 : Building Area (m²)
5 : Total Floor Area (m²)
6 : Structure
7 : Design Period
8 : Construction Period
9 : Collaborator

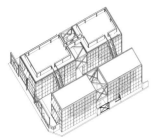
Kyoto College of Art, Takahara Campus

Boutique COLLECTION'S

Boutique DIMAGGIO

Interior Design of Nagano Natural History Museum

1982

ワイン・グロッサリー
Liquor Shop "WINE GROCERY"
1：Shimogyo-ku, Kyoto
2：liquor shop
5：120.41
6：interior design
7：1982.04 − 1982.05
8：1982.06 − 1982.07

京都芸術短期大学高原校舎
**Kyoto College of Art,
Takahara Campus**
1：Sakyo-ku, Kyoto
2：college
3：1,254.60
4：420.75
5：633.75
6：steel frame, 2 stories
7：1982.03 − 1982.05
8：1982.07 − 1982.10

1984

M House
M House
1：Sakyo-ku, Kyoto
2：one-family house
3：435.49
4：215.61
5：320.99
6：reinforced concrete / steel frame,
  2 stories
7：1983.01 − 1983.04
8：1983.07 − 1984.02

スイミング・クラブ「コア 25」
Swimming Club CORE25
1：Kusatsu, Shiga
2：swimming club
3：2,009.70
4：704.00

5：1,498.21
6：reinforced concrete, 3 stories
7：1983.11 − 1984.01
8：1984.04 − 1984.09

リカーショップ「ヤマノウチ」
Liquor Shop YAMANOUCHI
1：Minami-ku, Kyoto
2：liquor shop
5：78.42
6：interior design
7：1984.05 − 1984.06
8：1984.08 − 1984.10

ブティック「コレクションズ」
Boutique COLLECTION'S
1：Sumiyoshi-ku, Osaka
2：retail shop
5：58.49
6：interior design
7：1984.06 − 1984.08
8：1984.10 − 1984.11

ブティック「ディマジオ」
Boutique DIMAGGIO
1：Sumiyoshi-ku, Osaka
2：retail shop
5：57.33
6：interior design
7：1984.08 − 1984.09
8：1984.11 − 1984.12

1985

長野市立博物館分館茶臼山自然史館
**Interior Design of Nagano
Natural History Museum**
1：Nagano, Nagano
2：natural history museum
5：684.95
6：display design
7：1984.10 − 1985.08
8：1985.08 − 1985.09

1987

KIM HOUSE
KIM HOUSE
1：Ikuno-ku, Osaka
2：one-family house
3：53.43
4：38.03
5：69.07
6：steel frame, 2 stories
7：1986.03 − 1986.08
8：1986.12 − 1987.03

彦根古城博
オーミケンシ・ミカレディ・ブース
**Installation 'Cloth and yarn'
World Ancient Castle Festival**
1：Hikone, Shiga
2：exhibition
5：50.00
7：1986.10 − 1987.01
8：1987.03 − 1987.05

世界歴史都市博イベント・ゾーン
**Event Zone for World Historic
Cities Exposition**
1：Fushimi-ku, Kyoto
2：exposition event space
4：384.00
5：432.00
6：space frame made of steel frame
  scaffolds
7：1987.03 − 1987.10
8：1987.11 − 1987.11

1989

洛北の家
House in Rakuhoku
1：Sakyo-ku, Kyoto
2：one-family house
3：121.28
4：59.92

5：90.11
6：reinforced concrete / steel frame,
  2 stories
7：1987.08 − 1988.05
8：1988.07 − 1989.02

PARADE
PARADE
1：Higashiyama-ku, Kyoto
2：bar
5：65.54
6：interior design
7：1989.01 − 1989.05
8：1989.06 − 1989.07

TS chair
TS chair
2：chair
6：aluminum cantilever
7：1989.01 − 1989.07
8：1989.08 − 1989.09

都築Flat
TSUZUKI Flat
1：Chiyoda-ku, Tokyo
2：house + office
5：105.13
6：interior design of house and working
  space
7：1988.03 − 1989.04
8：1989.03 − 1989.11

AUTO LAB
AUTO LAB
1：Ukyo-ku, Kyoto
2：automobile showroom
3：1,890.00
4：220.50
5：220.50
6：steel frame, 1 story
7：1989.01 − 1989.06
8：1989.08 − 1989.11

Event Zone for World Historic Cities Exposition

House in Rakuhoku

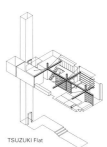
TSUZUKI Flat

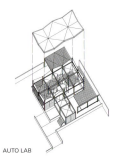

AUTO LAB

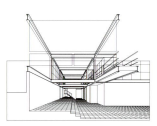

Kyoto Kagaku Research Institute

House in Kamigyo

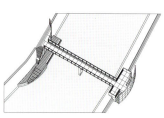

Yunoka Bridge

1990

京都科学・開発センター
Kyoto Kagaku Research Institute
1：Kizu-cho, Kyoto
2：research office
3：4,654.96
4：588.00
5：945.00
6：steel frame / reinforced concrete walls, 2 stories
7：1987.11 − 1989.06
8：1989.11 − 1990.08

上京の家
House in Kamigyo
1：Kamigyo-ku, Kyoto
2：one-family house
3：52.01
4：30.45
5：99.71
6：reinforced concrete, 3 stories
7：1988.11 − 1990.04
8：1990.06 − 1990.11

1991

湯の香橋
Yunoka Bridge
1：Ashikita-cho, Kumamoto
2：pedestrian bridge
5：L: 40.80m W: 3.50m
6：pre-stressed concrete beam with 1 center column
7：1989.12 − 1990.08
8：1990.11 − 1991.04

1992

日本橋の家
House in Nipponbashi
1：Naniwa-ku, Osaka
2：one-family house

3：42.74
4：32.50
5：112.60
6：steel frame, 4 stories
7：1990.03 − 1991.04
8：1991.07 − 1992.03

Weekend House in Tateshina
Weekend House in Tateshina
1：Tateshina, Nagano
2：weekend house
3：874.74
4：147.73
5：147.73
6：wood frame, 1 story
7：1991.04 − 1992.06

1993

Watch "Ecclo"
Watch "Ecclo"
2：watch
7：1993.05 − 1993.06

中京の家
House in Nakagyo
1：Nakagyo-ku, Kyoto
2：house + shop
3：66.60
4：44.89
5：124.57
6：reinforced concrete, 3 stories
7：1992.11 − 1993.03
8：1993.04 − 1993.10
9：KOHSEKI CO., LTD

園部 SD Office
Sonobe SD Office
1：Sonobe-cho, Kyoto
2：office
3：1,887.99
4：192.03
5：541.69

6：steel frame / reinforced concrete, 2 stories + 1 basement level
7：1991.08 − 1992.12
8：1993.02 − 1993.11

1994

下鴨の家
House in Shimogamo
1：Sakyo-ku, Kyoto
2：one-family house
3：104.42
4：99.40
5：80.52
6：steel frame, 2 stories
7：1992.12 − 1994.04
8：1994.05 − 1994.09

霜華
Restaurant "SOHKA"
1：Abeno-ku, Osaka
2：restaurant
5：95.73
6：interior design
7：1993.11 − 1994.06
8：1994.07 − 1994.10

Y HOUSE
Y HOUSE
1：Shiga-cho, Shiga
2：house + workshop
3：501.00
4：81.98
5：129.19
6：wood frame, 2 stories
7：1994.05 − 1994.12

Max Mara Headquaters project
Max Mara Headquaters project
1：Reggio nel l'Emilia, Italy
2：office complex
3：310,000.00
4：28,091.00

5：36,084.00
6：steel frame / reinforced concrete, 3 stories + 8 buildings
7：1994.12 − 1995.05

1995

紫野和久傳
Restaurant "Murasakino Wakuden"
1：Kita-ku, Kyoto
2：Japanese restaurant
3：55.17
4：35.87
5：103.98
6：reinforced concrete, 3 stories
7：1994.02 − 1994.12
8：1995.01 − 1995.08
9：KOHSEKI CO., LTD

宝塚花の道プロジェクト
Hananomichi project
1：Takarazuka, Hyogo
2：complex
3：4,500.00
4：3,600.00
5：26,000.00
6：reinforced concrete, 12 stories + 2 basement levels
7：1995.06 − 1995.08

宝塚の家
House in Takarazuka
1：Takarazuka, Hyogo
2：one-family house
3：209.37
4：90.71
5：148.40
6：steel frame / reinforced concrete, 2 stories
7：1994.02 − 1995.02
8：1995.03 − 1995.09

House in Nipponbashi

Weekend House in Tateshina

House in Nakagyo

Sonobe SD Office

● Project Data

House in Shimogamo

Restaurant "SOHKA"

Max Mara Headquaters project

Restaurant "Murasakino Wakuden"

1996

国立国会図書館関西館
**National Library
Kansai Division project**
1 : Seika-cho, Kyoto
2 : library
3 : 37,600.00
4 : 11,018.00
5 : 59,032.00
6 : steel frame / reinforced concrete, 5 stories + 1 basement level
7 : 1996.03 — 1996.06

1997

**N Resort project
N Resort project**
1 : Hakone-cho, Kanagawa
2 : resort house
3 : 7,843.34
4 : 1,900.00
5 : 3,063.45
6 : reinforced concrete / steel frame, 4 stories
7 : 1996.12 — 1997.02

山口大学医学部
創立50周年記念会館
Memorial Hall in Yamaguchi
1 : Ube, Yamaguchi
2 : memorial hall
3 : 92,631.18
4 : 329.53
5 : 626.77
6 : steel frame / reinforced concrete, 3 stories
7 : 1994.03 — 1996.03
8 : 1996.08 — 1997.04

東大阪の家
House in Higashi-Osaka
1 : Higashi-Osaka, Osaka

2 : one-family house
3 : 115.71
4 : 69.32
5 : 186.68
6 : steel frame, 3 stories
7 : 1995.05 — 1996.04
8 : 1996.07 — 1997.04

東灘の家
House in Higashinada
1 : Higashinada-ku, Kobe
2 : one-family house
3 : 71.62
4 : 40.16
5 : 117.25
6 : reinforced concrete, 3 stories + 1 basement level
7 : 1995.08 — 1996.06
8 : 1996.07 — 1997.04

**I project
I project**
1 : Nakagyo-ku, Kyoto
2 : shop annex
3 : 76.90
4 : 15.07
5 : 15.07
6 : wood frame, 1 story
7 : 1996.10 — 1997.04

**Jyvaskyla Music and Arts Center
Jyvaskyla Music and Arts Center**
1 : Jyvaskyla, Finland
2 : museum + concert hall
3 : 4,780.00
4 : 3,300.00
5 : 1,450.00
6 : steel frame + reinforced concrete, 4 stories + 2 basement levels
7 : 1997.06 — 1997.08

**VIA BUS STOP PRESS ROOM
VIA BUS STOP PRESS ROOM**
1 : Shibuya-ku, Tokyo
2 : office + press room
5 : 79.24
6 : interior design
7 : 1997.06 — 1997.07
8 : 1997.07 — 1997.09

**VIA BUS STOP MEN'S 新宿丸井店 I
VIA BUS STOP MEN'S, Shinjuku, I**
1 : Shinjuku-ku, Tokyo
2 : retail shop
5 : 87.82
6 : interior design
7 : 1997.08 — 1997.09
8 : 1997.09 — 1997.09

1998

VIA BUS STOP なんばCITY店
VIA BUS STOP, Namba
1 : Chuo-ku, Osaka
2 : retail shop
5 : 211.88
6 : interior design
7 : 1997.12 — 1998.02
8 : 1998.02 — 1998.03

VIA BUS STOP ACCESSORY
渋谷パルコ店
VIA BUS STOP ACCESSORY, Shibuya-parco
1 : Shibuya-ku, Tokyo
2 : retail shop
5 : 165.39
6 : interior design
7 : 1997.12 — 1998.02
8 : 1998.02 — 1998.03

VIA BUS STOP JEANS 宮下公園前
VIA BUS STOP JEANS, Miyashitakoen-mae
1 : Shibuya-ku, Tokyo
2 : retail shop
5 : 306.80
6 : interior design
7 : 1998.01 — 1998.02
8 : 1998.02 — 1998.03

VIA BUS STOP
新潟ビルボートプレス店
VIA BUS STOP, Niigata
1 : Niigata, Niigata
2 : retail shop
5 : 92.28
6 : interior design
7 : 1998.01 — 1998.03
8 : 1998.03 — 1998.03

苦楽園の家 I
House in Kurakuen I
1 : Nishinomiya, Hyogo
2 : one-family house
3 : 365.01
4 : 142.33
5 : 214.65
6 : reinforced concrete, 2 stories + 1 basement level
7 : 1996.01 — 1997.02
8 : 1997.03 — 1998.04

荒木組新本社 I + II
Araki Gumi New Headquarters I+II
1 : Okayama, Okayama
2 : office
3 : 3,200.00
4 : 1,331.80
5 : 3,547.55
6 : reinforced concrete, 4 stories + 1 basement level
7 : 1996.10 — 1998.04

House in Takarazuka

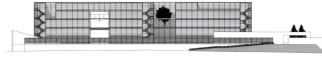
National Library Kansai Division project

Memorial Hall in Yamaguchi

House in Higashi-Osaka

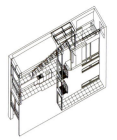
House in Higashinada

House in Kurakuen I Araki Gumi New Headquarters I+II

VIA BUS STOP 福岡店
VIA BUS STOP, Fukuoka
1：Chuo-ku, Fukuoka
2：retail shop
5：92.28
6：interior design
7：1997.12 − 1998.03
8：1998.04 − 1998.04

VIA BUS STOP 大丸
神戸ジニアスギャラリー店
VIA BUS STOP, Kobe
1：Chuo-ku, Kobe
2：retail shop
5：219.79
6：interior design
7：1997.12 − 1998.04
8：1998.04 − 1998.04

朱雀の家
House in Suzaku
1：Nara, Nara
2：one-family house
3：303.93
4：126.70
5：178.32
6：reinforced concrete,
 2 stories + 1 basement level
7：1996.06 − 1997.06
8：1997.10 − 1998.10
9：KOHSEKI CO., LTD

VIA BUS STOP MEN'S 新宿丸井 II
VIA BUS STOP, Shinjuku
1：Shinjuku-ku, Tokyo
2：retail shop
5：140.00
6：interior design
7：1998.08 − 1998.10
8：1998.11 − 1998.11

1999

iCB Paris
iCB Paris
1：Rue des Rosiers, Paris
2：shop
5：108.90
6：interior design
7：1998.06 − 1998.07
8：1998.09 − 1999.01

VIA BUS STOP JEANS 博多
VIA BUS STOP, Hakata
1：Hakata-ku, Fukuoka
2：retail shop
5：643.70
6：interior design
7：1998.08 − 1998.09
8：1998.12 − 1999.02

VIA BUS STOP 名古屋
VIA BUS STOP, Nagoya
1：Naka-ku, Nagoya
2：retail shop
5：423.30
6：interior design
7：1998.11 − 1998.12
8：1999.01 − 1999.03

VIA BUS STOP 小樽
VIA BUS STOP, Otaru
1：Otaru, Hokkaido
2：retail shop
5：368.70
6：interior design
7：1998.12 − 1998.12
8：1999.01 − 1999.03

VIA BUS STOP ACCESSORY 神戸店
VIA BUS STOP ACCESSORY, Kobe
1：Chuo-ku, Kobe
2：retail shop
5：149.00

6：interior design
7：1999.01 − 1999.01
8：1999.03 − 1999.03

VIA BUS STOP JEANS お台場
VIA BUS STOP JEANS, Odaiba
1：Kouto-ku, Tokyo
2：retail shop
5：233.26
6：interior design
7：1998.11 − 1999.02
8：1999.05 − 1999.06

Roswell Hotel project
Roswell Hotel project
1：Roswell, New Mexico
2：hotel
3：7,200.00
4：6,320.00
5：18,840.00
6：reinforced concrete,
 14 stories + 1 basement level
7：1999.07 − 1999.09

2000

青森県立美術館
Aomori Museum project
1：Aomori, Aomori
2：museum
3：129,536.37
4：10,656.84
5：14,776.40
6：reinforced concrete / wood roof
 frame, 3 stories + 1 basement level
7：1999.10 − 2000.01

かづらせい・寺町
Antique Gallery "Kazurasei"
1：Nakagyo-ku, Kyoto
2：antique gallery
3：176.10
4：121.10

5：335.72
6：reinforced concrete, 3 stories
7：1998.08 − 1999.02
8：1999.03 − 2000.03
9：KOHSEKI CO., LTD

苦楽園の家 III
House in Kurakuen III
1：Nishinomiya, Hyogo
2：one-family house
3：293.64
4：90.62
5：155.56
6：reinforced concrete, 2 stories
7：2000.01 − 2000.04

苦楽園の家 IV
House in Kurakuen IV
1：Nishinomiya, Hyogo
2：one-family house
3：297.83
4：116.48
5：197.64
6：steel frame / reinforced concrete,
 3 stories
7：2000.01 − 2000.04

苦楽園の家 V
House in Kurakuen V
1：Nishinomiya, Hyogo
2：one-family house
3：346.04
4：121.56
5：240.45
6：steel frame / reinforced concrete,
 3 stories
7：2000.01 − 2000.04

20 × 22 HOUSE
20 × 22 HOUSE
1：Sonobe-cho, Kyoto
2：two-family house
3：1,273.28

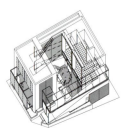
House in Suzaku

iCB Paris

VIA BUS STOP, Otaru

Roswell Hotel project

● Project Data

Antique Gallery "Kazurasei"

4：322.00
5：322.00
6：steel frame, 1 story
7：1999.11 − 2000.05

The Urban Planning of the Teresitas Beachfront in Santa Cruz de Tenerife
The Urban Planning of the Teresitas Beachfront in Santa Cruz de Tenerife

1：Canary Islands, Spain
2：shops + sports facilities + hotel + condominium
3：304.77
4：123.79
5：295.760
6：steel frame and reinforced concrete composite, 6 stories + 2 basement levels
7：2000.03 − 2000.07

文京の家
House in Bunkyo

1：Bunkyo-ku, Tokyo
2：two-family house
3：497.40
4：277.55
5：214.16
6：wood frame, 1 story
7：1999.03 − 1999.08
8：2000.01 − 2000.08

Louis Vuitton Building project in Tokyo
Louis Vuitton Building project in Tokyo

1：Minato-ku, Tokyo
2：shop + office
3：594.87
4：245.97
5：2,881.27
6：8 stories + 2 basement levels
7：2000.09 − 2000.10

House in Fukaya

The Urban Planning of the Teresitas beachfront in Santa Cruz de Tenerife

2001

苦楽園の家 II
House in Kurakuen II

1：Nishinomiya, Hyogo
2：one-family house
3：268.46
4：241.63
5：268.46
6：steel frame / reinforced concrete, 2 stories
7：1996.11 − 1997.10
8：2000.03 − 2001.02

スタジアム1100
Stadium 1100

1：Chigusa-ku, Nagoya
2：pachinko parlor
5：1,506.30
6：interior design
7：2000.11 − 2001.02
8：2001.03 − 2001.04

京都池田記念庭園
Kyoto Memorial Garden project

1：Kita-ku, Kyoto
2：religious facility
3：47,525.46
4：2,644.80
5：6,208.70
6：wood frame, 1 story, reinforced concrete, 1 story + 1 basement level
7：2001.04

深谷の家
House in Fukaya

1：Fukaya, Saitama
2：one-family house
3：343.89
4：146.87
5：186.72
6：steel frame / reinforced concrete, 2 stories
7：1999.08 − 2000.02
8：2000.08 − 2001.05

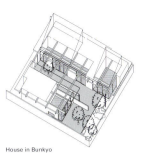

House in Bunkyo

六甲山の家
House in Rokko Mountains

1：Nada-ku, Hyogo
2：one-family house
3：2,211.00
4：257.50
5：257.50
6：reinforced concrete, timber frame roof
7：2000.11 − 2001.05

心斎橋の家
House in Shinsaibashi

1：Chuo-ku, Osaka
2：house + shop
3：29.93
4：25.80
5：88.81
6：steel frame, 4 stories
7：2001.03 − 2001.09

Stadium600
Stadium 600

1：Chigusa-ku, Nagoya
2：pachinko parlor
3：1,158.86
4：1,079.02
5：1,591.75
6：steel frame, 2 stories
7：2000.12 − 2001.08
8：2001.08 − 2001.11

2002

宮城県白石市プロジェクト
S Community Center project

1：Shiraishi, Miyagi
2：community center
3：2,035.75
4：470.00

House in Shinsaibashi

House in Kurakuen II

5：470.00
6：steel frame, 1 story
7：2001.12 − 2002.01

浅井町健康パーク
Azai-cho Welfare Facilities competition

1：Azai-cho, Shiga
2：welfare facilities
3：13.00
4：2,210.00
5：1,950.00
6：reinforced concrete / wood frame, 1 story
   reinforced concrete/steel frame, 2 stories
7：2002.02

平和橋
Heiwabashi Bridge

1：Hiroshima, Hiroshima
2：automobile and pedestrian bridge
5：L: 97.00m W: 25.80m
6：pre-stressed concrete beam with 2 columns
7：1995.12 − 2000.03
8：1999.04 − 2002.03

堺の家
House in Sakai

1：Sakai, Osaka
2：one-family house
3：151.46
4：78.48
5：85.68
6：wood frame, 2 stories
7：2001.02 − 2001.08
8：2001.10 − 2002.03

岐阜県営北方住宅
Gifu Kitakata Housing

1：Kitakata-cho, Gifu
2：condominium

House in Sakai

SUMOTO Housing project

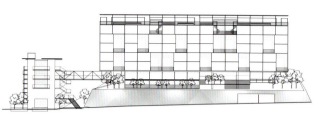
Eda Housing project

5：2,700.00
6：reinforced concrete, 30 units
7：2002.01 − 2004.11

6：steel frame, 3 stories
7：2001.01 − 2001.08
8：2001.11 − 2002.08

5：9,000.00
6：2 stories + 2 basement levels
7：2003.01 − 2003.02

6：steel frame, 1 story
7：2002.05 − 2003.02
8：2003.03 − 2003.09

南船場プロジェクト
Minami-senba Commercial Building project
1：Chuo-ku, Osaka
2：shops + restaurants + condominium
3：583.00
4：381.90
5：3,012.90
6：9 stories + 1 basement level
7：2002.05

Hu-tong House
Hu-tong House
1：Western Japan
2：one-family house
3：331.80
4：215.80
5：248.00
6：wood frame, 3 stories
7：2001.03 − 2001.12
8：2002.03 − 2002.08

東大津の家
House in Higashi-Otsu
1：Otsu, Shiga
2：one-family house
3：198.37
4：118.10
5：222.39
6：wood frame, 3 stories
7：2001.10 − 2002.07
8：2002.08 − 2003.04

京都・小野
Zen Lounge I
1：Nakagyo-ku, Kyoto
2：shop + gallery
5：78.71
6：interior design
7：2003.04 − 2003.06
8：2003.07 − 2003.09

洲本売建プロジェクト
SUMOTO Housing project
1：Sumoto, Hyogo
2：one-family house
3：172.71
4：71.57
5：115.11
6：wood frame
7：2002.04 − 2002.06

ROOM435
ROOM435
1：Atami, Shizuoka
2：studio
5：43.50
6：interior design
7：2002.01 − 2002.05
8：2002.05 − 2002.08

K邸別棟
K Residence Annex project
1：Showa-ku, Nagoya
2：audio room
3：1,830.63
4：84.49
5：94.28
6：reinforced concrete
7：2002.11 − 2003.06

住吉区複合施設
Sumiyoshi Community Hall project
1：Sumiyoshi-ku, Osaka
2：community hall
3：44,000.00
4：6,350.00
5：16,000.00
6：steel frame / reinforced concrete, 5 stories + 1 basement level
7：2003.09 − 2003.10

江田集合住宅プロジェクト
Eda Housing project
1：Aoba-ku, Yokohama
2：condominium + shop
3：3,195.30
4：1,397.90
5：5,649.10
6：steel frame / reinforced concrete, 10 stories + 1 basement level
7：2002.06

2003

北大阪計画プロジェクト
North-Osaka Development project
1：Kita-ku, Osaka
2：cultural facilities + condominium
3：24.00ha
4：11.00ha
5：85.20ha
6：steel frame + reinforced concrete, 40 stories + 2 basement levels
7：2002.12 − 2003.01

Nam June Paik Museum project
Nam June Paik Museum project
1：Kyonggi, Korea
2：museum
3：33,000.00
4：2,700.00
5：5,000.00
6：steel frame and reinforced concrete, 1 story + 2 basement levels
7：2003.07 − 2003.08

熊野古道情報センター
Kumano-kodo Information Center project
1：Owase, Mie
2：information center
3：32,500.00
4：4,150.00
5：2,840.00
6：timber masonry, 1 story
7：2003.11 − 2003.12

和歌山の家
House in Wakayama
1：Wakayama, Wakayama
2：one-family house
3：346.00
4：168.10
5：339.10

日田市プロジェクト
Hita City project
1：Hita, Oita
2：welfare facilities
3：9,500.00
4：5,000.00

子午線ライン明石船客ターミナル
Akashi Meridian Line Ferry Terminal
1：Akashi, Hyogo
2：ferry terminal hall
3：443.40
4：330.00
5：334.00

ルナ ディ ミエーレ 表参道ビル
Luna de Miele
1：Minato-ku, Tokyo
2：shop + office
3：30.90
4：23.81
5：108.35
6：steel-panel structure / reinforced

House in Wakayama

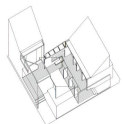
Hu-tong House

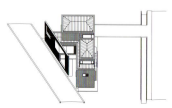
House in Higashi-Otsu

Akashi Meridian Line Ferry Terminal

Zen Lounge I

Luna de Miele

concrete, 6 stories
7：2003.05 − 2003.12
8：2004.03 − 2004.11

2004

Paju SW Office
Paju SW Office
1：Seoul, Korea
2：office
3：1,322.30
4：583.70
5：2,021.20
6：steel frame, 4 stories + 2 basement levels
7：2001.01 − 2002.09
8：2002.12 − 2004.02

標準住宅2004
House-Standard 2004
1：Sakyo-ku, Kyoto
2：one-family house
3：94.55
4：53.89
5：120.47
6：wood frame, 3 stories
7：2003.02 − 2003.05
8：2003.09 − 2004.02

Dior project
Dior project
1：Chuo-ku, Osaka
2：shop
5：W: 16.30m H: 16.00m
6：facade design of retail shop
7：2004.02 − 2004.03

住田歯科診療院
Sumida Dental Clinic
1：Amagasaki, Hyogo
2：dental clinic
3：237.30
4：141.10

5：126.20
6：wood frame, 1 story
7：2002.05 − 2003.05
8：2003.09 − 2004.04

AQUA CUBE
AQUA CUBE
2：furniture
6：steel + acrylic acid resin
7：2002.04 − 2004.05
9：CASSINA IXC. Ltd.

TITTOT GLASS ART MUSEUM
TITTOT GLASS ART MUSEUM
1：Taipei, Taiwan
2：museum
3：5,050.00
4：4,200.00
5：14,000.00
6：steel frame / reinforced concrete, 9 stories + 2 basement levels
7：2004.07 − 2004.08

中之島新線駅プロジェクト
Nakanoshima New Line Design project
1：Nishi-ku, Osaka
2：station building
5：double track line 2.9km
7：2004.10 − 2004.12

2005

代々木上原の家
House in Yoyogi-Uehara
1：Shibuya-ku, Tokyo
2：one-family house
3：85.21
4：51.12
5：105.24
6：wood frame, 3 stories
7：2003.04 − 2004.02
8：2004.06 − 2005.04

N2B project
N2B project
1：Chiyoda-ku, Tokyo
2：hotel + office
3：7,938.25
4：4,900.00
5：88,939.00
7：2005.06 − 2005.07

武蔵野段丘の家
House on Musashino-Hills
1：Setagaya-ku, Tokyo
2：one-family house
3：348.01
4：69.12
5：151.72
6：reinforced concrete, 1 story + 2 basement levels
7：2003.01 − 2003.10
8：2004.09 − 2005.10

Asian Culture Complex
International project Competition
Asian Culture Complex
International project Competition
1：Gwangju, Korea
2：welfare facilities
3：118,170.00
4：55,420.00
5：140,045.00
6：steel frame, 4 stories + 1 basement level
7：2005.09 − 2005.11

Laurel Restaurant
Laurel Restaurant
1：Shanghai, China
2：restaurant
5：708.50
6：interior design
7：2005.04 − 2005.07
8：2005.08 − 2005.12
9：ACDC

京都パープルサンガスタジアム
Kyoto Soccer Stadium project
1：Sakyo-ku, Kyoto
2：soccer stadium
7：2005.10 − 2005.12

2006

清澄の家
Kiyosumi Housing
1：Koto-ku, Tokyo
2：one-family house + apartment
3：188.53
4：127.18
5：577.11
6：steel frame, 6 stories + 1 basement level
7：2004.02 − 2004.10
8：2005.04 − 2006.02

翠松園の家
House on Jade-Garden Hills
1：Moriyama-ku, Nagoya
2：one-family house
3：752.00
4：271.15
5：327.81
6：steel frame, 2 stories
7：2005.06 2006.02

ライカ銀座店
Leica Ginza Showroom
1：Chuo-ku, Tokyo
2：shop + gallery
5：208.00
6：interior design
7：2005.07 − 2006.01
8：2006.02 − 2006.04

京都N別邸
Kyoto N House
1：Sakyo-ku, Kyoto
2：one-family house

Sumida Dental Clinic

House in Yoyogi-Uehara

House on Musashino-Hills

Laurel Restaurant

Kiyosumi Housing

Leica Ginza Showroom

Inter-office Showroom

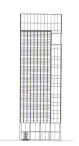
GLASHAUS

3：330.63
4：107.12
5：155.87
6：reinforced concrete, 3 stories
7：2005.06 − 2006.06

HKDI project
HKDI project
1：Tiu Keng Leng Tseung Kwan O, Hong Kong
2：university
3：14,000.00
4：9,200.00
5：41,950.00
6：steel frame + reinforced concrete, 11 stories
7：2006.07 − 2006.07

T-6 プロジェクト
T-6 project
1：Kita-ku, Osaka
2：residential + retail
3：381.53
4：242.18
5：2,355.25
6：reinforced concrete, 12 stories
7：2006.05 − 2006.06

天満橋プロジェクト
Temmabashi project
1：Miyakojima-ku, Osaka
2：condominium
3：811.50
4：481.08
5：2,762.09
6：reinforced concrete, 8 stories
7：2006.04 − 2006.06

インターオフィス／大阪
Inter-office Showroom
1：Nishi-ku, Osaka
2：office + showroom
5：466.00

6：interior design
7：2006.06 − 2006.08
8：2006.09 − 2006.10

2007
GLASHAUS / 靱公園
GLASHAUS
1：Nishi-ku, Osaka
2：shop + apartment
3：356.25
4：245.94
5：2,466.45
6：reinforced concrete, 14 stories
7：2005.06 − 2005.09
8：2006.07 − 2007.10

Suzhou Vanke Villa
Suzhou Vanke Villa
1：Suzhou, China
2：shophouse
5：288.90
6：interior design
7：2007.04 − 2007.07
8：2007.08 − 2007.12
9：ACDC

京都東急ホテル7階・8階改装
Kyoto Tokyu Hotel 7F&8F Room Renovation
1：Shimogyo-ku, Kyoto
2：accommodations of hotel
5：3,777.00
6：interior design
7：2007.01 − 2007.12
8：2007.08 − 2007.10

Fitness & Spa Rhino
Fitness & Spa Rhino
1：Ukyo-ku, Kyoto
2：fitness center
5：1,815.00
6：interior design

7：2007.06 − 2007.08
8：2007.10 − 2007.11

北京アートホテル
Hotel in Beijing
1：Beijing, China
2：hotel
6：interior design
7：2007.10 − 2007.12

2008
麻布十番プロジェクト
Azabu-juban Commercial Complex
1：Minato-ku, Tokyo
2：shop + apartment
3：171.32
4：111.22
5：920.02
6：steel frame, 8 stories + 1 basement level
7：2005.11 − 2006.12
8：2006.05 − 2008.03

House in Freiburg
House in Freiburg
1：Freiburg, Germany
2：one-family house
3：893.71
4：292.25
5：566.26
6：reinforced concrete, 3 stories
7：2006.03 − 2007
8：2007 − 2008

博多の家
House in Hakata
1：Chuo-ku, Fukuoka
2：one-family house
3：198.69
4：119.12
5：320.10
6：reinforced concrete, 4 stories

7：2004.09 − 2005.11
8：2007.05 − 2008.02
9：KOHSEKI CO., LTD

なかい歯科
Nakai Dental Clinic
1：Nakagyo-ku, Kyoto
2：dental clinic
5：110.68
6：interior design
7：2007.06 − 2007.12
8：2008.02 − 2008.04

Haneda TR 3階 project
Haneda TR project
1：Ota-ku, Tokyo
2：retail shop
6：interior design of shop area
7：2007.11 − 2008.01

Wujiang New City Planning project, China
Wujiang New City Planning project, China
1：Wujiang, China
2：urban plan
3：5,900,000.00
7：2008.01 − 2011.04

京都東急ホテル 2階・3階改装
Kyoto Tokyu Hotel 2F&3F Room Renovation
1：Shimogyo-ku, Kyoto
2：hotel
5：3,196.07
6：interior design
7：2008.02 − 2008.03
8：2008.06 − 2008.07

Suzhou Vanke Villa

Kyoto Tokyu Hotel Room Renovation

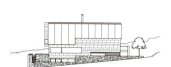
House in Freiburg

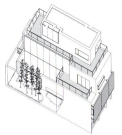
House in Hakata

Wujiang New City Planning project, China

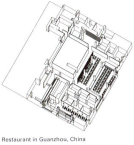
Restaurant in Guanzhou, China

Kamiya House

2009

Restaurant in Guanzhou, China
Restaurant in Guanzhou, China
1：Guangzhou, China
2：restaurant
5：2,000.00
6：interior design
7：2008.04 − 2008.07
8：2008.10 − 2009.10
9：ACDC

紙屋 HOUSE
Kamiya House
1：Shibuya-ku, Tokyo
2：dental clinic + apartment
3：174.56
4：119.38
5：627.04
6：steel frame, 7 stories
7：2007.01 − 2007.09
8：2008.03 − 2009.01

Tearoom project in the Center of Tokyo
Tearoom project in the Center of Tokyo
1：Minato-ku, Tokyo
2：tea ceremony pavilion
3：3,984.27
4：197.78
5：176.76
6：steel frame / reinforced concrete, 1 story
7：2008.08 − 2009.01

書院 / Penthouse
Zen Lounge II
1：Western Japan
2：guest house
5：167.00
6：interior design
7：2008.11 − 2008.12

8：2009.02 − 2009.05

書院 / Third-place
Zen Lounge III
1：Chiyoda-ku, Tokyo
2：tea ceremony studio
5：77.89
6：interior design
7：2008.12 − 2009.02
8：2009.03 − 2009.06

Office Headquarters project, Yentai, China
Office Headquarters project, Yentai, China
1：Yentai, China
2：head office
3：154,700.00
5：162,000.00
7：2009.09 − 2009.11

立礼卓
Ryurei Style Tea Table
2：Ryurei-style tea ceremony table
7：2008.12 − 2009.02
8：2009.03 − 2009.06

2010

東京国際空港ターミナル商業ゾーン
Tokyo International Air Terminal Commercial Zone
1：Ota-ku, Tokyo
2：event space + shopping mall + restaurants
5：4,000.00
6：interior design
7：2005.11 − 2008.10
8：2008.04 − 2010.10
9：KOHSEKI CO., LTD

KIT HOUSE
KIT HOUSE
1：Sakyo-ku, Kyoto
2：student union building
3：73,385.28
4：983.95
5：1,605.11
6：steel frame, 2 stories
7：2009.02 − 2009.07
8：2009.10 − 2010.03
9：YASUI ARCHITECTS & ENGINEERS, INC.

羽田物販ゾーン
Haneda Product Sales Area
1：Ota-ku, Tokyo
2：shop
5：376.86
7：2009.06 − 2010.04

ちゅーピーパーク
Chupi Park
1：Hatsukaichi, Hiroshima
2：2,220,931,357.00
7：2007.12 − 2010.02

福山田島プロジェクト
Fukuyama Tajima project
1：Fukuyama, Hiroshima
3：11,450.00
4：319.16
5：678.47
7：2010.01 − 2010.12

2011

御所西の家
House near Kyoto Gosho
1：Kamigyo-ku, Kyoto
2：one-family house
3：73.37
4：43.93
5：127.75

6：reinforced concrete, 3 stories + 1 basement level
7：2009.11 − 2010.07
8：2010.08 − 2011.03

東急ホテル4-6階改装
Kyoto Tokyu Hotel 4F-6F Room Renovation
1：Shimogyo-ku, Kyoto
2：hotel
5：6,363.00
6：interior design
7：2010.04 − 2010.07
8：2010.12 − 2011.02

日東薬品構内景観整備計画1
-Cento anni Hall
NITTO PHARMA Landscape project 1-Cento anni Hall
1：Muko, Kyoto
2：hall + meeting rooms
5：326.51
6：steel frame, 2 stories
7：2010.10 − 2010.11
8：2011.01 − 2011.02

Spiretec Office Headquarters project
Spiretec Office Headquarters project
1：Delhi, India
2：head office
3：85.029
4：62,750.00
7：2010.12 − 2011.01

象彦漆美術館
Zohiko Urushi Museum
1：Sakyo-ku, Kyoto
2：museum
5：371.00
6：interior design
7：2010.07 − 2011.05
8：2011.06 − 2011.09

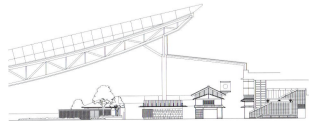
Tokyo International Air Terminal Commercial Zone

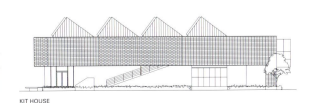
KIT HOUSE

House near Kyoto Gosho

NITTO PHARMA Landscape project 1-Cento anni Hall

Zohiko Urushi Museum

KIM HOUSE 2011
KIM HOUSE 2011
1 : Ikuno-ku, Osaka
2 : one-family house
3 : 69.14
4 : 47.63
5 : 74.98
6 : steel frame, 2 stories
7 : 2011.05 – 2011.08
8 : 2011.08 – 2011.11

2012

東京ステーションギャラリー
Tokyo Station Gallery
1 : Chiyoda-ku, Tokyo
2 : gallery
5 : 3,088.09
7 : 2008.06 – 2009.06
8 : 2010.04 – 2012.10
9 : JR EAST DESIGN CORPORATION

曹洞宗 仏光山 喜音寺
Kionji Temple
1 : Takarazuka, Hyogo
2 : temple
3 : 957.39
4 : 391.05
5 : 499.86
6 : reinforced concrete / steel frame / wood frame, 3 stories
7 : 2009.11 – 2010.06
8 : 2010.12 – 2012.03

Xuancheng project
Xuancheng project
1 : Anhui, China
2 : meeting hall
3 : 118,337.00
5 : 3,243.14
7 : 2011.07 – 2012.11

Villa in Shanghai
Villa in Shanghai
1 : Shanghai, China
2 : one-family house
3 : 416.84
4 : 157.50
5 : 274.59
7 : 2011.08 – 2012.02

2013

GLA近畿会館
GLA Osaka Hall
1 : Suita, Osaka
2 : religious facility
3 : 1,632.98
4 : 1,035.21
5 : 3,200.15
6 : south building: steel frame, 6 stories
   north building: reinforced concrete / wood frame, 2 stories
7 : 2011.09 – 2012.01
8 : 2012.04 – 2013.03

日東薬品構内景観整備計画2
NITTO PHARMA Landscaping project 2
1 : Muko, Kyoto
2 : research facility
5 : 231.00
6 : light gauge steel frame, 2 stories
7 : 2013.05 – 2013.06
8 : 2013.09 – 2013.11

2014

山野井の家
House in Yamanoi
1 : Himeji, Hyogo
2 : one-family house
3 : 796.45
4 : 499.91
5 : 876.81

6 : steel frame (partially)/ reinforced concrete, 2 stories
7 : 2011.07 – 2013.06
8 : 2013.06 – 2014.07
9 : SOTOJI CONSTRUCTION

生方記念文庫
Ubukata Memorial Museum
1 : Numata, Gunma
2 : museum
3 : 736.00
4 : 119.72
5 : 239.44
6 : wood frame, 2 stories
7 : 2011.09 – 2013.03
8 : 2013.10 – 2014.05

京都大学北部グラウンド運動部部室棟
Kyoto University Student Clubhouse, north campus
1 : Sakyo-ku, Kyoto
2 : athletic clubhouse
3 : 199,530.05
4 : 418.88
5 : 654.19
6 : steel frame, 2 stories
7 : 2012.04 – 2012.08
8 : 2013.10 – 2014.05

GLA八ヶ岳 人生祈念館納骨室改装
GLA Yatsugatake Charnel House
1 : Hokuto, Yamanashi
2 : charnel house
5 : 189.00
6 : floor part under the ground: reinforced concrete,
   2 stories + 1 basement level
7 : 2012.09 – 2013.06
8 : 2013.07 – 2014.04

白鳳堂京都本店
Hakuhodo
1 : Nakagyo-ku, Kyoto

2 : shop
3 : 158.09
4 : 125.49
5 : 227.47
6 : reinforced concrete, 2 stories
7 : 2013.09 – 2013.12
8 : 2013.03 – 2014.10

代々木公園の家
House near Yoyogi Park
1 : Shibuya-ku, Tokyo
2 : residence
3 : 249.65
4 : 146.68
5 : 430.88
6 : reinforced concrete / steel frame,
   3 stories + 1 basement level
7 : 2013.04 – 2014.05

瓜生山学園造形芸術大学 図書館
Library for Kyoto University of Art and Design
1 : Sakyo-ku, Kyoto
2 : library
3 : 1,800.00
4 : 895.52
5 : 2,883.28
6 : reinforced concrete, 3 basement levels
7 : 2013.12 – 2014.05
8 : 2014.05 –
9 : Kenichi Kishi

京都ホテル オークラ 桃李改装
Restaurant "TOH-RI", Kyoto Hotel Ohkura
1 : Nakagyo-ku, Kyoto
2 : restaurant
5 : 600.00
6 : interior design, renovation
7 : 2013.12 – 2014.03
8 : 2014.05 – 2014.08

KIM HOUSE 2011

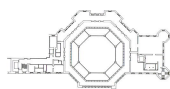
Tokyo Station Gallery

Kionji Temple

GLA Osaka Hall

House in Yamanoi

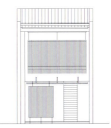
Hakuhodo

象彦 寺町店
Zohiko Teramachi
1：Nakagyo-ku, Kyoto
2：shop
3：178.24
4：139.84
5：109.18
6：interior design of retail shop
7：2013.12 – 2014.01
8：2014.03 – 2014.04

"1888" 京都高島屋
"1888", Kyoto, Takashimaya Department store
1：Shimogyo-ku, Kyoto
2：shop, delicatessen
5：17.19
6：interior design
7：2014.02 – 2014.04
8：2014.05 – 2014.05

象彦 本店
Zohiko Office + Shop
1：Kita-ku, Kyoto
2：head office
5：296.13
6：renovation
7：2014.03 – 2014.06
8：2014.04 – 2014.08

京都市庁舎プロポーザル
Kyoto City Government Office proposal
1：Nakagyo-ku, Kyoto
2：city hall
7：2014.04 – 2014.07

2015-

GLA 名古屋
GLA Nagoya Hall
1：Naka-ku, Nagoya
2：religious facility

3：1,511.19
4：1,305.39
5：6,411.27
6：steel frame, 9 stories + 1 basement level
7：2013.01 – 2015.02
8：2015.03 –
9：Design Department, Nagoya Branch, Takenaka Corporation

Spa project in Peony-Garden
Spa project in Peony-Garden
1：Shanghai, China
2：spa
5：2,000.00
6：renovation
7：2013.10 –
9：Kazuhira Nagasaki

Warehouse Renovation at Minsheng-road
Warehouse Renovation at Minsheng-road
1：Shanghai, China
2：office + shopping mall
3：8,525.64
4：3,455.56
5：10,222.06
6：renovation
7：2013.12 – 2015.03
8：2015.03 –
9：Kazuhira Nagasaki, Masahiro Kinoshita

京都市美術館新館計画案
Kyoto City Musium Annex project
1：Sakyo-ku, Kyoto
2：museum
3：24.33
4：6,396.00
5：11,907.00
existing area: 11,311.00
(the extension of main building and annex)
6：reinforced concrete
existing area: 2 stories + 1 basement level
annex: 1 story + 2 basement levels
7：2015.05 – 2015.07
9：Yukio Tahara; NIHON SEKKEI, INC.; Kishi Studio, Department of Architecture and Engineering, Kyoto University (Mao Sugiyama)

南泉禅寺再建計画
Nanquan Temple project
1：Anhui, China
2：temple complex
3：200,000.00
4：main area: 913.52
  zen area: 1,765.83
  tower area: 596.16
  hillside area: 2,185.55
7：2014.08 – 2014.11
9：Kazuhira Nagasaki; Kishi Studio, Department of Architecture and Engineering, Kyoto University (Mao Sugiyama)

略歴

岸 和郎
建築家・京都大学大学院教授
http://www.k-associates.com/

略歴

1950	横浜市生まれ
1973	京都大学工学部電気工学科卒業
1975	同大学工学部建築学科卒業
1978	同大学院修士課程建築学専攻修了
1981	岸和郎建築設計事務所を設立
1993	岸和郎建築設計事務所をK.ASSOCIATES／Architectsに改組改称
1981→1993	京都芸術短期大学にて教鞭を執る
1993→2010	京都工芸繊維大学にて教鞭を執る
2000→2010	同大学大学院工芸科学研究科造形科学域建築設計学専攻教授
2003	カリフォルニア大学バークレー校客員教授
2004	マサチューセッツ工科大学客員教授
2010→	京都大学大学院工学研究科建築学専攻教授
2013→	京都造形芸術大学客員教授
	現在に至る

主な受賞歴

1983	商空間デザイン賞優秀賞
1987	SD Review 入選
1991	くまもと景観賞受賞
1993	日本建築家協会新人賞
1994	京都市地域住宅HOPE賞
1995	ケネス・F・ブラウンアジア太平洋デザイン賞功労賞
	日本建築学会作品選奨
1996	日本建築学会賞
	日本建築学会作品選奨
2002	愛知まちなみ建築賞
2004	明石市都市景観賞
	兵庫県人間サイズのまちづくり賞
2006	デダロ・ミノス国際賞審査員賞
2007	グッドデザイン賞
2008	アジアパシフィックインテリアデザイン賞金賞
2009	大阪市ハウジングデザイン賞
2012	香港デザイナー協会グローバルデザイン賞金賞
2014	フリッツヘーガー賞ブリックアーキテクチャー部門特別賞
	平成26年度京都景観賞建築部門奨励賞

主な出版物

1983	建築とポップ・カルチュア／レイナー・バンハム著（訳書）　鹿島出版会
1992	WARO KISHI architectural works 1987-1991（作品集）　大龍堂書店
	CRITIC vol.1 Waro Kishi（作品集）　大伸社
1995	Waro Kishi（作品集）　Editorial Gusutavo Gili, S.A.（Spain）
1996	waro kishi（作品集）　ELcroquis 77 II（Spain）
1997	ケース・スタディ・ハウス／case study house（著書）　住まいの図書館出版局
	WARO KISHI CONCEPTION/PRAXIS（作品集）　建築文化 Vol.52, No.609
2000	WARO KISHI PROJECTed Realities（著書）　TOTO出版
	Waro Kishi（作品集）　Edition Axel Menges GmbH（Germany）
	WARO KISHI store design 5 bus stops + 1（作品集）　LOGOS ART s.r.l.（Italy）
2001	Waro Kishi recent works（作品集）　2G nexus Vol.19（III）（Spain）
2003	建築を旅する（著書）　共立出版
2004	Pro Architect（作品集）　ARCHIWORLD Co., Ltd.（Korea）
	建築の終わり（共著）　TOTO出版
2005	Waro Kishi（作品集）　Mondadori Electa spa（Italy）
2007	逡巡する思考（著書）　共立出版
2008	イームズ・ハウス／チャールズ＆レイ・イームズ（著書）　東京書籍
	ヘヴンリーハウス―20世紀名作住宅を巡る旅2
	イームズ・ハウス／チャールズ＆レイ・イームズ（著書）　東京書籍
2009	updates01@warokishi Hu-Tong House（著書）　藍風館
	updates02@warokishi House in Fukaya（著書）　藍風館
2012	updates03@warokishi KIM HOUSE 1987/2011（著書）　藍風館
	updates04@warokishi House in Nipponbashi（著書）　藍風館
	重奏する建築（著書）　TOTO出版
2013	CA Waro Kishi（作品集）　CA Press（Korea）
2014	Waro KISHI+K.ASSOCIATES（作品集）　Equal Books（Korea）
2015	デッドエンド・モダニズム（著書）　LIXIL出版

Profile

Waro Kishi
Architect / Professor, Kyoto University

Biography
2013-	Visiting professor, Kyoto University of Art and Design, Kyoto, Japan
2010-	Professor, Kyoto University
2004	Visiting professor, Massachusetts Institute of Technology, Cambridge, USA
2003	Visiting professor, University of California, Berkeley, USA
2000-2010	Professor, Kyoto Institute of Technology
1993-2010	Taught Architecture Design in Kyoto Institute of Technology
1981-1993	Taught Architectural Design in Kyoto College of Art
1993	Organized, Waro Kishi + K. ASSOCIATES/Architects, Kyoto
1981	Principal, Waro Kishi, Architect & Associates, Kyoto
1978	Completed Post-Graduate Course of Architecture, Kyoto University
1975	Graduated from Department of Architecture, Kyoto University
1973	Graduated from Department of Electronics, Kyoto University
1950	Born in Yokohama, Japan

Awards
2014	"Special Mention, Fritz-Höger-Preis 2014 für Backstein-Architektur" Germany
	"Honorable mention in Building category of Kyoto Cityscape Awards" Kyoto, Japan
2012	"Gold Award, Global Design Awards 2011, HKDA" Hong Kong
2009	"Housing Design Award for Osaka" Osaka, Japan
2008	"Gold Award, 16th Asia Pacific Interior Design Awards" Hong Kong
2007	"Good Design Award 2007" Tokyo, Japan
2006	"Commendation of the Jury, Dedalo Minosse International Prize" Italy
2004	"Award for Townscape of Hyougo Prefecture" Hyogo, Japan
	"Award for Townscape of Akashi" Hyogo, Japan
2002	"Award for Townscape of Aichi Prefecture" Aichi, Japan
1996	"Annual Architectural Design Commendation of the Architectural Institute of Japan" Architectural Institute of Japan Tokyo, Japan
	"The Prize of Architectural Institute of Japan for Design" Architectural Institute of Japan Tokyo, Japan
1995	"Annual Architectural Design Commendation of the Architectural Institute of Japan" Architectural Institute of Japan Tokyo, Japan
	"Kenneth F. Brown Asia Pacific Culture and Architecture Merit Award" University of Hawaii Honolulu, U.S.A
1994	"Hope Award for Excellent House in Kyoto" Kyoto, Japan
1993	"JIA (Japan Institute of Architects) Award for the Best Young Architect of the Year" Japan Institute of Architects Tokyo, Japan
1991	"Award for Townscape of Kumamoto Prefecture" Kumamoto, Japan
1987	"SD Review Award" Kajima Institute Publishing Co., Ltd. Tokyo, Japan
1983	"Commercial Space Design Award in Excellence" Japanese Society of Commercial Space Designers Tokyo, Japan

Monographs/Books
2015	*Dead-end Modernism*, LIXIL Publishing: LIXIL Corporation, Japan
2014	*WARO KISHI + K.ASSOCIATES*, EQUAL BOOKS, Korea
2013	*CA Waro Kishi*, CA Press, Korea
2012	*updates04@warokishi : House in Nipponbashi*, Lampoon House, Japan
	multi-storied buildings, TOTO Publishing, Japan
	updates03@warokishi : KIM HOUSE 1987/2011, Lampoon House, Japan
2009	*updates02@warokishi : House in Fukaya*, Lampoon House, Japan
	updates01@warokishi : HU-TONG HOUSE, Lampoon House, Japan
2008	*Heavenly House No2: Eames House*, Tokyo Shoseki.Co.,Ltd.,Japan
2007	*Waro Kishi Writings 1982-2007*, Kyoritsu Suppan., LTD., Japan
2005	*Waro Kishi, Electa*, Mondadori Electa spa, Italy
2004	*Waro Kishi, Pro Architect*, ARCHIWORLD Co., Ltd., Korea
	The END of architecture, TOTO Publishing, Japan
2003	*Journey Through Architecture*, Kyoritsu Suppan., LTD., Japan
2001	*Waro Kishi Recent works*, GG, N.19, Editorial Gustavo Gili, S.A, Spain
2000	*Waro Kishi Store Design 5bus Stops + 1*, Logos Art s.r.l., Italy
	Waro Kishi Projected Realities, TOTO Publishing, Japan
	Waro Kishi, Axel Menges, Germany
1997	*Waro Kishi Conception/Plaxis*, Kenchiku bunka, Vol.52, No.609, Shokoku-sha Co., Ltd., Japan
	Case Study Houses, Sumaino Toshokan Publishing Co., Ltd., Japan
1996	*Waro Kishi 1987-1996*, El Croquis 77- II, El Croquis Editorial, Spain
1995	*Waro Kishi*, GG, Editorial Gustavo Gili, S.A, Spain
1992	*Waro Kishi: Architectural Works 1987-1991*, Tairyu-do Co., Ltd., Japan
	Critic Vol.1, Daishin-sha Co., Ltd., Japan
1983	Translation: *Design by Choice*, Reyner Banham, Kajima Institute Publishing Co., Ltd., Japan

クレジット
Credits

写真　Photographs

宗教法人狐蓬庵
Religious corporation KOHOAN
p. 016

浄土真宗本願寺派 本山 本願寺
Jodo Shinshu Honganji sect Motoyama Honganji
p. 017

新建築社写真部
Shinkenchiku-sha
pp. 027-033

平井広行
Hiroyuki Hirai
pp. 035-039, pp. 051-070, p. 071 top, pp. 073-085, pp. 087-143, pp. 146-167, pp. 169-177, pp. 180-203

小川重雄
Shigeo Ogawa
pp. 044-045, p. 046 top right, p. 046 bottom, p. 047, p. 048 top, p.048 bottom right, pp. 243-267, pp. 293-317, pp. 323-347

市川靖史
Yasushi Ichikawa
p. 046 top left, p. 048 bottom left, p. 049, p. 269, pp. 271-273, pp. 281-287, p. 388

Minghong
p. 071 bottom

鈴木久雄
Hisao Suzuki
pp. 211-213, pp. 234-237, pp. 239-241

CHINA VANKE CO., LTD.
p. 215

ALAN CHAN DESIGN CO.
pp. 216-221

上田 宏
Hiroshi Ueda
pp. 223-231, pp. 319-321

上記以外はケイ・アソシエイツ
Images / figures other than the above were provided by
Waro Kishi + K.ASSOCIATES/Architects

英訳協力　English translation support

マチダ・ゲン
Gen Machida

スタッフリスト　Staff list

佐藤真理子
Mariko Sato

松尾しのぶ
Shinobu Matsuo

田辺美和
Miwa Tanabe

山下裕美子
Yumiko Yamashita

中村祥子
Shoko Nakamura

竹内麻子
Asaco Takeuchi

鈴木 恵
Megumi Suzuki

北野新吾
Shingo Kitano

山瀬健一郎
Kenichiro Yamase

小嶋雄之
Yushi Kojima

宮本直子
Naoko Miyamoto

松井雅永
Masanaga Matsui

榊田倫之
Tomoyuki Sakakida

岸 研一
Kenichi Kishi

村川美紀
Miki Murakawa

永田 真
Makoto Nagata

山下恭司
Kyoji Yamashita

町田 彩
Aya Machida

郭 銀貞
Kwak Eun Jung

大澤さおり
Saori Ozawa

弓張久留美
Kurumi Yumihari

吉田美智留
Michiru Yoshida

川上美奈
Mina Kawakami

倉本優香子
Yukako Kuramoto

大久保 隆
Takashi Okubo

宮﨑 梢
Kozue Miyazaki

小坂田雄介
Yusuke Osakada

田原俊平
Shumpei Tahara

浅野さえ子
Saeko Asano

西田理恵
Rie Nishida

遠山律子
Ritsuko Toyama

協力　Special thanks to

大石義一
Yoshikazu Oishi

鬼丸貞利
Sadatoshi Onimaru

森迫清貴
Kiyotaka Morisako

門藤芳樹
Yoshiki Mondo

梅田 潔
Kiyoshi Umeda

アラン・チャン
Alan Chan

中村義明
Yoshiaki Nakamura

田原幸夫
Yukio Tahara

中村 潔
Kiyoshi Nakamura

朽木順綱
Yoshitsuna Kutsuki

杉山真魚
Mao Sugiyama

長崎和平
Kazuhira Nagasaki

木下昌大
Masahiro Kinoshita

乾 陽亮
Yosuke Inui

室野和子
Kazuko Murono

WARO KISHI
岸 和郎の建築

2016年1月27日　初版第1刷発行

著者／岸 和郎
発行者／加藤 徹
発行所／TOTO出版（TOTO株式会社）
〒107-0062 東京都港区南青山1-24-3 TOTO乃木坂ビル2F
［営業］TEL　03-3402-7138　FAX　03-3402-7187
［編集］TEL　03-3497-1010
URL　http://www.toto.co.jp/publishing/
アートディレクション／山口信博
デザイン／宮巻 麗
印刷・製本／図書印刷株式会社

落丁本・乱丁本はお取り替えいたします。
本書の全部又は一部に対するコピー・スキャン・デジタル化等の無断複製行為は、
著作権法上での例外を除き禁じます。
本書を代行業者等の第三者に依頼してスキャンやデジタル化することは、
たとえ個人や家庭内での利用であっても著作権上認められておりません。

定価はカバーに表示してあります。

© 2016 Waro Kishi

Printed in Japan
ISBN978-4-88706-356-3